Ficino
and
Renaissance Neoplatonism

Ficino
and
Renaissance
Neoplatonism

Edited by
Konrad Eisenbichler
and
Olga Zorzi Pugliese

University of Toronto Italian Studies   1

Dovehouse Editions Canada
1986

We gratefully acknowledge the cooperation and financial assistance of the Italian Embassy, Ottawa, and the support of Mr. Remo Rapetti, in the publication of this volume.

Canadian Cataloguing in Publication Data

Main entry under title:
 Ficino and renaissance neoplatonism

ISBN 0-919473-59-8

1. Ficino, Marsilio, 1433-1499 2. Neoplatonism.
I. Pugliese, Olga, 1941-   II. Eisenbichler, Konrad

B785.F43F43 1986   195   C86-090172-6

Copyright © 1986, Dovehouse Editions Canada

For information on distribution and for all orders write to:
 Dovehouse Editions Canada
 32 Glen Ave.
 Ottawa, Canada
 K1S 2Z7

Table of Contents

Introduction

This volume contains the revised texts of the papers which were delivered at a conference held on October 13-14, 1984 at Victoria College in the University of Toronto on the topic 'Ficino and Renaissance Neoplatonism.' The conference was organized by the Department of Italian Studies (University of Toronto), together with the Centre for Reformation and Renaissance Studies (Victoria University, Toronto) to commemorate the 500th anniversary of the publication of Ficino's translation of Plato's works in 1484, and was made possible through the substantial funding provided by the Social Sciences and Humanities Research Council of Canada and through the generous contributions made by various bodies at the University of Toronto: the President's Office, the Deans of the Faculty of Arts and Science and the School of Graduate Studies, the Principal of Victoria College, the Department of Italian Studies, and the Centre for Reformation and Renaissance Studies.*

The two-day event attracted a large number of participants, and not exclusively from the Toronto area, some attending from as far away as Alberta and California. The thirteen speakers — from Canada, the United States, and Italy — included historians of philosophy, art, and music and also critics who work on the English, French, Hebrew, and Italian literatures of the Renaissance. With their varied backgrounds, diverse interests, and differing approaches, these scholars provided a truly international and interdisciplinary exchange of ideas quite appropriate to the topic of discussion, for, indeed, the impact of Ficino and Renaissance Neoplatonism was felt in many disciplines, throughout Europe, and for centuries.

The leading thinker of Italy in his day, and the spiritual leader of the Platonic Academy of Florence during the time of the Medici, Marsilio Ficino (1433-99) occupies an important place in the history of philosophy. Through his translation into Latin of the works of Plato, Plotinus, and the Hermetic writers, he introduced their doctrines into the mainstream of Western thought. In the formulation of his own system, especially in his *Theologia Platonica* and in his commentary on Plato's *Symposium* or *De Amore*, he incorporated, into a basic Platonic structure, a broad spectrum of doctrinal and literary traditions which, once brought together and refashioned, produced Ficino's own syncretic brand of Christian Neoplatonism. Of particular resonance were his view of a hierarchically arranged but man-centred cosmos, and his complex theory of what he was the first to term 'Platonic' love, with its carefully worked out mechanics and physiology, its insistence on the myth of the two Venuses, and its purpose as a means to reach contemplation of the divine. These, along with other principal tenets of his thought, exerted extraordinary influence on many fields in addition to that of philosophy — on music, fine art, and literature, for example.

The broad reaches of this fundamental aspect of Renaissance culture are well represented in the papers read and discussed at the Toronto conference and collected in this volume. Arranged for convenience under the scholars' names in alphabetical order, the individual pieces approach the subject from a multiplicity of perspectives, thus illustrating the very richness of the theme under investigation. They cover a number of the areas singled out by P.O. Kristeller as requiring further investigation,[1] and they respond to the view forcefully presented by W.G. Craven that the old theses we have inherited must be reexamined.[2]

One of the principal features of Ficino's philosophy is the central place he assigns to man in the hierarchy of beings, viewing him as the veritable link of the universe. Charles Trinkaus's paper (No. 10) focusses on Ficino's concept of man's autonomy which, according to Trinkaus, an expert on humanist thought, is the fullest and most far-reaching exposition of the idea to come out of the Renaissance. Using direct references to the texts he shows how Ficino develops his vision of human autonomy beginning with the belief in man's intelligence and in the power of choice exercised by his rational soul. Not compelled even by divinity or Divine Providence, or by the heavens, the human will can choose to descend into corporeal forms and matter or to ascend to the angels and to God. It dominates matter and the body controlling even the humours through the art of medicine. The climax of Ficino's argumentation, and of Trinkaus's exposition, is provided by Ficino's elaboration on the traditional concept of *homo faber*, of man the artist who imitates the works of divine nature and perfects and corrects those of lower nature. Trinkaus's analysis demonstrates how Ficino's praise of man's ability to utilize and beautify earthly things reflects the world of Renaissance art, how it brings man to a level equalling that of God, and also how it places in order of increasing merit the industrial, civil, and liberal arts which characterize man and illustrate his autonomy. Trinkaus's clear and tightly-argued exposition proves the important contribution Ficino made to later thinking on man and it also gives us an inroad to understanding the pattern of reasoning which governs his writings.

The contribution by William Bowen (No. 1) is designed to expound another aspect of Ficino's thought, namely his theory of music as it revolves around the concept of *harmonia*, not simply in a general sense, however, but in its technical meaning, that is as the proper collocation of consecutive sounds which is a reflection of the order of the cosmos. To show the connection between the sensible experience of harmony and true knowledge of the metaphysical principle, Ficino makes use of number, Bowen shows, conveniently summarizing the data provided in Ficino's commentaries and epistolary tracts with the aid of a diagram. Ficino's measurement of the ratios which define the musical intervals is based on the *tetraktys* but it results on different occasions in two contradictory scales — one which adheres to the traditional Pythagorean theory, the other indicating, instead, some concern for contemporary musical practice too. Ficino was a musician himself, of course; nevertheless, Bowen concludes, he was ultimately governed by his overriding interest in the role of harmonic science as a means of philosophical ascent to the One.

The question of Ficino's debt to Plotinus in the formulation of his theory of love is debated by Al Wolters and Laura Westra in their respective papers (Nos. 13 and 12). Wolters argues that Ficino's concept of 'Platonic love' is actually that of Plotinus because Ficino, like other Renaissance philosophers, read Plato through the glasses of Neoplatonism, more specifically, through *Enneads*, III, 5 ('On Eros'). Wolters studies the relations between this text and Ficino's translation of and commentary on it, as well as his reference to Plotinus's ideas in his original writings. First Wolters analyzes the manner in which Plotinus had read his own elaborate ontology into Plato's *Symposium* and he parallels this to Ficino's Christianized adaptation of Plotinus in his own commentary on the *Symposium*. Using a philological approach, Wolters makes use of the manuscripts of Plotinus used by Ficino, as well as evidence of Plotinian influence to be found in his major work, the *Theologia Platonica*, and in other writings such as his correspondence. The deep familiarity Ficino had with Plotinus is evidenced, Wolters shows with abundant and precise examples, in the accuracy of Ficino's translation of Plotinus, that is, in his ability to capture both grammatical subtleties and points of argumentation in the original Greek text.

Since Ficino defines love as the desire for beauty, it is fitting that Westra should concentrate on the concept of beauty as well as on that of love in her study of the relation between Ficino and Plotinus and of their respective views on the soul's relation to God and its mode of ascent to Him. However, Westra's aim is to attenuate the traditional view of Ficino's heavy reliance on Plotinus since she sees significant differences between the two thinkers. Although the same terms may be used by both, the meanings and implications can be far different: for example, the two wings involved in the flight of the soul are philosophy *and religion*, for Ficino. Indeed Ficino's concept of beauty is more spiritual, more intimately tied with goodness, than is the case for Plotinus. His concept of love is more religious, based as it is on man's natural and enflamed desire for God, whereas Plotinus describes love as a more intellectualized experience. Westra finds certain parallels between Ficino and Avicenna more convincing. She concludes by stressing Ficino's Christian, rather than Plotinian, Platonism and by stating that the monotheistic Platonism of Avicenna appears to be closer to the spirit of Ficino's thought than the pagan ascent that Plotinus outlines in the *Enneads*.

Since the sources for Ficino's ideas were not strictly philosophical in nature, it is important to trace the connections between him and earlier literary traditions too. Massimo Ciavolella (No. 3) deals with Guido Cavalcanti's *canzone* 'Donna me prega' — a difficult poem written in the thirteenth century which was analyzed by many commentators in the Middle Ages and in the Renaissance. Ficino mentions it in his commentary on the *Symposium* but distorts its basic meaning, by turning what was a scientific description of sensual love, based on natural philosophy, into an exposition of Neoplatonic doctrine. Ficino achieves this forced interpretation, Ciavolella convincingly illustrates, by glossing over the medical details on *ereos*, or erotic melancholy, for example, and by adding imagery which was extraneous to the poem. Since Ficino's views, erroneous though they might have been, were adopted by later theorists of love who used Cavalcanti's poem as their point of departure, Ficino came to have an impact on Renaissance literary criticism: he altered the way Cavalcanti was to be viewed for centuries, that is, as a full-fledged philosopher and not simply as a poet interested also in natural philosophy.

In addition to looking at Ficino in relation to the currents which preceded him, one must inevitably consider what followed, what constituted the extensive influence of his Neoplatonism. Giovanni Pico della Mirandola (1463-94) was one contemporary philosopher who also operated in the Florentine milieu and who absorbed much of Ficino's teachings. However, while developing certain of Ficino's tenets (e.g. the freedom and dignity of man), he also deviated from other Ficinian convictions, by attempting a complete fusion of Platonism and Aristotelianism, for instance. One of the areas of interest he shared with the master was that of the occult sciences.

In his paper (No. 11) Louis Valcke provides a detailed analysis of Pico's ideas on magic and miracles, placing these in the history of thought to show the relationships between Pico and various philosophical currents. In an earlier phase, represented by his oration on the dignity of man and the defence of his 900 theses of 1486, Pico had made a distinction between natural magic and black magic in order to include the latter among the rational sciences. On this point Pico had relied on Plotinus but had departed from him on the question of determinism since this would exclude the possibility of divine miracles. To salvage such intervention by God, Pico relied on arguments Valcke believes are Augustinian. However, at a later stage, in his treatise against astrologers (1493), Pico abandoned Neoplatonism and rejected magic completely. This evolution in his thought, Valcke argues, shows that Pico, far from being engaged heroically in free scientific research, was actually being guided by apologetic concerns. His separation of the sacred from the profane is what really constitutes the mark he leaves on the history of thought.

Another thinker who followed in the wake of Ficino, and who was also steeped in Cabalistic culture, was Leone Ebreo (Yehuda Abravanel). He was the author of the very successful and oft translated *Dialoghi d'amore*, first published in 1535 and subsequently to become the source of inspiration for many literary figures. A Portuguese Jew who went to Italy after the expulsion in 1492, Leone Ebreo came into contact with humanist classicism and with Neoplatonism, evidence of which is to be found in his *Dialoghi*. The result is a complex work which has puzzled scholars, faced as they inevitably are with the vexatious problem of determining in what language the work was originally written, exactly what type of syncretism its ideas reflect, and what the meaning of its composition had for its author. Riccardo Scrivano and Arthur M. Lesley have proposed their solutions to these questions in papers 9 and 5.

Scrivano judiciously assesses the information available on the author's life and on the milieu in which he operated in the late fifteenth and early sixteenth centuries. He adds some new unpublished data attesting to the high esteem in which Leone was held as a physician and showing perhaps that he was still alive in 1533. Scrivano supplements his insightful observations on the style and structure of Leone's prose and poetic writings and his elucidation of Leone's views on astrology (a field in which he proves to be closer to Ficino than to Pico) and on his concepts of macrocosm and microcosm, with a useful review of traditional and more recent research on Leone, stressing the difficulties of studying Hebrew culture of the Renaissance and of defining the peculiar blends of Cabalistic, orthodox Hebrew, and classical elements devised by Renaissance thinkers. The environment in which Jewish scholars operated in this period was wrought by conflict between the rationalist tendencies of official Hebraism and the search for mystical ardour present in the more heretical Cabala. In this environment Leone produced a syncretist system which was quite original in the weight and superiority it attributed to the Hebrew tradition. What the author, a believer and extremely cultured intellectual, was trying to prove was that, beyond existing divisions, everything, including classical mythology, stems from the unique truth which lies in Hebraism. In the *Dialoghi*, Leone shows, for example, that the Platonic myth of Androgyne is simply an adaptation of the Biblical account of the creation of Adam and Eve. According to Scrivano, then, Leone was writing for Christian members of the intellectual world, in order to persuade them of the truth contained in the ancient Biblical matrix. Thus the original text was probably composed in Latin, or even in the vernacular.

Lesley, instead, sides with the other school of criticism, which maintains that Leone was addressing a Jewish audience and that he wrote his treatise in Hebrew over 30 years before it was published in Italian. (The fact that the various vernacular manuscripts of the *Dialoghi* bear variants which are not of substance but of wording, convinces these critics that they are versions of a common base text.) Comparing Leone's situation and experience in the social and intellectual context of the Jewish community to the emblematic one of Yohanan Alemanno some years earlier, Lesley finds evidence suggesting that Leone's text must have created quite a stir and been the object of criticism. Even though, as Lesley agrees, the *Dialoghi* gave pride of place to Judaism, making Platonism and Cabala subservient to it, nevertheless, it was probably rejected by Jewish intellectuals because of its union of reason and revelation and because of its very attempt to reach syncretism and to use Platonism at all. It fell into oblivion until Christians in Rome published it and gave it a place in European literature.

It was Pontus de Tyard, the poet studied by Eva Kushner in essay No. 4, who was responsible for translating Leone's text into French in 1551. Distinct from the other members of the Pléiade in the philosophical depth of his Platonism, Kushner shows that Tyard adapted the thought of Ficino and Leone, not in succession, but contemporaneously right from the early stages of his writing career. Tyard was able to overcome Platonic dualism by adopting Leone's type of syncretism — one with a long history and tradition from Philo of Alexandria onwards — with its stress on the value of the temporal world. The subtle differences which ensued between the role of beauty in Ficino's system and that of Tyard are evident in the latter's poetry where, as the quotations Kushner cites indicate, the circle of love is made to begin and end in the beauty of the beloved, whereas in Ficino it had originated and terminated in God. Even the dialogue structure of Leone's treatise was adapted by the French poet for its philosophical value, since, as

Kushner observes, it placed the two speakers on equal footing, thus overcoming a strict hierarchical arrangement.

Similar attempts are made in two other papers to determine the exact impact made by Ficino and Neoplatonism but, in these cases, on some unlikely artistic and literary works of the Renaissance. In No. 2, Francis Broun offers a fresh interpretation of the enigmatic Louvre painting, known as the *Concert champêtre*, usually attributed to Giorgione and / or Titian, and generally recognized as having contributed substantially to the development of the genre of idyllic landscape. In his witty analysis, Broun rejects the traditional view that the painting tells no story at all; he finds, instead, strong evidence pointing to the influence of Ficino's commentary on the *Symposium*. The intensity of the gaze that passes between the two young men recalls the emphasis Ficino places on the eyes in the perception of beauty and the transmission of love. The two figures — one unkempt and bearing a naked foot, the other more fashionable — represent the dual aspects of Love, born of Poros and Penia, according to the myth included in Ficino's discussion. Light seems to emanate from one male figure to illuminate the face of the other, and for this detail too, Broun finds corroborating passages in Ficino's text. The two female figures in the painting represent the twin nature of Venus, since one, to be identified as the Source, pours water from a pitcher into a well, and the second is firmly connected with earth and has a wooden flute, not a heavenly instrument. On the basis of the parallels to be found with Ficino's writings, Broun proposes a new title for the masterpiece: *Allegory of Neoplatonic Love and Beauty*.

After documenting Ariosto's early interest in Neoplatonism, Peter Marinelli too (No. 6) offers an original interpretation of the hybrid creature, the aerial horse or hippogriff which is the vehicle of transport for two of the major heroes in *Orlando furioso*. Even this image, which springs from earlier chivalric literature and whose germ was in Boiardo, bears elements, Marinelli cogently argues, which relate to Ficinian love-theory. The magician Atlante who rides the hippogriff is invested with attributes of Amor which include Ovidian *otium* and militancy, talons mentioned by Boccaccio, and old age as in Petrarch. However, the elements of light and flight show that Ariosto was adapting to the new theories outlined by Ficino. The downward and upward flight, taken by the riders Ruggiero and Astolfo, signify the two loves: generative and cognitive. Orlando, who does not fly at all, represents lust and the disease of love. The various types of love are represented by the degree of control exercised by the riders on the steed, a traditional symbol of the passions, just as their respective views from on high indicate their varying degree of attachment to earth.

More obvious and widely accepted is the Neoplatonism found in the texts analyzed by Dennis J. McAuliffe and Olga Z. Pugliese. However, both essays offer new qualifications to the subject. In paper 7, McAuliffe prefaces his analysis of Vittoria Colonna's poetry with a description of the cultural, intellectual, and emotional circumstances in which this influence first manifests itself. Highlighting the grief caused Vittoria by her husband's death in 1525 and the tragic political events in Rome in subsequent years, and also the tension she felt as a religious thinker, torn as she was between attraction to a contemplative life of prayer and an active life of good works, McAuliffe successfully shows how distinct Vittoria was among sixteenth-century Petrarchists in basing her poetry on lived experience, how philosophy and theology were the media through which she filtered her experience in her poetry. In the poems themselves McAuliffe detects Neoplatonic images of light and dark, and the recurring Neoplatonic concept of the winged soul which attempts to break away from the prison of the present life in order to reach the world of the spirit. The will to die so as to be reunited with her husband gives way in the later poems to a desire to be united with Christ. In one sonnet discussed the theme of flight also signifies poetic inspiration. Generally, though, it has spiritual meaning and, in its later mystical versions, takes place without any reliance on earthly beauty.

Through a comparison with Ficino's *De Amore* Pugliese shows (No. 8) how, through omissions and additions, Girolamo Benivieni and Baldassar Castiglione modify Ficino's love-theory in the 'Canzona d'amore' (written in the 1470s and later commented upon by Pico) and in Book IV of *Il libro del cortegiano* respectively. What these texts offer are two particularly stimulating variations. The ethereal doctrine in Benivieni's poem bears a peculiar 'reforming' stage in the steps of contemplation and other elements which are not pure Ficino but hark back perhaps to Bonaventure. Castiglione's version is more earth-bound and appears to question the validity of Neoplatonism in an ironical manner. Pugliese's analysis also treats the basic rhetorical structure of the two hymns and the concern both authors express for the problems of verbal inadequacy in attempting to express divine love. The *persona* of each text is not a lover, but a theorist of love, who is providing what are essentially commentaries on Ficino's pre-text in a selfconscious manner. Through the statements negating expression in the envoy of Benivieni's poem, and the skeptical voices heard at the beginning and end of Bembo's speech, both texts come to be framed ironically. The doubts and uncertainties which characterize the poetry and prose of Benivieni and Castiglione, absent in Ficino's own commentary, constitute the type of displacement of their model these authors effect.

The preceding summaries should indicate clearly how the Toronto conference addressed (as this volume of the proceedings also aims to do) some of the major issues involved in the study of Ficino and Renaissance Neoplatonism. And these are approached from a variety of points of view — from that of the philologist to that of the historian of ideas to, further, that of the literary critic, all sensitive to the nuances of the concepts and the style of their objects of investigation. Certain questions, like the connection between Ficino and Plotinus, or the definition of Leone Ebreo's Neoplatonic syncretism have elicited contrary conclusions from two scholars. Both are supported, nevertheless, by equally valid arguments.

What all thirteen contributions bear evidence of is the earnest attempt on the part of modernday students of Renaissance Neoplatonism to go beyond traditional views and sometimes outdated clichés. It has been their intention to reassess the data, old and new, and to reread the Neoplatonic texts — in their verbal and visual and auditory forms — afresh and with open minds. The volume which their efforts have created does not pretend to exhaust this inexhaustible topic, but it is a step in the right direction — one which established scholars like Kristeller and more recent arrivals on the scholarly scene like Craven have been pointing to in recent years.

The Editors

* The Editors wish to express their deepest gratitude to Kiloran McRae and A. Manuela Scarci, who were of great assistance in running the Conference and in preparing the proceedings for publication.

NOTES

1 Paul Oskar Kristeller, 'L'Etat présent des études sur Marsile Ficin,' in *Platon et Aristote à la Renaissance. XVI Colloque Internationale de Tours* (Paris: Vrin, 1976), pp. 59-76, provides a long list of topics for further study needed on Ficino.
2 William George Craven, *Giovanni Pico della Mirandola, Symbol of His Age: Modern Interpretations of a Renaissance Philosopher* (Geneva: Droz, 1981), points out the pitfalls in all theories presented to date on Pico.

William R. Bowen

Ficino's Analysis of Musical *Harmonia**

Ficino's discussion of music is too complex to treat adequately in a single paper. Therefore, the subject of this essay will be limited to an aspect of his thought that up to this point has received little attention, his analysis of musical *harmonia*. It should be mentioned that the Latin word *harmonia* is used in preference to its English cognate, 'harmony,' because Ficino follows ancient tradition and primarily considers *harmonia* in terms of the proper collocation of consecutive sounds, or, more abstractly, as the scale structure underlying true melody, rather than in terms of the simultaneous combination of sounds commonly associated with 'harmony.'[1] This analysis takes place in the mathematical discipline known today as harmonic science, or by its classical name, *harmonikē*.[2]

The identification of the intrinsic nature of music as *harmonia*, that is, as the fitting or joining together of diverse but mutually adaptable elements, is one of the richest notions in the history of ideas,[3] and one which figures prominently in Renaissance Platonism.[4] For Ficino and his contemporaries, the *harmonia* embodied in music, specifically, in the mutual adjustment of high and low pitch, is a structural principle that has unlimited manifestations throughout the universe. Thus, as audible *harmonia*, instrumental and vocal music come to have cosmological significance.

Indeed, in definitions of music, Ficino consistently points out that audible music merely imitates its metaphysical archetypes. For example, in the letter, *De Rationibus Musice* (*On the Principles of Music*), he defines true music (*vera musica*) as the agreement of the powers (*vires*) and of the motions (*motus*) belonging to the rational soul (*animus*). Audible music is but an image of true music.[5] Further, in the letter *De Divino Furore* (*On Divine Madness*), Ficino elaborates the Platonic conception of music that serves as the foundation for his own thought:

Through the ears, however, the soul draws in the sweetest concords and numbers, and by these images is reminded of, and called forth to, the divine music which has to be contemplated by a certain more acute and profound sense of mind. Moreover, according to the Platonists, divine music is twofold. They think that the one, certainly, exists in the eternal mind of

God; [that] the other, in truth, [exists] in the order and motions of the heavens through which the heavenly spheres and orbits effect a wonderful concord; in fact, that our soul was a participant of both before it was imprisoned in [our] bodies. Yet [the soul] uses the ears as certain gaps and entire [chinks] in this prison and by these, as we have already said many times, perceives the images of that incomparable music. By which [images] [the soul] is led back to a certain profound and silent recollection of the *harmonia* in which it earlier enjoyed itself . . .[6]

In this analysis, divine music originates in God's mind, the source of all Ideas, and is revealed in the disposition and motion of the celestial spheres: the rational or incorporeal soul has a natural affinity for this music but is held back by the imperfection inherent in corporeal being. Hence, it appears that the archetype of music is ultimately located in God's mind and is manifested throughout the hierarchy of souls, including the World Soul, the lesser cosmic souls associated with the celestial bodies, and, finally, the souls of men. Ficino goes on to observe that, driven by the desire to recover the pure state of his soul and to enjoy true or divine music, man strives to imitate the ideal *harmonia* through audible music and poetry.[7]

Ficino's conviction that the corporeal world is imperfect because of its mutability is a fundamental thesis in his understanding of the hierarchy of being,[8] a hierarchy which corresponds precisely with a hierarchical classification of knowledge (*scientia, epistēmē*) or philosophy (*philosophia*).[9] Since Ficino, with Renaissance Platonists, locates true knowledge and wisdom (*sapientia*)[10] in speculative thought whose objects are purely intelligible, he seeks to reach ultimate truths by determining the real essences exhibited in sensible particulars.[11] For him, knowledge of the essence of things and the structure of the universe cannot reside in the uncertainty of experience, the basis of empirical science. Experience of sensible objects provides a primitive and inferior source for insights into, and recollection of, purely intelligible objects. Therefore, while speculative science aims to save the appearance of natural phenomena, it must explain them through the principles of metaphysics. In other words, the mind, not the ear, is the judge of music.

The key to bridging the gap between the sensible experience of *harmonia* and true knowledge of its nature lies in number. For Ficino and, indeed, for many writers throughout the Middles Ages and the Renaissance, the Biblical verse, *omnia in mensura, et numero et pondere disposuisti*[12] (You have ordered all things in measure, and number, and weight), provides divine authority for a tenet of their epistemology, which is, in order to reason about all that we perceive, we must quantify.[13] Numbers are intermediaries between the corporeality and mutability of particulars and the incorporeality and immutability of essences;[14] the numbers themselves, with their unchanging properties, give certainty of knowledge of the reality behind the world of sense perception.[15] Thus, regardless of whether an individual theorist subscribes to the extreme position of the Pythagorean school which reduces all things to number, or to the more moderate Platonic and Aristotelian characterization of numbers as forms and formal causes, arithmological or numerological studies are vital to grasping the principles of God's creation.[16]

Given Ficino's hierarchical theories of being and knowledge, the study of *harmonia* at any one of its levels or manifestations presupposes principles confirmed in superior disciplines. Further, because numbers, or, to be more precise, whole numbers in certain ratios, define the essence of *harmonia*, the scientific analysis of *harmonia* found in *harmonikē* is subsumed under arithmetic in the quadrivium.[17] This analysis must not be confused with the examination of the physical properties of sound itself, the subject of acoustical physics. In *harmonikē*, theorists study audible *harmonia* with a view to uncovering purely intelligible (not physical) causes. Thus, any theorist whose aim is to establish those musical ratios that define and govern musicality or the *harmonia* evident in the combination of sounds must consider arithmological arguments about number itself. Furthermore, if the theorist subscribes to a Platonic conception of music like the one espoused by Ficino, wherein vocal and instrumental music imitate divine archetypes, philosophical arguments concerning the structure of the soul and of the cosmos are not mere adjuncts to the scientific discussion of music; they are essential components.

In this way the study of audible *harmonia* begins with sensible objects but ascends to the contemplation of intelligible causes. The interdisciplinary character of this ascent is immediately apparent if one lists the different stages. First, harmonic science analyses melody by reducing it to its most basic sensible phenomena, namely, certain intervals formed by the arrangement of individual pitches[18]: in so far as melody does not consist in a single sound, but in the interrelations of pitches, the basic musical phenomenon is the interval, not the note. Next, in order to measure musical intervals, *harmonikē* relies on physical or natural science. Because the classical acoustical physics assumed by the Renaissance lacked a theory for establishing absolute pitch, it had no means to quantify a single isolated sound.[19] However, this science was able to quantify the arrangement of two discrete pitches forming a musical interval. The theory is simple. By measuring the lengths of two sonant strings which produce a specific interval, one can quantify the interval as a numerical ratio.[20] Such information allows us to define and, therefore, reproduce a specific interval. Thus the theory does not aim to reproduce the same pitches, but rather their relationship as a musical interval. In short, the acoustical physics accepted by Ficino and his contemporaries gave harmonic science its foundation in relative, not absolute, quantity.

After quantifying intervals as ratios of whole numbers, the analysis continues and ascends from the discussion of sounds to their ultimate formal principles. In other words, harmonic science moves from the consideration of the sensible to the purely intelligible elements of melody, from sounds and intervals to the ratios which define the intervals, and then from these ratios to the numbers which define them. By crossing the boundary into the superior disciplines of arithmetic and metaphysics, the analysis arrives at a specific set of elementary numbers which contains within itself all musical ratios. Once the numbers have been established by arithmological and metaphysical argument, *harmonikē* proceeds by synthesis. First, from this set of numbers, harmonic theory derives a limited set of elementary ratios. Next, from these ratios are deduced, according to well established rules, the remaining melodic ratios. Finally, since ratios are the essence of intervals and scales are sequences of intervals, the synthesis culminates, in effect, with the derivation and justification of scale structure.

By emphasizing the explanatory character of harmonic science in the context of the ascent to wisdom, it becomes propaedeutic to metaphysics.[21] Although such a philosophical purpose is prominent in the history of harmonic science, and appears in certain writers as Ficino, Renaissance musicians tend to emphasize the sterility of such a purpose if pursued exclusively, that is, without returning to the practical ramifications.[22] Because the science has the authority of a systematic or scientific derivation from first principles, it also prescribes musicality and establishes a canon for the criticism of music practice. Hence, knowledge of *harmonikē* is considered essential to the perfect musician who, ideally, combines the contemplation of music with its practice.[23] In other words, harmonic science belongs to philosophical inquiry and to the study of music practice, and so serves both the philosopher and the musician.

Having completed this summary of the structure of the harmonic science associated with Ficino and, indeed, with Renaissance Platonism as a whole, his analysis of *harmonia* can be further characterized by examining a significant inconsistency in his account of musical scales. Ficino describes two scales, the first in his commentary on Plato's *Timaeus*, and the second in the *De Rationibus Musice*. The inconsistency is that, even though both scales derive from the same ultimate elements, they differ in their structure.

The ultimate elements themselves deserve attention. Although Ficino demonstrates considerable flexibility in his arithmology, in the context of his music theory he relies on the primacy of the *tetraktys* of the decad. Because integers after the number ten or decad repeat the progression from one to nine, the decad came to be recognized as containing the elements of number and, in Pythagorean and Neoplatonic sources, as a paradigm for the cosmos: the members of the decad form elements not only of arithmetic, but of all things measured, and indeed, constituted by number.[24] The *tetraktys*, here understood as the numbers 1, 2, 3, and 4, has several unique properties, of which the most obvious is that the addition of its constituent numbers (1 + 2 + 3 + 4) makes ten.[25] According to the Pythagorean tradition, the *tetraktys* represents the decad and is an inseparable manifestation of it. For Ficino, then, the first four numbers constitute first principles of the universe.[26] From these four numbers, he derives the ratios which are the purely intelligible principles of music.

In the chapters on Pythagorean and Platonic music theory, Ficino establishes 2:1, 3:2, and 4:3 as the primary ratios, defining the most pleasing concords, or intervals, of the octave, fifth and fourth.[27] Given that these ratios are the intelligible elements of *harmonikē*, all other musical ratios (including those which define discordant intervals) and, eventually, all musical scales must derive from them. For our purposes, it is not necessary to go over the methods involved in producing scales; indeed, Ficino himself glosses over the subject. However, by elaborating Plato's construction of the World-Soul, commonly referred to as the *Timaeus* scale, Ficino supplies an adequate model.[28] Essentially, the procedure involves the partition of the scale by the elementary concords, followed by their manipulation in order to collocate and derive other musical intervals. To be more specific, this manipulation occurs in two ways: either by the addition and subtraction of the primary concords, which is equivalent to the compounding and division of their ratios, or by the insertion of arithmetic and harmonic means into musical ratios. The net result of the operations mentioned in the commentary is the Pythagorean scale outlined in the following diagram.

Note in particular that the Pythagorean scale acknowledges three primary concords, the octave, fifth and fourth; and further, that the smaller intervals of the tone and semitone have the ratios 9:8 and 256:243 respectively.

The musical elements of the second scale, known as the syntonic diatonic, again derive from the *tetraktys* of the decad. Yet, in this case, the relationship of the first four numbers to the primary ratios is less direct than in the Pythagorean scale. Here, Ficino justifies the musical elements by referring to the relative lengths of sonant strings. Given two strings of equal length, one string is extended so that the relative lengths can be described as (greater : lesser), or, in Ficino's terms, (whole + added part : whole). Whether or not the resulting interval is a concord depends on the commensurability of the whole and the added part. Ficino concludes that, if the added part is a ¼, ⅓, ½, ⅟₁ of the whole, the strings produce one of the elementary concords.[29]

string lengths	musical ratio	interval
1 + 1 / 4 : 1	5:4	third
1 + 1 / 3 : 1	4:3	fourth
1 + 1 / 2 : 1	3:2	fifth
1 + 1 / 1 : 1	2:1	octave

The connection with the *tetraktys* is inescapable, even though Ficino does not specifically mention it in this particular portion of the letter. Whereas in the Pythagorean scale the *tetraktys* was the source for both terms of ratio (4:3, 3:2, 2:1), here the significant number is the partition of the string represented by the added part, or, equivalently, the lesser term in the whole-number ratio.

On the basis of this procedure, Ficino names the octave (2:1), fifth (3:2), fourth (4:3) and major third (5:4) as concords. Moreover, by using arithmological arguments, Ficino reorders the concords so that the major third stands before the fourth, as it was recognized in music practice. The resulting scale is outlined in the diagram. Note that the two scales differ not only in the number of elementary concords, but also in the fact that the syntonic diatonic has two different tones.

To appreciate the conflict, one may recall the context in which these scales are discussed. The Pythagorean scale is found in a commentary which concentrates solely on a venerable tradition. The syntonic diatonic (a scale also know in antiquity) appears in an unpublished, personal letter which evidences concern for contemporary musical practice and, at the same time, adheres to the traditional choice of ultimate elements. Viewed in this light, the conflict shows Ficino accommodating the requirements of traditional theory to contemporary musical practice and signals a characteristic problem of Renaissance harmonic science which was eventually resolved by abandoning traditional theory altogether. That Ficino does not directly address this conflict is a function of his over-riding interest in the role of harmonic science as a means of philosophical ascent to the One. Hence he dwells at greater length on the first principles of harmonic science rather than the derivation of musical phenomena from them.

Centre for Reformation and Renaissance Studies
Victoria University

Notes

* I here express my sincere thanks to Dr. Alan C. Bowen and Prof. Paul Oskar Kristeller for their detailed comments on this article. I also acknowledge with gratitude the support of the Social Sciences and Humanities Research Council of Canada; the final version of this paper was completed during my tenure of a Postdoctoral Fellowship.

 1 That harmonic science traditionally explains proper scale structure underlying musical melody does not, of course, exclude it from being relevant to the judgement of simultaneously (as opposed to consecutively) sounded pitches. Nevertheless, because the word 'harmony' is predominantly associated with the analysis of music in terms of tonality and chordal structure, an analysis that is essentially anachronistic to the music theory of the fifteenth century, it should be avoided.

 2 Renaissance theorists, including Ficino, do not consistently employ a single name for *harmonikē*. In most cases, they refer to it as *musica theorica* or *speculativa*, and as the *scientia* or *philosophia* of music. See William R. Bowen, 'Music and Number: An Introduction to Renaissance Harmonic Science' (Ph.D. dissertation, University of Toronto, 1984), pp. 14-16.

 3 The perception of music as *harmonia* has attracted the most attention in the study of classical authors. For an introduction to the concept and its interpretation, see W.A. Anderson, *Ethos and Education in Greek Music: The Evidence of Poetry and Philosophy* (Cambridge, Mass.: Harvard University Press, 1966), pp. 191-5; L. Spitzer, *Classical and Christian Ideas of World Harmony*, ed. A.G. Hatcher (Baltimore: John Hopkins Press, 1963); E.A. Lippman, *Musical Thought in Ancient Greece* (New York: Columbia University Press, 1964), Ch.1 *et passim*, and 'Hellenic Conceptions of Harmony,' *Journal of the American Musicological Society* 16 (1963) 3-35; T.J. Mathiesen, 'Problems of Terminology in Ancient Greek Theory: 'APMONIA,' in *Festival Essays for Pauline Alderman*, ed. B.L. Karson (Provo, Utah: Brigham Young University Press, 1976), pp. 3-17.

 4 Two recent studies contain valuable discussions of *harmonia* in Renaissance thought: S.K. Heninger, Jr., *Touches of Sweet Harmony* (San Marino, Calif.: The Huntington Library, 1974), and D. Koenigsberger, *Renaissance Man and Creative Thinking* (Atlantic Highlands, N.J.: Humanities Press, 1979).

5 Ficino, *De Rationibus Musice*, in *Supplementum Ficinianum*, P.O. Kristeller, ed., 2 vols. (Florence: Leo S. Olschki, 1973), I, 51.

6 Ficino, *De Divino Furore* in *Epistolae* (Venice, 1495), f. 4r-v.

... per aures vero concentus quosdam numerosque suavissimos animus haurit. Hisque imaginibus admonetur atque excitatur ad divinam musicam acriori quodam mentis & intimo sensu considerandam. Est autem apud platonicos interpretes divina musica duplex: alteram profecto in eterna dei mente consistere arbitrantur, alteram vero in coelorum ordine ac motibus qua mirabilem quendam coelestes globi orbesque concentum efficiunt, utriusque vero animum nostrum ante quam corporibus clauderetur participem extitisse: verum iis in tenebris auribus velut rimulis quibusdam ac cunctiis utitur hisque imagines ut saepe iam diximus musicae illius incomparabilis accipit. Quibus in eius qua antea fruebatur harmoniae intimam quandam ac tacitam recordationem reducitur ...

Punctuation marks have been added to clarify the sentence structure. Compare *Epistolarum* I in *Opera omnia*, 2 vols. (Basel, 1576; facsimile edition, Turin: Bottega d'Erasmo, 1962), I, 614. The translation is my own; for another translation, see Ficino, *The Letters of Marsilio Ficino*, trans. by members of the Language Department of the School of Economic Science, London (London: Shepheard-Walwyn, 1975), I.7, 45. On the history of the letter, see S. Gentile, 'In margine all'Epistola "De divino furore" di Marsilio Ficino,' *Rinascimento* 23 (1983) 33-77.

7 Ficino, *De Divino Furore, Epistolarum* I in *Opera* I, 614.

8 For an introduction to Ficino's hierarchy of being, see P.O. Kristeller, *The Philosophy of Marsilio Ficino*, trans. V. Conant (Gloucester, Mass.: Peter Smith, 1964; repr. of New York, 1943), Chs. 5-6. The concept of a hierarchical and continuous order in the universe can be traced from antiquity to the Renaissance: A.O. Lovejoy, *The Great Chain of Being. A Study of the History of an Idea* (Cambridge, Mass.: Harvard University Press, 1936), Chs. 1-4; E.P. Mahoney, 'Metaphysical Foundations of the Hierarchy of Being According to Some Late-Medieval and Renaissance Philosophers,' in *Philosophies of Existence, Ancient and Medieval*, ed. P. Morewedge (New York: Fordham University Press, 1982), pp. 165-257 (on Ficino, see pp. 188-92).

9 The scholastic division of philosophy appears to be the most common model: for example, see Ficino's *Summa Philosophie* and *Divisio Philosophie* presented by P.O. Kristeller, 'The Scholastic Background of Marsilio Ficino,' in *Studies in Renaissance Thought and Letters* (Rome: Edizioni di Storia e Letteratura, 1956), pp. 56, 95-6; also Ficino, *Théologie platonicienne de l'immortalité des âmes*, ed. and trans. R. Marcel, 3 vols. (Paris: Les Belles Lettres, 1964-70), II, 225-6, and *De Lumine* 12 in *Opera* I, 982.

10 Ficino occasionally uses *sapientia, scientia, prudentia*, and *ars*, to parallel the scholastic hierarchy of metaphysical, natural (physical), practical (moral), and productive sciences: *Theol. Plat.* VIII.3, Marcel ed., I, 296, and *Epistolarum* V, *Opera* I, 657. But note, the meaning of the terminology is not rigid — in other circumstances, *scientia*, as the knowledge of divine things, is synonymous with *sapientia*: *In Theaetetum Platonis, Opera* II, 1281. For a general study of the hierarchy of knowledge, see E.F. Rice, Jr., *The Renaissance Idea of Wisdom* (Cambridge, Mass.: Harvard University Press, 1958), especially Ch. 3.

11 Ficino considers this progression from natural to divine things to be fundamental to both Platonic and Aristotelian philosophy: *Compendium in Timaeum, Opera* II, 1438.

12 Wisdom 11:21. For example, Ficino cites the verse in *Epistolarum* VI, *Opera* I, 822.

13 Plato, *Epinomis* 977b-978 with Ficino, *In Epinomidem*, *Opera* II, 1526. Also Ficino, *In Philebum Commentariorum* I.28, *Opera* II, 1236. I am grateful to Prof. Charles Trinkaus for discussing this point with me after the conference. His evaluation of Ficino's approach to measuring and numbering supports my analysis: see C. Trinkaus, 'Protagoras in the Renaissance: An Exploration,' in *Philosophy and Humanism. Renaissance Essays in Honor of Paul Oskar Kristeller*, ed. E.P. Mahoney (New York: Columbia University Press, 1976), p. 207.

14 In this framework, mathematics is the mean between metaphysics and physics: see Ficino, *Compendium in Timaeum*, *Opera* II, 1438, with Kristeller, *The Philosophy of Marsilio Ficino*, pp. 222-3, 301-4, and E. Garin on the *pia philosophia*, *Italian Humanism. Philosophy and Civic Life in the Renaissance*, trans. P.Munz (Oxford: Basil Blackwell, 1965), pp. 92-3. Consult C. Trinkaus on Cusanus and Ficino, 'Protagoras in the Renaissance,' in *Philosophy and Humanism*, ed. E.P. Mahoney, pp. 199-207. Also see G. Boas's discussion of number as the key to knowledge of order and beauty, 'Philosophies of Science in Florentine Platonism,' in *Art, Science, and History in the Renaissance*, ed. C.S. Singleton (Baltimore: John Hopkins Press, 1967), pp. 242-4.

15 On account of its precision and certainty, mathematics is used to advance the study of physical phenomena and to reach a greater understanding of God: M. Boas, *The Scientific Renaissance 1450-1630* (New York: Harper Torchbooks, 1966; c. 1962), pp. 197-9; E. Cassirer, *The Individual and the Cosmos in Renaissance Philosophy*, trans. M. Domandi (Philadelphia: University of Pennsylvania Press, 1972; c. 1963), pp. 52-4, 153-4 *et passim*; P.L. Rose, *The Italian Renaissance of Mathematics* (Geneva: Librairie Droz, 1975), p. 6 *et passim*.

16 As Kristeller points out in a discussion of the impact of Platonism on the mathematical sciences, such speculative (nonempirical) studies generally focus either on the symbolic or mathematical properties of numbers. 'Renaissance Platonism,' in *Renaissance Thought. The Classic, Scholastic, and Humanist Strains* (New York: Harper Torchbooks, 1961), p. 66.

17 In both the division of philosophy (see sources cited n. 9 *supra*) and in the liberal arts, *harmonikē* was usually assigned to the quadrivium: N.C. Carpenter, *Music in the Medieval and Renaissance Universities* (New York: Da Capo Press, 1972; repr. of Norman, Oklahoma, 1958); P.O. Kristeller, 'The Modern System of the Arts,' in *Renaissance thought and the Arts* (Princeton, N.J.: Princeton University Press, 1980), pp. 163-89; E.A. Lippman, 'The Place of Music in the System of the Liberal Arts,' in *Aspects of Medieval and Renaissance Music*, ed. J. LaRue (New York: W.W. Norton & Company, Inc., 1966), pp. 545-59; G.W. Peitzsch, *Die Klassifikation der Musik von Boethius bis Ugolino von Orvieto* (Halle: Max Niemeyer Verlag, 1929). However, when combined with music practice, the classification of music was less consistent, at times suggesting a conception of fine arts: see Ficino, *Epistolarum* XI, *Opera* I, 944 with A. Chastel, *Marsile Ficin et l'art* (Geneva: Librairie Droz, 1975, c. 1954), p. 61. Ficino follows traditional accounts of the mathematical sciences when he characterizes music (with stereometry and astronomy) as less pure, or less abstract, than arithmetic and geometry because of the association with a physical phenomenon, sound: Ficino, *De Republica* VII, *Opera* II, 1411.

18 The other parts of melody, rhythm and text, have no part in this science. The separation of the subjects is traditional: see R.L. Crocker, '*Musica Rhythmica* and *Musica Metrica* in Antique and Medieval Theory,' *Journal of Music Theory* 2 (1958) 2-3.

19 For an introduction to the acoustical physics assumed by Ficino, see Bowen, 'Music and Number,' pp. 45-8 and 63-9.

20 On the meaning of musical ratios, see Bowen, 'Music and Number,' pp. 73-8.

21 The conception of the music treatise as a *protreptikos* is considered in L. Schrade, 'Music in the Philosophy of Boethius,' *Musical Quarterly* 33 (1947) 188-200; A. Seay, 'Ugolino of Orvieto,' *Musica Disciplina* 9 (1955) 145-51. Also see L.A. Gushee's discussion of the classification of music treatises, 'Questions of Genre in Medieval Treatises on Music,' in *Gattungen der Musik in Einzeldarstellungen*, ed. W. Arlt, E. Lichtenhahn, & H. Oesch (Bern: Francke, 1973), pp. 365-433.

22 For example, see Gioseffo Zarlino, *Le istitutioni harmoniche* (Venice, 1558; facs. ed., New York: Broude Brothers, 1965), I.3-4 & 11.

23 Ficino, *De Rationibus Musice, Suppl.* I, 51.

24 Ficino consistently refers to the *denarius* as the *numerus universus*: *In Phaedrum Commentum* 25, *Opera* II, 1379; *De Republica* VIII.3, *Opera* II, 1415-16; *In Timaeum* 28, *Opera* II, 1451.

25 Ficino, *De Republica* VIII.7, *Opera* II, 1418 and *In Timaeum* 20, *Opera* II, 1446.

26 The comprehensiveness of Ficino's treatment of the *tetraktys* is indicated at *In Timaeum* 20, *Opera* II, 1446-7.

27 The central discussion of Pythagorean and Platonic music theory is found in chapters 29-32 of the *Timaeus* commentary, *Opera* II, 1453-8. The primacy of the octave, fifth, and fourth is assumed throughout this commentary and, indeed, throughout all of his writings: for example, see *In Timaeum* 32, *Opera* II, 1456 and *De Republica* VIII.12-13, *Opera* II, 1420-2. However, Ficino does not always make a clear distinction between the primary concords and the intervals derived from them, that is, their compounds and the discords: *De Republica* III, *Opera* II, 1400 and *In Philebum* I.28, *Opera* II, 1235-6.

28 Ficino, *In Timaeum* 33-6, *Opera* II, 1458-61 with Plato, *Timaeus* 35a-36b.

29 Ficino, *De Rationibus Musice, Suppl.* I, 53-4.

Francis Broun

The Louvre 'Concert Champêtre': A Neoplatonic Interpretation

The subject of this paper is one of the most celebrated works in the history of art, the *Concert champêtre* in the Louvre.[1] It is one of the most beautiful and at the same time one of the most influential of all Venetian paintings, an evocation of pastoral bliss that inspired an entire type of picture — the idyllic landscape.

For several centuries the authorship of Giorgione was rarely questioned, but lately there has been a tendency to favour his slightly younger contemporary, Titian.[2] In fact both of them may have had a hand in it. After Giorgione's tragically early death in 1510 some of the pictures left unfinished in his studio were completed by Titian, the best known being the Dresden *Venus* to which Titian contributed parts of the landscape and a Cupid that has since been painted out.[3] My own feeling is that Giorgione was responsible at least for the conception of the *Concert champêtre*, and I would still like to believe that he executed most of it as well.

However controversial the picture's attribution may be, even more discussion has surrounded the question of its interpretation. One school of thought maintains, sometimes vehemently, that the artist's sole motivation was to give pleasure to his friends, those 'young Venetian aristocrats who loved good painting and were indifferent to subject matter.'[4] Kenneth Clark suggested that 'although it tells no story, and the most determined iconologists have been unable to saddle it with a subject, its theme is not altogether new, for artists had enjoyed painting picnics since the fourteenth century.'[5] This attitude can be summed up in the words of Charles Blanc: 'quelle absence de sujet!'[6]

Other writers speak in very general terms of playful nymphs and balmy air, but more serious consideration has to be given to the few scholars who have tried to analyse the picture in terms of Renaissance thought. Foremost among these is Patricia Egan, who compared the painting to representations of *Poesia*.[7] Her arguments are too persuasive to be dismissed lightly, although she fails to provide an adequate explanation for the two youths who, by compositional and other means, are accorded equal value with their female companions. What

this present analysis will demonstrate is that the primary source of inspiration for the *Concert champêtre* was Marsilio Ficino's *Commentary on
Plato's 'Symposium'*, the *De Amore*, although Giorgione's genius was such
that he was quite capable of incorporating several sources and several
levels of meaning in a single work.[8]

Some of the suggestions that have been made for an interpretation
of the *Tempest* provide an idea of the complexity of Giorgione's art: the
painter and his family; Paris being suckled; Apollo being suckled;
Adrastos with Hypsipyle suckling Opheltes; the Finding of Moses; Dio-
nysus in his role as Messiah; Jupiter and Io; Venus and Adonis; the
legend of Geneviève; a pastoral allegory involving *Fortezza*, *Carità* and
Fortuna; an allegory of Venus Genetrix from the *Hypnerotomachia
Poliphili*. To complicate matters still further, x-rays have shown that
beneath the standing male figure is a second naked female, and so it is
even possible that Giorgione made this picture up as he went along,
with no specific meaning in mind beyond the picture's electric mood.[9]

This confusion is partly due to the fact that Giorgione was never
content merely to illustrate a particular idea. The intellectual content is
certainly present in paintings like these — and presumably would have
been perfectly clear to his educated contemporaries — but his prime
motivation as an artist was to produce images that were aesthetically
pleasing. In this way he could avoid an exclusive appeal either to the
mind or to the senses, and approach, rather, the faculty that lies pre-
cariously between the two, the faculty that Walter Pater has so aptly
labelled the 'imaginative reason.'[10]

The *Concert champêtre* is typical of a work that has endured because
of its lyrical beauty, even though, as the title currently in use suggests,
the original meaning has been lost. The scene is simply described. In
an idyllic landscape setting, four figures hold centre stage: two naked
women, one of them seated and carrying a pipe or flute, the other
standing and pouring water from a pitcher into a well; beyond them
two youths, one richly attired and playing a lute, the other shabbily
dressed and having nothing. This juxtaposition of clothed and naked
forms, combined with the young men's total disregard of the women,
strongly suggests that the mode of representation is allegorical rather
than realistic.

The most striking single feature of the *Concert champêtre*, and the focal point of the entire composition, is the gaze that passes with almost
palpable intensity between the two young men. If one looks carefully,
though, one can see that the eyes of the youth on the right are not directed towards his companion, but are lowered modestly to the ground. It
is therefore interesting to compare the picture in its present condition
(which is generally poor and over-painted) with the engraving in

Crozat's 1742 catalogue of the French royal collection.[11] Here the stare is most emphatically returned, and it is impossible to determine whether this was the original intention of the artist or whether the engraver has inferred it from the positioning of the heads.

When reading the *De Amore*, it is difficult to ignore the emphasis placed by Ficino on the eyes. Taken first in an abstract sense, they are compared with the Angelic Mind in that the eyes are attracted to the light of the sun in the same way that the Angelic Mind turns towards God. The eye 'at first dark and . . . formless, loves the light while it looks toward it; in so looking it is illuminated; in receiving the ray, it is informed with the colors and shapes of things.' (I,3)[12]

In a more practical vein, the role that the eye is said to play in the transmission of love is as ingenious as it is unlikely. The blood of a young man, being 'thin, clear, warm, and sweet' (VII,4; p. 159), is transformed into a vapour called spirit which 'sends out rays like itself through the eyes which are like glass windows' (VII,4; p. 159). The spirit, 'since it is very light, flies out most to the highest parts of the body, and its light shines out more copiously through the eyes since they themselves are transparent and the most shining of all the parts' (VII,4; p. 159). On entering the body of the 'wounded man,' the spirit passes immediately to the heart where it is condensed and turned back into blood (VII,4; p. 160). In this way, assuming that the love is reciprocated, there is a mutual exchange of identity by which 'this one has himself, but in that one. That one also possesses himself, but in this one' (II,8; p. 56). All this happens very quickly, and is said to be as easily contracted as other contagious diseases like 'the itch, mange, leprosy, pneumonia, consumption, dysentery, pink-eye, and the plague' (VII,5; p. 162).

Lovers are best charmed therefore, when 'by very frequent gazing, directing their sight eye to eye, they join lights with lights and drink a long love together, poor wretches. As Musaeus says, the whole cause and origin of this illness is certainly the eye' (VII,10; p. 166). The eye is most effective when it is large, blue, and shining, while the 'harmony of the other parts besides the eyes seems not to have the power to cause this disease but only a tendency to occasion it' (VII,10; p. 166).

The function of the eye is to allow an appreciation of beauty, this being not so much a material entity but rather an image of it, 'comprehended or grasped by the soul through the sight' (V,3; p. 87). Beauty emanates from God, passes across the Angelic Mind and the World-Soul, and finally lodges in the body. From there 'it shines out, especially through the eyes, the transparent windows of the soul' (VI,10; p. 126), so that 'anyone who is beautiful bewitches us with his youthful eyes' (VI,10; p. 127).

Final evidence of the overwhelming power of the eyes can be found in the recommended cure for love. Apart from the more mundane suggestions of the Arabian physician, Rhazes, who prescribed 'coitus, fasting, inebriation, and walking' (VI,9; p. 122), we are told that the lover can be saved only if he is 'especially careful lest the lights of [his] eyes be joined' with those of the beloved (VII,11; p. 167).

The two youths in the *Concert champêtre* seem to illustrate well enough Ficino's emphasis on the eyes, but so far nothing has been said to suggest that they are anything other than ordinary mortal lovers. However, if we return to the *De Amore*, it will be possible to establish that they are far more than this: they are personifications of Love itself.

'On the birthday of Venus, while the Gods were feasting, Porus, the son of Counsel, drunk with nectar, lay with Penia in the garden of Jupiter. From this union was born Love' (VI,7; p. 116). The child of Porus and Penia (Plenty and Poverty), Love is thus vested with a dual personality which is represented in the *Concert champêtre*.

As the son of Poverty, Love is described as 'dry, thin, and squalid, bare-footed, humble, without a home, without a bed, and without any cover: sleeping on doorsteps, on the road, under the sky; and finally, . . . always needy' (VI,9; p. 120). As the son of Plenty, 'he lies in wait for the beautiful and the good. He is manly, bold and high-strung, impetuous, a crafty and keen-scented hunter, always laying new traps, devoted to prudence, eloquent, philosophizing all of his life, a sorcerer, an enchanter, powerful, a magician, and a sophist' (VI,9; p. 120).

Had Giorgione been a lesser artist, he might have been tempted to introduce so many of these ingredients that he would have produced nothing more than dry and unimaginative stereotypes. His prime concern as we have seen was to maintain the aesthetic unity of the picture, and this he did by selecting only those elements that can most naturally be included in such an idyllic scene. From these, if one has the necessary knowledge, the rest of the information can be inferred.

That one of the young men is the son of Poverty is indicated by his costume and unkempt hair, both of which are in striking contrast to the more fashionable and colourful appearance of his companion. He is shown to be humble by the downward direction of his head, and also by the eyes which are probably lowered. The identification of this figure is so far inconclusive, but one piece of evidence assures the plausibility of the other details. This is the naked foot that protrudes in an awkward manner from the back of the seated woman. As a compositional device it continues the diagonal line of the small hill at the left of the picture, but to achieve this continuity of design the artist could have used a wide variety of equally effective motifs. This seems to be a determinedly naked foot, and so some special significance can presumably be attached to it. Love is bare-footed, says Diotima in the *De Amore*, because the 'lover is so much occupied with matters of love that in the other affairs of life, public as well as private, he does not proceed as cautiously as he should, but, without any anticipation of dangers, is rashly carried anywhere. For this reason in his travels he encounters frequent dangers, not unlike those who do not protect their feet with leather. Whence they are hurt by frequent thorns and pebbles' (VI,9; p. 123).

Love as the son of Plenty is depicted in the same laconic manner, although again Giorgione could have easily over-loaded the figure with all the attributes of his rank. His identity is suggested by his rich clothing and also by such details as the fact that he is shown in profile, a device which adds authority to his pose. Again, there is one single element that helps to clarify the others, and here it is his action of serenading his companion. In affairs of the heart, the son of Plenty is 'clever and crafty . . . , so that in marvelous ways he goes bird-catching for the beloved's favor, whether he snares him with traps, or captures him with attentions, or appeases him with eloquence, or soothes him with song' (VI,10; p. 125). Giorgione selects from this list the element which can be most successfully incorporated into a 'concert,' and in this way he continues to maintain the overall unity of the picture.

Music is perceived by the sense of hearing which, together with the mind and sight, is one of the faculties that enables us to enjoy beauty (I,4; p. 41). In this context Orpheus speaks of the three graces; Splendour, Viridity and Abundant Joy. 'That grace and beauty of the soul which consists in brightness of truth and virtue he calls "Splendor." Pleasantness of shape and color he calls "Viridity," for this flourishes most in the greenness of youth. Finally, that pure, powerful, and perpetual pleasure which we experience in musical melody he calls "Joy"' (pp. 86-87). In Agathon's speech, 'Love is said to soothe with his song the minds of gods and men' (V,9; p. 98), while those depressed by love because of adverse humours are advised that the 'pleasures of music and love are [reliefs] of this kind. For we can devote our energy to no other pleasures so continuously as to the charms of music and voices and the attractions of beauty' (VI,9; p. 122).

Having thus established the identity of the two male figures, attention can now be focused on their female counterparts. As might be expected, their true identities are revealed by seemingly minor details of pose and gesture. By analysing these it will be discovered that, just as the youths represent the dual personality of Love, so the females represent the twin nature of Venus.

'The first Venus, which is in the Mind, is said to have been born of
Uranus without a mother, because *mother*, to the physicists is *matter*.
But that Mind is a stranger to any association with corporeal matter'
(II,7; p. 53). As pure 'intelligence,' which relates her to the son of
Plenty (who is also the grandson of Counsel), she is contrasted to the
second Venus, the daughter of Jupiter and Dione, who is 'the power of
procreation attributed to the World Soul' (II,7; p. 54). The first 'is en-
tranced by an innate love for understanding the Beauty of God'; the
second, 'by her love for procreating that same beauty in bodies. The
former Venus first embraces the splendor of divinity in herself; then
she transfers it to the second Venus. The latter Venus transfers sparks
of that splendor into the Matter of the world' (II,7; p. 54). These Venuses, with their twin Loves, are present in the human soul so that
when the beauty of a physical body meets the eye it appeals first, via
the Heavenly Venus, to the mind, and secondly, via the Earthly Venus,
to the power of generation within us which wishes to recreate a similar
beauty. The Love in each case is thus the desire to contemplate beauty
and the desire to propagate it.

An important change takes place here. Whereas the Earthly Venus
had previously been held reprehensible because of her association with
physical love, she is now elevated by Ficino so that both loves are 'virtuous and praiseworthy, for each follows a divine image' (II,7; p. 54). We
learn later that in direct contrast to Plato's distinction between benevo-
lent and malevolent spirits, 'in reality both are good, since the procreation of offspring is considered to be as necessary and virtuous as the
pursuit of truth' (VI,8; p. 119). It is mainly because of this new interpretation of the Earthly Venus that I consider Ficino, rather than Plato
himself, to have been the primary source of the iconography of the
Concert champêtre.

The Venuses shown here are so closely related in physical type that
they can be seen as two views of one physical model, in the same way
that their characters are two facets of the same being. The left figure
stands facing the viewer, her torso slightly twisted as she empties water
from a pitcher into a well. Her erect stance makes her appear superior
to her 'sister,' but it is the gesture of pouring which identifies her most
clearly as the Heavenly Venus. This action classes her as the Source, a
title which she merits as being closest to *the* source, God, whom Ficino
describes as the 'fountain of Counsel' (VI,7; p. 116). It is from her, as
we have seen, that the glory of God descends into the World-Soul and
thence to earthly matter, and so it is perhaps her privileged rank that
draws her slightly apart from the close grouping of the other figures.

The pose of the second Venus, while hardly leading us to believe
that 'we stand on the verge of the lascivious,' as was suggested a hun-

dred years ago,[13] is nevertheless sensual enough to have inspired
Dante Gabriel Rossetti's poem 'For a Venetian Pastoral by Giorgione':

> Whither stray
> Her eyes now, from whose mouth the slim pipes creep
> And leave it pouting, while the shadowed grass
> Is cool against her naked side?[14]

She is thus as firmly connected with the earth as the Heavenly Venus,
balanced on only one visible foot, seems almost to float above it.

As a kind of included footnote, this seems to be an appropriate place
to mention the fact that the poses of Giorgione's Venuses can be helpful in the identification of similar figures. The *Venus* from Dresden has
only one visible foot; Titian's *Venus of Urbino* has two — though only
just![15] From this evidence alone it can perhaps be inferred that the
former is Heavenly, the latter Earthly. In the case of Titian's famous
Sacred and Profane Love, there has been some disagreement about
which woman is sacred and which is profane.[16] Again using the precedent of Giorgione's types, there can be little doubt that the seated figure is earthly, or profane, while her companion, minimally in contact
with the ground, is heavenly, or sacred.

Returning to the *Concert champêtre*, there is again one specific detail
which provides the key to the identity of the second Venus. This is the
wooden flute which, by its nature, places her in opposition to the more
highly favoured lute held by the son of Plenty. The *De Amore* mentions
two types of melody in music, one serious, the other playful: 'Plato . . .
judges the former to be beneficial to users and the latter harmful'
(III,3; p. 67). The flute is related by Plato to sensuous behaviour.
Aristotle is more lenient, claiming that although it is unsuitable for education, it is nevertheless useful for the relief of passions, and in this
he concurs more readily with the opinions of Agathon quoted above.[17]
It seems quite reasonable for Giorgione's Venus, who had already been
'vindicated' by Ficino, to carry an instrument previously associated with
her Platonic character, but which was also considered by many to be
less blameworthy.

One final figure remains to be explained: the shepherd who appears
in the middleground at the right of the picture. A shepherd is one of
the very few characters who could have been included in the *Concert
champêtre* without disturbing the essential harmony of the scene, and
his presence can once again be attributed to the *De Amore*. There we
are told that 'the true lover, like a shepherd, protects his flock of lambs
from the abyss and plague of false lovers, or wolves' (VII,16; p. 173).

The fact that the main group has been pushed to one side to accommodate this figure suggests that Giorgione wanted to stress the protective element in love.

In conclusion, I would like to focus on one small detail of the *Concert champêtre* which seems to epitomise Giorgione's extraordinary genius. In it we shall see his ability to combine several 'quotations' from the *De Amore* in a single motif, and thus to form a chain of associated ideas which adds immeasurably to the effectiveness of the work. I refer to the way in which the face of the right-hand youth is lit. Rather than stemming from the setting sun, the light seems to emanate from his companion, and it does so in such a way that it appears almost literally to dawn upon his features. This poetic passage alludes initially to the relationship which exists between the sons of Poverty and Plenty, with the former, as the 'inferior' of the two, being the recipient of the other's wisdom or illumination. However, its implications lead us far beyond this. I have already cited the lines which describe the eye receiving the glow of the sun as it is transformed from a blind to a receptive organ. This in turn relates to the soul, which, 'immediately after [it] is born from God, it turns toward Him as its parent by a certain natural instinct . . . Having turned toward Him, the soul is illuminated by His rays' (IV,4; p. 75). The radiating glow is connected also with physical beauty which is 'a certain grace shining' (V,6; p. 93) in the body, and which, in its perfect state, illumines with its own rays those things which are attracted to itself (VI,10; p. 130).

As a final example of this cumulative process of association we may cite a sentence from the discussion of the general nature of the eyes: 'it is said that the deified Augustus had eyes so bright and shining that when he stared at someone very hard, he forced him to lower his eyes, as if before the glow of the sun' (VII,4; pp. 159-60).

In suggesting a new interpretation for a work of art, a new title should also be proposed. The complexity and subtlety of the *Concert champêtre* cannot be summarised in a few words, but it seems logical to call this masterpiece an *Allegory of Neoplatonic Love and Beauty*.

Art Gallery of Ontario

Notes

1 Oil on canvas; 109 x 137 cm. I am happy to have the opportunity to express my thanks to Professor John Rupert Martin, for whom an earlier version of this paper was written. I also owe a considerable debt to Professor S.R. Jayne for his valued comments and advice.

2 A summary of attributions can be found in Terisio Pignatti, *Giorgione* (London: Phaidon, 1971), pp. 132-3, No. A42.

3 Pignatti, pp. 108-9, No. 23, Plates 103-5.

4 Lionello Venturi, *Four Steps Toward Modern Art* (New York: Columbia University Press, 1956), p. 8.

5 *The Nude* (New York: Pantheon Books, 1956), p. 121.

6 *Histoire des peintres de toutes les écoles: Ecole vénitienne* (Paris: Renouard, 1877), 'Le Giorgione,' p. 4.

7 *'Poesia* and the *Fête Champêtre'*, *Art Bulletin*, 41 (December, 1959), pp. 303-13.

8 Giorgione or his advisor presumably made use of the original Latin version of Ficino's text, published as part of the *Opera Platonis* in 1484 and re-issued in Venice in 1491.

9 Pignatti, pp. 101-2, No. 13.

10 *The Renaissance* (New York: Mentor Books, 1959), p. 93.

11 *Recueil d'Estampes dans le Cabinet du Roy* (Paris: 1742), II, Plate 138.

12 Marsilio Ficino, *Commentary on Plato's 'Symposium' on Love*, trans. Sears Jayne. (Dallas, TX: Spring Publications, 1985), p. 39; see also pp. 134-35, 144. Further references to Jayne's translation are made by means of page numbers inserted in the text. The original Latin references, taken from the critical edition (Marsile Ficin, *Commentaire sur le Banquet de Platon*, ed. Raymond Marcel. Paris: 'Les Belles Lettres', 1956) are the following:

'obscurus primo et ... informis lumen amat, dum aspicit; irradiatur aspiciendo; radium accipiendo rerum coloribus figurisque formatur' (p. 141);
'subtilis est, clarus, calidus atque dulcis' (p. 246);
'Ad altissimas quippe corporis partes spiritus, maxime cum sit levissimus, evolat, eiusque lumen per oculos, cum ipsi perspicui sint atque omnium partium nitidissimi, uberius emicat' (p. 247);
'saucii hominis' (p. 248);
'habet seipsum uterque et habet alterum. Iste quidem se habet sed in illo. Ille quoque se possidet, sed in isto' (pp. 156-57);
'si pruritum, si scabiem, si lepram, pleuresim, phtisim, disenteriam, lippitudinem, epidimiam' (p. 249);
'frequentissimo intuitu aciem visus ad aciem dirigentes, lumina iungunt luminibus et longum, miseri, combibunt amorem. Huius profecto morbi, ut Museo placet, causa omnis et origo est oculus' (p. 254);
'Reliquorum preter oculos membrorum concinnitas non cause vim ad egrotationem huiusmodi, sed occasionis impulsum videtur habere' (p. 254);
'eius imago per visum ab animo capitur vel concipitur' (p. 183);
'presertim per oculos, animi phenestras lucidissimas, emicat' (p. 219);
'formosus quisque teneris non fascinat oculis' (p. 221);
'cohitu, ieiunio, ebrietate, deambulatione' (214);
'Summopere vero cavendum ne lumina oculorum luminibus coniungantur' (p. 256);
'In Veneris natalibus, discumbentibus diis, Consilii filius Porus, potu nectaris ebrius, cum Penia in Iovis orto se miscuit. Ex eo congressu natus est amor' (p. 208);
'aridus est macilentus et squalidus, nudis pedibus, humilis, sine domicilio, sine stramentis et tegmine ullo, ad fores in via, sub divo dormiens ac denique semper egenus' (p. 213);
'pulchris ac bonis insidiatur.Virilis est, audax feroxque, vehemens, callidus, sagaxque venator, nova semper machinamenta contexens, prudentie studiosus, facundus, per omnem vitam philosophans, incantator fascinatorque, potens, veneficus atque sophista' (p. 213);

'amator adeo in rebus amatoriis occupatus est ut in ceteris vite officiis tam privatis quam publicis non cautus quidem incedat, ut decet, sed absque ulla discriminum providentia temerarius quocumque feratur. Ideo in suis progressibus frequentia incurrit pericula, non aliter quam qui pedes suos corio non suffulciunt. Unde crebris sentibus et calculis offenduntur' (p. 216);

'astutum . . . et calidum, qui miris modis amati gratiam aucupetur, seu dolis implicet, seu captet obsequiis, sive eloquio mulceat sive cantu delineat' (p. 218);

'Splendorem vocat gratiam illam et pulchritudinem animi que in veritatis et virtutis claritate consistit. Viriditatem vero, figure colorisque suavitatem. Hec enim summopere in iuventutis viriditate florescit. Letitiam denique sincerum illud et salubre et perpetuum, quod in musica melodia sentimus oblectamentum' (p. 182);

'dicitur amor cantu suo mentes deorum hominumque mulcere' (p. 194);

'Huiusmodi sunt musice amorisque delitie. Nullis enim aliis oblectamentis tam assidue operam impendere possumus quam musice vocumque delinimentis pulchritudinisque illecebris' (p. 215);

'Venus prima, que in mente est, celo nata sine matre dicitur, quoniam mater apud Physicos materia est. Mens autem illa a materie corporalis consortio est aliena' (p. 154);

'intelligentia' . . . 'vis generandi anime mundi tributa' (p. 154);

'amore ingenito ad intelligendam dei pulchritudinem rapitur' . . . 'amore suo ad eamdem pulchritudinem in corporibus procreandam. Illa divinitatis fulgorem in se primum complectitur; deinde hunc in Venerem secundam traducit. Hec fulgoris illius scintillas in materiam mundi transfundit' (p. 154);

'Amor uterque honestus atque probandus. Uterque enim divinam imaginem sequitur' (p. 155);

'Revera utrique sunt boni, quoniam tam sobolis procreatio quam indagatio veritatis necessaria et honesta censetur' (p. 211);

'consilii fons' (p. 208);

'Illud utentibus utile, hoc noxium . . . Plato iudicat' (p. 164);

'verus amator, utpote pastor, agnorum gregem a falsorum amantium ceu luporum voragine ac peste tutatur' (p. 261);

'Porro anima statim ex deo nata, naturali quodam instinctu in eum, parentem suum, convertitur . . . Conversa in eum, eius radiis illustratur' (p. 172);

'gratia quedam . . . in ipso refulgens' (p. 188);

'Fertur et divus Augustus oculos adeo claros et nitidos habuisse ut, cum acrius quemquam intueretur, cogeret eum quasi ad Solis fulgorem vultum submictere' (p. 247).

13 J.A. Crowe and G.B. Cavalcaselle, *A History of Painting in Northern Italy*, ed. Tancred Borenius. (London: John Murray, 1912), III, p. 28.

14 D.G. Rossetti, *Poems* (Boston: Roberts Brothers, 1870), p. 258.

15 Harold E. Wethey, *The Paintings of Titian*, III, *The Mythological and Historical Paintings* (London: Phaidon, 1975), pp. 203-4, No. 54.

16 Wethey, pp. 175-9, No. 33.

17 Egan, p. 309.

Massimo Ciavolella

Eros / Ereos: Marsilio Ficino's Interpretation of Guido Cavalcanti's 'Donna me prega'

Discussing the concepts of will and love in Ficino's philosophy Paul Oskar Kristeller remarks that

... with the concept of Platonic love Ficino enters into a large historical perspective comprising not only philosophy and theology but also poetry and literature. In his concept of love he combines the will of St. Augustine, the charity of St. Paul, the friendship of Aristotle and the Stoics with love in Plato's sense of the term into a new and fertile idea. Moreover, Ficino's speculation on love was foreshadowed (as has been repeatedly observed) by the old Provençal and Tuscan lyric to which he himself consciously refers. In this respect the explicit quotation of Guido Cavalcanti in the *De Amore* is of great importance ....[1]

Kristeller, however, and most of the critics who have studied Ficino,[2] mention the reference to Cavalcanti only *en passant*, and fail to perceive that Ficino distorts Cavalcanti's meaning completely. This study will direct its attention upon this distortion, and especially on the effect that it had upon later critical perception of Cavalcanti's text.

The poetry of Guido Cavalcanti has emphatically influenced Italian letters from the very time it was written. This influence is chiefly attributed to one of his *canzoni*, 'Donna me prega,' considered by many critics as one of the most doctrinaire and difficult poems in the history of Italian poetry. What ensured Cavalcanti's fame was the fact that the *canzone* was a learned disquisition upon the causes, symptoms, and effects of love, and that Cavalcanti, apart from being acknowledged by Dante — for a time at least — as 'primo de li miei amici,'[3] was also considered by the poets of the *dolce stil nuovo* as the leading spokesman for their group.[4] It is symptomatic that 'Donna me prega' elicited glosses from the moment it appeared, giving rise to lengthy commentaries like those of the Florentine physician Dino del Garbo and of the learned philosopher Egidio Colonna.[5] In the course of history, 'Donna me prega' became the departure-point for many of the writers who dealt with the subject of love: Boccaccio, Petrarch, Lorenzo de' Medici, Pico della Mirandola, and Marsilio Ficino.

Ficino's reference to Cavalcanti occurs in the first chapter of the seventh and last speech of his *Commentarium in Convivium Platonis de Amore*, entitled 'Conclusio Supradictorum, et Opinio Guidonis Cavalcantis Philosophi.' Its brevity and obvious importance in the context of this paper allow for a full citation:

Finally, Cristoforo Marsuppini, a man who is very thoughtful, as he was about to take the part of Alcibiades, turns to me with these words:

Marsilio, I certainly congratulate very much the family of your Giovanni [Cavalcanti] which has produced, among many knights famous for both learning and deeds, Guido, the philosopher, who, having deserved well of his country, and surpassing everyone of his era in the subtleties of logic, and having imitated this Socratic love in conduct as well as in poetry, touched briefly upon everything you have said.

For Phaedrus discussed the origin of love, emanating from the viscera of Chaos. Pausanias divided love, once born, into two kinds, namely heavenly and vulgar. Eryximachus revealed its breadth when he showed that, divided into two kinds, it is found in all things. Aristophanes then explained what the presence of this so powerful god does in everything, showing that through him men who were split are put back together. Agathon discussed how great is love's influence and power, when he argued that only by it do men become blessed. Finally, Socrates, taught by Diotima, briefly explained what love is; what its nature is; whence it arose, how many parts it has, what its purpose is, and what it is worth.

All of these things Guido Cavalcanti, the philosopher, seems to have put very artfully into his verses. Just as a mirror, struck in a certain way by a ray of the sun, shines back, and by that reflection of the splendor sets on fire a piece of wool placed next to it, so he thinks that the part of the soul which he calls the dark fancy and the memory (like the mirror) is struck by a certain image (like a ray) of beauty itself (taking the place of the sun), taken in through the eyes; in such a way that from that it makes another image for itself (a splendor, as it were, of the first image) by which the force of desire (like the wool) is kindled and loves. He adds that this first love, kindled in the appetite of sense, is created by the form of the body seen through the eyes, but that this form itself is not impressed on the fancy in the same way in which it exists in the matter of the body, but without matter; yet in such a way that it is the image of a certain particular man placed in a definite place and time.

Then, he says, there immediately appears in the intellect another species of this image, which no longer seems to be a likeness of one particular human body, as it was in the fancy, but a common Reason or definition of the whole human race equally. And so, just as from the fancy's image, taken from the body, there arises in the appetite of sense, devoted to the body, a love inclined toward the senses, so from the intellect's universal species or Reason, which is very remote from the body, there arises in the will another love which is very foreign to commerce with the body.

The former he placed in lust, the latter in contemplation. The former he thinks revolves around the particular beauty of a single body, the latter around the universal beauty of the whole human race. He says that these two loves certainly oppose each other in man, and that the former drives him down to the bestial or voluptuous life, whereas the latter raises him up to the angelic or contemplative life. The latter he says is free from perturbation and is found in few people; the former is troubled by many passions, and seizes most people. For this reason he dismisses the latter in a few words, and is more prolix in explaining the passions of the other.

But since he explains very clearly the same things which you also have discussed above, I did not think it necessary to review them at present. But let it suffice to have learned that this philosopher included in the procreation of love a certain formlessness of Chaos, such as you have posited above, when he said that the dark fancy is illuminated, and that from the mixture of that darkness and this light love takes its origin. Moreover, who does not see in his words that double love, namely, heavenly and vulgar? But he also places the first origin of that in the beauty of divine things, the second in the beauty of bodies, for by *sun* he means the light of God; by *ray*, he means the beauty of bodies. Finally, he says that its end corresponds to its beginning, so long as the incitement of love carries some people to the beauty of the body and others to the beauty of God.[6]

Guido Cavalcanti, whom Boccaccio had called 'un de' migliori loici che avesse il mondo e ottimo filosofo naturale'[7] is transformed by Ficino into a veritable Neoplatonic philosopher. Looking closely at Ficino's text we cannot fail but notice that, although only a very brief excerpt from the *canzone* is discussed (or perhaps for this very reason), the underlying motif is an implied comparison between Socrates's explanation of the essence, nature, origin, parts, purposes, and effects of love, and the questions formulated in the *dedicatoria* to the canzone:

> Donna me prega, — per ch'eo voglio dire
> d'un accidente — che sovente — è fero
> ed è sí altero — ch'è chiamato amore:
>   sí chi lo nega — possa 'l ver sentire!
> Ed a presente — conoscente — chero,
> perch'io no spero — ch'om di basso core
>   a tal ragione porti canoscenza:
> ché senza — natural dimostramento
> non ho talento — di voler provare
> là dove posa, e chi lo fa creare,
>   e quali sia sua vertute e sua potenza,
> l'essenza — poi a ciascun suo movimento,

e 'l piacimento — che 'l fa dire amare,
e s'omo per veder lo pò mostrare.[8]

Cavalcanti's text, at least from the point of view of the division of the
discussion of love, seems indeed to follow that of Socrates. Ficino, having established this formal comparison, freely comments upon Cavalcanti's answer to the first question, where love resides:

In quella parte — dove sta memora
prende suo stato — sí formato, — come
diaffan da lume, — d'una scuritate . . . .

In his attempt to force his particular meaning upon Cavalcanti's
poem, Ficino goes so far as to add to the text of the *canzone* the simile
of the rays of the sun ('Quemadmodum solis radio speculum modo
quodam percussum splendet iterum, et proxime sibi appositam lanam
reflexione illa splendoris inflammat; ite ille partem animae . . .') which
he derives from the commentary by Egidio Colonna:

Prende suo stato si formato come diaffan dal lume d'una oscuritate. Quasi dica:
come il diaffano essendo prima sotto una oscuritate isguardato dal sole et
illuminato dal suo raggio prende suo stato perfetto e luminoso, cossì
l'animo essendo prima quasi sotto una oscuritate isguardato da la cosa de
fuori per la vertù de la ditta ymagine prende suo stato perfetto, cio è stato
d'amore, nela qual simigliança asomiglia l'autore la cosa de fuori al sole, la
ymagine de la cosa al raggio del sole, l'amore al lume, la privation del
amore ala oscuritate.[9]

There is no doubt that Ficino purposely forces the meaning of
Cavalcanti's poem. By extrapolating from the *canzone* one of the most
obscure passages, the only one in fact open to a symbolic interpretation, and by ignoring almost completely Cavalcanti's lengthy discussion
of *ereos*, or erotic melancholy, he can carry out the fusion of Socratic
love and poetic love, and establish a direct link between the poet and
Renaissance Florence. (Ficino's only concession to this problem is the
remark that Guido recognizes two types of love, one that he locates in
voluptuousness, the other in contemplation.) Cavalcanti, the poet-
philosopher epitomizing the Tuscan lyric tradition under the banner
of the revived Platonism, becomes the bard of Ficino's concept of love.

*   *   *   *   *

Ficino's brief chapter on Cavalcanti not only went against every previous and contemporary opinion on 'Donna me prega,' but it also exerted a profound influence on later interpretations of the *canzone*.

All early interpreters of the poem described Cavalcanti's love as sensual, as a negative force capable of leading the lover into a state of melancholic delirium and to psychological and physical destruction. The first commentator, the physician Dino del Garbo, interpreted the poem in the light of the mediaeval concept of erotic-melancholy, or *ereos*. Illustrating his opinions with examples drawn from Aristotle and from Arabic physician / philosophers, that is to say from natural philosophy, Dino del Garbo took Cavalcanti's advice to heart: (vv. 8-9): 'ché senza — natural dimostramento / non ho talento ....'[10] Egidio Colonna's commentary, also written in the first quarter of the fourteenth century, echoes that of Dino del Garbo in considering Cavalcanti's love as a purely sensual phenomenon:

Dice l'autore che l'amore non è vertù naturale né vertù morale, e cio è che dice *Non è vertute*. Unde rimane che l'amore è passione del apetito e cio è che l'autor dice non è vertute e prova spitialmente che non è vertù morale però che non se genera de la ragiona.[11]

Boccaccio, rather than explain in his *chiose* to the *Teseida* the nature of the love between Arcita and Emilia, refers the reader to 'Donna me prega' and to the commentary by Dino del Garbo:

... amore volere mostrare come per le sopradette cose si generi in noi, quantunque alla presente opera forse si converrebbe di dichiarare, non è mio intendimento di farlo, perciò che troppo sarebbe lunga la storia: chi disidera di viderlo, legga la canzone di Guido Cavalcanti 'Donna mi priega etc.', e le chiose che sopra vi fece Maestro Dino del Garbo. Dice adunque sommariamente che questo amore è una passione nata nell'anima per alcuna cosa piaciuta e di poterla avere.[12]

Filippo Villani in his *Liber de Civitatis Florentiae Famosis Civibus* also feels he must mention 'Donna me prega' while discussing Cavalcanti, to whom he attributes, just like his predecessors, a sensual concept of love:

He [Guido Cavalcanti] published a very elegant and remarkable *canzone* which very subtly discusses love, which consists of sensuality rather than reason, and its nature, qualities and affection. In this *canzone* he treated most ingeniously and abundantly matters of natural science previously unheard of. The natural philosopher Dino del Garbo, whom I mentioned above, and Egidio Romano, the renowned natural philosopher, having admired its remarkable understanding deigned to comment it.[13]

Giovanni Pico della Mirandola himself, in his vernacular commentary upon Girolamo Benivieni's *Canzone d'amore* — in which the Florentine poet undertook 'to summarize in a few verses that which Marsilio in many pages most elegantly describes' — explains that the love which Benivieni describes is heavenly love, and not the sensual, vulgar love expounded in Cavalcanti's 'Donna me prega':

Il trattare dell'uno et dell'altro amore s'apartiene a diverse scientie. Dello amore volgare, tratta el philosopho naturale et el philosopho morale. Dello amore divino, tratta el theologo, o volendo parlare ad modo de paripathetici, el Metaphisico .... Di questi due amori hanno trattato specificamente duo poeti in lingua Toscana. Dello amore volgare Guido Cavalcanti in una sua canzona. Dell'altro, cioè del celeste, el poeta nostro nell'opera praesente, nella quale quantunque tratti dell'uno et dell'altro, nondimeno principalmente tratta del celeste, né dell'altro parla se non inquanto è una debole imagine di quello.[14]

It is well-known that Ficino's commentary on the *Symposium* began the literary genre of the Platonic *trattato d'amore*, a genre very much in vogue in the Cinquecento. Ficino's reading of Cavalcanti's text also created a trend for further commentaries on the *canzone*, at the same time forcing them in the direction of the *trattati d'amore*. As a result, the commentaries, instead of focussing on the poem, merely used the poem as a point of departure for lengthy discussions on Platonic love.

With the exception of the 1568 commentary by Fra' Paolo del Rosso — who follows the tradition of the medical-philosophical treatises begun by Dino del Garbo, and thus considers Cavalcanti's love 'desiderio vitioso di bellezza ... mortifero spesse volte a la ragione e pieno di diverse perturbationi' while asserting that true love is 'quello che risolve nel Convito di Platone'[15] — all other commentaries owe their existence to Ficino's brief chapter: the two lectures delivered by Francesco de' Vieri and only recently transcribed and edited under the title *Lezzioni d'amore*,[16] the unpublished *espositione* by Iacopo Mini commissioned by Annibal Caro,[17] the commentary by Girolamo Fracchetta,[18] and all the many references to the *canzone*, from that in Mario Equicola's *Libro de natura de amore* to the one found in Jacques Ferrand's *Traicté de la maladie d'amour*.[19]

One example will suffice. Francesco de' Vieri, in the Proem to the first of his lectures, gives the reason for his choice of Cavalcanti's *canzone*:

Tra questi generosi spiriti, i quali hanno cerco di compiacer al desiderio di quelli i quali desiderano per ragione havere conoscenza d'amore, è stato Guido Cavalcanti in quella canzone nella quali egli tratta d'amore con somma gravità e dottrina, come filosofo di maniera che il suo discorso è lodato da le persone che intendono.[20]

Cavalcanti was a 'sommo poeta et eccellentissimo filosofo,' or rather 'sommo poeta' because he was an 'eccellentissimo filosofo.' The poetic illustration of the text belongs to Petrarch's lyric poetry, while its *raison d'être* is offered by 'Donna me prega.' From this moment onward the reputation of Cavalcanti was indissolubly bound to his *philosophy* of love. So much so, in fact, that all discussions of 'Donna me prega' after Ficino, with the exception, as already mentioned, of Fra' Paolo del Rosso's, deal almost exclusively with the problem of Cavalcanti's philosophical position. This means that Ficino did not just force a Neoplatonic reading of Cavalcanti's text — that, after all, could only last as long as Neoplatonism remained in vogue — but that he also established the reputation of Cavalcanti as a moral philosopher, against the early interpretations which saw him as a natural philosopher. In critical terms, this has meant that readers of the *canzone* have struggled ever since to reconstruct Cavalcanti's philosophy, a problem which still absorbs critics of 'Donna me prega,' from Salvadori and Vossler to Shaw, Nardi, Favati, Contini, Marti, Corti, just to name a few.[21] Was Cavalcanti a Thomist; was he influenced by Aristotle mediated through the Arabic philosophers, especially Ibn Sina; or was he an Averroist, as most critics today seem to believe following Nardi's relentless defence of his thesis against Favati?[22]

However, once we consider how Cavalcanti's fame as a philosopher came about, how Ficino's interpretation of 'Donna me prega' not only radically changed the way in which the *canzone* was interpreted but also the reputation of its author, we should be prompted to return to the text in order to meditate on a Cavalcanti 'ottimo filosofo naturale.' In sum, we should re-read and re interpret his text in relation to those of the *filosofi naturali* and *physici*, that is to say in the light of the well-established mediaeval concept of *amor ereos*.

Carleton University

NOTES

1 P.O. Kristeller, *The Philosophy of Marsilio Ficino* (Gloucester, Mass.: Peter Smith, 1964; 1st ed. New York: Columbia University Press, 1943), p. 287. See also p. 27.

2 See for example J. Festugière, *La Philosophie de l'amour de Marsile Ficin* (Paris: J. Vrin, 1941), and R. Marcel, *Marsile Ficin* (Paris: Les Belles Lettres, 1958), who do not mention Cavalcanti at all. See also note 22 below.

3 Dante, *Vita nuova*, III.

4 One thinks of the influence Cavalcanti exerted upon Dante and the other poets of the *dolce stil nuovo*, especially Cino da Pistoia.

5 Egidio Colonna's authorship has been repeatedly contested by modern critics who consider the opinions expressed in the commentary unworthy of Colonna's philosophical stature. Early commentators such as Benvenuto da Imola, Lorenzo de' Medici, Pico della Mirandola, Mario Equicola, did indeed believe the commentary to have been written by Egidio Colonna. For a discussion of Colonna's authorship, see J.C. Nelson, *Renaissance Theory of Love* (New York and London: Columbia University Press, 1955), pp. 267-70.

6 M. Ficino, *Commentary on Plato's Symposium on Love*, trans., intro., & notes by Sears Jayne (Dallas, Tx: Spring Publications, 1985), pp. 153-55. The Latin original, to be found in *Commentaire sur le banquet de Platon*, ed. Raymond Marcel (Paris: Les Belles Lettres, 1956), pp. 240-1 reads:

Postremo Christophorus Marsupinus, vir humanissimus, Alcibiadis personam gesturus, his ad me verbis convertitur. Gratulor equidem, o Marsili, Iohannis tui familie plurimum, que inter multos et doctrina et rebus gestis clarissimos equites, Guidonem philosophum peperit, de re publica bene meritum et aculeis dialectice cunctis suo seculo precellentem, qui hunc amorem socraticum tam moribus quam carminibus imitatus, brevi quecumque a vobis sunt dicta perstrinxit.

Phedrus enim amoris originem tetigit ex cahos visceribus emanantem. Pausanias iam natum amorem, geminam divisit in spetiem, celestem scilicet et vulgarem. Eryximachus eius aperuit amplitudinem, dum cunctis in rebus eum sic .inesse monstraret in partes geminas distribuit.Aristophanes quid agat in singulis tam amplissimi dei presentia declaravit, ostendens per hunc fractos homines / refarciri. Agathon quanta sit eius virtus potentiaque tractavit, cum ab eo solo beatos fieri homines disputaret. Socrates tandem, a Diotima edoctus, summatim quid sit amor et qualis, unde ortus, quot habeat partes, quorsum tendat et quantum valeat explicavit.

Guido Cavalcantes philosophus omnia hec artificiosissime videtur carminibus suis inseruisse. Quemadmodum Solis radio speculum modo quodam percussum splendet iterum et proxime sibi appositam lanam reflexione illa splendoris inflammat, ita ille partem anime quam obscuram phantasiam vocat atque memoriam, ceu speculum, pulchritudinis ipsius Solis locum habentis simulacro tamquam radio quodam per oculos hausto, censet ita pulsari ut ipsa sibi ex illo alterum effingat simulacrum, quasi simulacri primi splendorem, quo appetendi vis non aliter quam lana accendatur et amet. Addit amorem / hunc primum in appetitu sensus accensum a forma corporis per oculos inspecta creari. Sed eam ipsam formam non eo modo quo in corporis materia est, in phantasiam imprimi sed sine materia, ita tamen ut certi cuiusdam hominis signato in loco et tempore positi sit imago. Rursus imaginis huiusmodi spetiem aliquam statim in mente lucere, que non amplius unius cuiusdam humani corporis, ut erat in phantasia, videatur esse similitudo, sed totius eque generis humani ratio communis et definitio. Itaque sicut ex phantasie imagine a corpore sumpta, in appetitu sensus corpori dedito, amor ad sensus proclivis exoritur, ita ex hac mentis spetie rationeque communi tamquam a corpore remotissima, amor alius in voluntate nascitur a commertio corporis alienissimus. Illum in voluptate, hunc in contemplatione locavit. Illum circa particularem corporis unius formam revolvi putat, hunc circa universalem / totius humani generis pulchritudinem. Hos utique amores sibi ipsis in homine repugnare et illum deorsum ad ferinam et voluptuosam depellere, hunc sursum ad angelicam vitam contemplativamque attollere. Hunc absque perturbatione vult esse et in paucis reperiri; illum multis passionibus anxium ac plurimos occupare. Ideo istum paucis verbis absolvit, in alterius passionibus enarrandis prolixior.

Quoniam vero eadem apertissime, que et vos in superioribus narravistis, hic explicat, ea in presentia recensere opus esse non censui. Verum cognovisse sufficiat philosophum hunc aliquam chaos informitatem, qualem supra vos posuistis, in amoris procreatione miscuisse, dum diceret obscuram phantasiam illuminari atque ex illius obscuritatis et huius luminis mixtione amorem originem ducere. Amorem preterea geminum illum / celestem scilicet et vulgarem quis in eius verbis non videat? Originem quin etiam illius primam in divinorum, secundam in corporum collocat pulchritudine. *Solem* namque dei lucem, *radium* corporum formam intelligit. Finem postremo suum vult eiusdem principiis respondere, dum alios usque ad formam corporis, alios usque ad dei spetiem, amoris provehit instigatio.

7 G. Boccaccio, *Decameron,* VI,9.

8 G. Contini, *Letteratura italiana delle origini* (Florence: Sansoni, 1970), pp. 172-3.

9 *Il canzoniere Vaticano Barberino Latino 3953,* ed. Gino Lega. Collezione di opere inedite o rare (Bologna: Reale Commissione pe' testi di lingua nelle provincie dell'Emilia, 1905), pp. 93-94. See also Nelson, p. 79 and n. 13, where he offers the following translation: 'It takes its state formed like a diaphanous body from the light of a darkness. As though he said, as the diaphanous body, being first in darkness, when beheld by the sun and illuminated by its ray takes its perfect and luminous state, so the soul, being first so to speak in darkness, when beheld by the outside thing takes its perfect state — that of love — by virtue of the said image. In this comparison the author likens the outside thing to the sun, the image of the thing to the sun's ray, love to light, the privation of love to darkness.'

10 'Donna me prega,' vv. 8-9.

11 *Il canzoniere Vaticano Barberino Latino 3953,* p. 102. 'Where the author says, "It is not a virtue," he means that love is neither a natural nor a moral virtue. Whence it follows that love is a passion of the appetite, since the author says that it is not a virtue and proves especially that it is not a moral virtue, because it is not generated by reason.' Transl. by Nelson, p. 39.

12 G. Boccaccio, *Teseida,* ed. A. Limentani (Milan: Mondadori, 1964), p. 464: 'Although it may be proper within the context of this work to discuss how love is generated in us through the above-mentioned things, I do not intend to do it because the matter would be too long. Whoever wants to see it, can read Guido Cavalcanti's poem "Donna me prega etc.," and the commentary that master Dino del Garbo wrote on the poem. In brief, he says that this type of love is a passion born in the soul for something perceived as pleasing and attainable.' My translation.

13 Nelson, p. 268. The Latin original reads:

Hic [Guido de Cavalcantibus] de amore qui in sensualitate potius, quam in ratione versatur, eiusque natura, moribus et affectu subtilissime disputando, elegantissimam et mirabilem edidit cantilenam, in qua physicae inaudita hactenus, ingeniosissime et copiose tractavit; cujus mirabilem intellectum mirati Dinus de Garbo physicus, de quo supra habui mentionem, et Aegidius Romanus, insignis physicus, commentare dignati sunt.

14 Giovanni Pico della Mirandola, *Opera omnia* (Basileae, 1557; repr. with an introduction by C. Vasoli, Hildesheim: Georg Olms, 1969), t. 1, p. 912. 'The discussion of the two loves belongs to difference sciences. The natural and moral philosophers deal with vulgar love. Heavenly love belongs to the theologian or, if we want to speak in the manner of the peripatetics, to the metaphysician . . . These two types of love have been discussed specifically by two poets in the Tuscan tongue. Guido Cavalcanti discussed earthly love in one of his poems. The other love, that is to say the heavenly kind, has been discussed by our poet in the present work. And although he deals with both kinds of love, he is mainly preoccupied with the heavenly one, and he speaks of the other only in so far as it is but a pale image of divine love.' My translation.

15 Florence, 1568. The commentary has never been republished. For a brief discussion of it, see Nelson, pp. 42-44 ff.

16 Francesco de' Vieri, *Lezzioni d'amore*, edited with an introduction by John Colanieri (Munich: Wilhelm Fink Verlag, 1973).

17 Jacopo Mini's commentary remains unpublished in a XVI century MS in the Biblioteca Laurenziana in Florence (XLI.20). It may be of interest to know that Mini offers to write a more detailed commentary on the *canzone* if the one he is writing should please Caro; since we do not possess this second *espositione*, we can speculate that Caro may have not thought much of the vague, superficial text prepared by the Florentine physician.

18 (Venice: Gioliti, 1585).

19 Mario Equicola, *Libro de natura de amore* (Venice, 1525), pp. 4v-5v; Jacques Ferrand, *Traicté de l'essence et guerison de l'amour, ou de la Melancholie Erotique* (Paris, 1623).

20 Francesco de' Vieri, *Lezzioni d'amore*, p. 79. 'Among those generous men who tried to fulfil the desire of those who wanted to know about love in a reasoned manner, was Guido Cavalcanti with his *canzone* in which he discusses love with great seriousness and doctrine, as a philosopher, so that his discussion is praised by those who understand.' My translation.

21 See the introduction by G. Contini to 'Donna me prega,' in *Letteratura italiana delle origini*, p. 172, and M. Corti, *Dante a un nuovo crocevia* (Florence: Le Lettere, 1982) and especially *La felicità mentale. Nuove prospettive per Cavalcanti e Dante* (Turin: Einaudi, 1983).

22 Contini, p. 172.

Eva Kushner

Pontus de Tyard entre Ficin et Léon l'Hébreu

Au sein du groupe connu dans l'histoire des lettres comme la Pléiade, Pontus de Tyard (1521-1605) fait figure d'isolé. Ses études à Paris datent de dix ans avant que ne s'y installent, sous la férule de Jean Dorat au collège de Coqueret, Ronsard, du Bellay et Jean-Antoine de Baïf (1547). Mais surtout, Tyard se distingue des autres poètes du groupe par le caractère continu de son platonisme et de son pétrarquisme. Sa longue existence, qui s'étend jusqu'au seuil du XVIIe siècle, est caractérisée par une activité continuelle de poète, philosophe, théologien et traducteur. Loin en effet d'être uniquement le poète amoureux au coeur brisé que mettent en scène les *Erreurs amoureuses* (1549, 1551, 1555), Tyard est aussi le philosophe qui a donné — en langue vernaculaire ce qui est en soi une innovation — six *Discours philosophiques* dont les deux premiers, le *Solitaire premier* (1552) et le *Solitaire second* (1555), contiennent une somme néo-platonicienne sur la poésie, la musique et leurs rapports réciproques ainsi que leurs rapports avec la vie morale de l'homme, la connaissance de l'univers, et les rapports de l'homme avec Dieu. S'ajoutant aux trois livraisons successives de *Erreurs amoureuses* et à la traduction en 1551 des *Dialoghi d'amore* de Léon l'Hébreu, ces deux discours appartiennent à la période franchement platonicienne tandis que Ronsard et Du Bellay, ayant chacun donné un *canzoniere* empreint de platonisme et de pétrarquisme, dans les *Amours* de 1552-53 et l'*Olive* respectivement, se sont vite dégagés de cette double tendance et l'ont même satirisée.

Après cette intense production platonicienne qui nous intéresse ici comme exemple de transformation et de réception, Tyard continue, dans ses quatre discours philosophiques subséquents, son tour d'horizon de l'encyclopédie du savoir, à la suite d'un tournant qui à première vue pourrait apparaître comme un abandon de la vision contemplative, une percée vers la pensée scientifique concrète, et une sorte de passage (qu'il faut analyser avec toutes les nuances historiques et philosophiques requises) de Platon à Aristote. En 1556, le *Discours du temps, de l'an et de ses parties* témoigne en effet d'une attention très particulière à la temporalité tant dans la vie humaine, et en particulier dans le langage qui nomme les divisions du temps, qu'au sein du cosmos. A partir de là, dans les deux discours formant *L'Univers* (1557), Tyard passe en revue les doctrines scientifiques existantes. D'une manière dialogique, c'est-à-dire remarquablement ouverte pour l'époque, les différents personnages du dialogue assumant des positions épistémologiques différentes, il aborde successivement une longue série de grands problèmes relatifs au cosmos et à l'homme. Il donne encore en 1558 *Mantice*, où sont condamnées, avec certaines nuances, les prédictions astrologiques: et, en 1573, à la faveur d'une réédition de l'oeuvre poétique passée, de *Nouvelles oeuvres poétiques* où se manifeste une recrudescence du pétrarquisme formel. Mentionnons encore, parmi les oeuvres tardives, le *De recta nominum impositione* (1603), oeuvre d'érudition onomastique en apparence, mais lourde surtout de réflexion platonicienne dans la mesure où Tyard est convaincu de ce que les mots représentant les concepts les plus fondamentaux correspondent aux choses qui les incarnent, et que les noms et les choses reçoivent de Dieu leur réalité et leur cohérence.

L'oeuvre de Tyard représente, en résumé, une sorte de laboratoire idéal où s'opère devant nos yeux la transformation des néo-platonismes, et plus particulièrement de l'apport de Ficin et de celui Léon l'Hébreu, dans la vision d'un poète et philosophe du XVIe siècle français destiné aussi à devenir un évêque de la Contre-réforme. Car la particularité de cette oeuvre, qui en fait un exemple privilégié, c'est de recommencer l'expérience ficinienne du 'miles Christi' tout d'abord dans la vision d'un jeune penseur laïque voué, dès ses débuts poétiques, à chercher, à travers l'amour humain, le vrai amour; et à ne jamais renier cette recherche alors qu'il s'ouvre progressivement à l'essor scientifique du monde qui l'entoure, et qu'il y participe, sachant par ailleurs reconnaître très vite quelles limites doit s'assigner l'imagination néo-païenne de la jeune Pléiade. Problème fort pertinent, sans être nouveau, puisqu'à tout moment, de l'Antiquité à la Renaissance, les topoï néo-platoniciens sont autant de pierres de touche de la spiritualité d'une époque, ou d'un courant donné. La valeur de l'exemple tyardien consiste donc en son exemplarité. Mais pourquoi le situer entre Ficin et Léon l'Hébreu? S'agit-il d'une transition qui ferait coïncider son ficinianisme primordialement avec la période de l'amour de Pasithée et de la sublimation de cet amour en une vision d'harmonie universelle figurée par la poésie et la musique? Ce serait la période allant de 1549 à 1555, que terminerait le *Discours de temps, de l'an et de ses parties* par une plongée dans la temporalité à travers la science d'abord, puis la vision et l'activité chrétiennes. Le rôle de Léon l'Hébreu aurait alors été, par sa récupération du processus cosmique et du processus humain, les deux étant d'ailleurs profondément liés, d'introduire au sein même de la vision théologique de Pontus de Tyard, lorsqu'en 1578 il deviendra évêque de Chalon, un néo-platonisme compatible avec la doctrine de l'Incarnation.

Cette interprétation évolutive, tentante par sa simplicité, est en réalité simplificatrice à l'excès, et ne tient pas compte du fait que Léon l'Hébreu est présent à la pensée de Tyard dès le début de sa carrière littéraire et philosophique puisque, si la publication de la traduction française des *Dialoghi d'amore* coïncide à peu près avec celle de la *Continuation des Erreurs amoureuses*, la préparation de cette traduction doit, vu son ampleur, remonter aux débuts même de la création poétique, c'est-à-dire à 1548 ou même plus tôt. Par ailleurs, dès 1552, la forme dialoguée des *Dialoghi d'amore* se retrouve dans le *Solitaire premier*, y instaurant un échange à plusieurs niveaux de signification entre un homme et une femme qui sont non seulement amant et amante mais aussi maître et élève sans que cette dernière soit pour autant en situation de dominée; au contraire plutôt: chez Tyard comme chez l'Hébreu le personnage féminin introduit à plusieurs reprises des éléments nouveaux et une alternative véritable. C'est dire que pour des raisons philosophiques et formelles à la fois l'influence de Léon l'Hébreu est opérante aussi tôt que celle de Ficin; et qu'on ne saurait parler d'un simple passage de l'un à l'autre, car une telle notion simplifierait à l'excès la pensée de Ficin aussi bien que celle de Léon, faisant de la pensée du premier un platonisme désincarné, dans lequel la Beauté elle-même, concept pourtant primordial, ne serait qu'une première approche vers l'idéal et en cela nierait la beauté attachée aux êtres; alors que la Pensée du second serait le véritable moteur d'une philosophie de l'Incarnation laquelle, ayant triomphé du dualisme, aurait aidé Tyard à vaincre sa tentation principale qui est, précisément, le dualisme. En réalité, il semble plutôt qu'une dialectique vivante et complexe se soit instaurée dès le début entre les deux modèles. Pas plus que Ficin que d'ailleurs il connaît, Léon l'Hébreu ne relève d'un système univoque ou même parfaitement isolable. L'un et l'autre reste en contact avec l'aristotélisme, et rêve de faire concorder Platon et Aristote. L'un et l'autre considère l'amour de Dieu comme la fin de l'homme et le moteur ultime de toute chose; pour cette raison, chacun à sa manière finit par superposer à la sagesse néo-platonicienne sa propre sagesse religieuse.

La spécificité de ce que Léon l'Hébreu propose à Tyard, par delà ce que l'on pourrait appeler un nouveau syncrétisme[1] néo-platonicien où Léon, tout autant que Ficin, plonge de toutes ses racines, c'est le sens de la valeur du temporel, puisque rien n'échappe à l'emprise créatrice de Dieu. Paradoxalement, ce trait judéo-chrétien fait que ce penseur hébraïque a fourni à Tyard ce qui manquait le plus à son christianisme

— le sens de l'Incarnation. Voilà qui illustre cette merveilleuse qualité préhensile du néo-platonisme, si riche en notions et symboles de portée universelle que les imaginaires les plus divers pouvaient s'y rencontrer, s'y nourrir, et même y développer leurs propre spécificités. Ce qu'il faut également se rappeler, c'est que Tyard en tant qu'humaniste avait mille raisons d'emboîter le pas à ceux qui, à la suite des Pères de l'Église eux-mémes, vivaient profondément et sans culpabilité les textes païens préfigurateurs, à leurs yeux, des textes sacrés du christianisme.

Léon l'Hébreu, en effet, s'est constitué un éclectisme bien à lui, nourri des multiples sources de syncrétisme hellénistique dont il est, à la suite de Ficin, un des héritiers ultimes:

Avant même l'apparition de Plotin, avec Philon d'Alexandrie, les bases de ce syncrétisme sont posées, mais il est certain que c'est le néo-platonisme qui lui donne sa consistance, puisque la philosophie de Plotin paraît la construction intellectuelle la plus apte à s'accorder avec les dogmes fondamentaux du judéo-christianisme ainsi qu'avec les Ecritures Saintes, les livres de l'Ancien et du Nouveau Testament, les textes de la Genèse, comme aussi bien les Evangiles selon Saint-Jean ou les Epîtres de Saint Paul ou sa lettre aux Corinthiens. Accrédité par les pères de l'Eglise, ce syncrétisme a traversé tout le Moyen Age, présidé aux synthèses cosmologiques des grands commentateurs d'Aristote, et finalement, il a atteint les philosophes du XVe et XVIe siècle, jouissant même auprès d'eux d'un regain de faveur. Des auteurs tels que Pic de la Mirandole, Marsile Ficin, Jérôme Benivieni, Giordano Bruno et notre Léon l'Hébreu, lui-même, en sont imprégnés.[2]

Il ne faut pas oublier en effet que déjà pour Philon d'Alexandrie, cet autre Israélite, Dieu se répercute par tout le sensible, le temps, le corporel; par ses puissances, même si en tant qu'essence il est intemporel et non localisé, le Logos, sans cesser d'être l'Un, génère la multiplicité des archétypes d'êtres actifs dans le monde concret, agent donc à la fois unificateur et générateur de différenciation.

La pensée judéo-chrétienne n'en finit pas de puiser aux sources grecques, c'est bien connu. Origène s'est saisi pour le christianisme des hypostases plotiniennes. La conception vétéro-testamentaire de la Parole de Dieu créatrice, révélatrice et judiciaire se trouve aussi chez Philon.[3] Et n'y a-t-il pas comparabilité et même coïncidence entres les hypostases plotiniennes et les noms partiels de Dieu en théologie hébraïque, incarnant les diverses puissances du nom total et indicible? Pontus de Tyard s'occupera à plusieurs reprises de l'unité et de la multiplicité du nom divin en hébreu, notamment dans ses *Homilies sur l'oraison dominicale* de 1585.

On ne saurait donc insister suffisament sur le fait que les néo-platonismes renaissants dont s'inspire Pontus de Tyard se relient au syncrétisme des premiers siècles de l'ère chrétienne par leur ouverture aux intuitions des penseurs non-chrétiens, et plus spécifiquement aux néo-platoniciens, préfigurateurs de la pensée chrétienne. Rappelons le mot de Jérôme qui répond à un rhéteur lui reprochant ses emprunts antiques que 'Moïse et Salomon ont fait des emprunts à la sagesse grecque' et que Saint-Paul a cité des vers d'Epiménide, de Ménandre et d'Aratus; et il ajoute encore:

Il est dit, dans le *Deutéronome*, que lorsqu'on veut épouser une femme cap-tive, il faut d'abord lui raser la téte et les sourcils, lui couper les poils et les ongles, et qu'on peut ensuite s'unir avec elle. Est-il surprenant que, moi aussi, charmé de la grâce et de la beauté de la sagesse profane, j'aie voulu en faire une Israélite, de servante et d'esclave qu'elle était? Après avoir retranché tout ce qu'elle avait de mortel . . . ne puis-je pas, en m'alliant avec elle, la rendre féconde pour le Seigneur?[4]

On voit, par exemple, quel usage un Saint Eusèbe, un Saint Augustin, Saint Basile ou Saint Cyrille font de la notion d'hypostase pour fonder ontologiquement la Trinité. Pour ce qui est de Grégoire de Nysse, sa notion de l'infini divin et de la finitude du microcosme humain se répercutera presque littéralement chez Léon l'Hébreu. Dans son traité *Sur l'âme et la résurrection*, il dit en effet:

Cette infinité de Dieu nous est analogiquement révélée par l'étendue incommensurable du ciel: Dieu nous illumine intérieurement comme les rayons du soleil, cependant si éloigné de nous, inondent toute chose; notre âme comme un microcosme merveilleux reflète en son exiguïté une image réduite des inexprimables propriétés de Dieu, comme un petit fragment de verre semble contenir le disque entier du soleil, non égal à la grandeur réelle de l'astre, mais proportionnel à celle du fragment lui même.[5]

Et, au *Troisième Dialogue*, Léon l'Hébreu fera dire à Philon:

Ainsi que l'oeil entre toutes les corporelles parties de l'homme (qui est un petit monde) est simulacre et imitateur de l'intellect divin entre les spiri-tuelz, et ainsi comme la lumiere et veüe de l'oeil de l'homme . . . est dependante de la veüe et lumiere intellectuelle: ainsi est la lumiere du Soleil, en respect de la premiere et vraye lumiere de l'intellect divin. Telle-ment que tu peux aisément croire que le Soleil est vray simulacre de l'en-tendement divin, luy ressemblant en beauté plus que autre chose, car ainsi que la souveraine beauté consiste en l'intellect divin, dans lequel tout l'univers est figuré en accomplie beauté: aussi la beauté du Soleil est celle qui embellit et fait lucide tout l'univers et monde corporel.[6] (La traduction est celle de Tyard).

Certes, chez Grégoire de Nysse comme chez Léon l'Hébreu le monde corporel — aussi bien le cosmos que l'homme dans sa corporéité — reflète l'entendement divin; toutefois Léon l'Hébreu complexifie cette conception fondamentale en faisant intervenir le rôle de l'oeil médiateur et actif dans la relation entre l'intelligence divine et l'intelligence humaine; et en attribuant au soleil un rôle plus que symbolique qui est de figurer la beauté divine; enfin en faisant appel à cette notion même de beauté qui permet à chacun des éléments de participer à l'harmonie de l'ensemble, donc à la beauté divine. En comparaison, dans le passage de Grégoire de Nysse, le petit fragment de verre qu'est l'homme, avec sa vision, n'a d'autre vocation que de servir d'analogue ou modèle infiniment réduit de l'immensité du monde, laquelle est à son tour analogue et modèle réduit — et appauvri — de l'infinie richesse de Dieu.

De Grégoire de Nysse à Pontus de Tyard se transmet à travers Léon l'Hébreu cette vision des échelons de l'être, lequel gagne en réalité à mesure qu'il s'approche de Dieu, et perd en réalité à mesure qu'il s'éloigne de Lui. Dans les *Homilies sur l'oraison dominicale*, Tyard étendra encore, s'il se peut, l'écart entre l'infini de Dieu et ses manifestations terrestres, en mettant l'accent sur l'inconnaissabilité de Dieu et de son vrai nom. Le nom — comme cela se voit quelques années plus tard dans le *De recta nominum impositione* — est symbolique de la chose. Donc, lorsqu'il s'agit de Dieu, il est impossible que l'homme s'approche du Nom véritable: c'est par ses manifestations qu'il sera connu, donc par les noms partiels révélant différents attributs de la divinité. Sabaoth, par exemple, dénote la toute-puissance de Dieu maître des 'armées terrestres et célestes; Jéhovah, le punisseur des orgueilleux,' etc. 'Car le nom de Dieu,' dit Tyard 'c'est Dieu mesme, lequel nous recognoistrons par ses effects puisque nous sommes incapables de le comprendre par son essence . . . Nous donques l'appellerons Eternel, avant tout temps et commencement, qui toutefois a créé au commencement le Ciel, la Terre, et tout leur contenu.'[7] Tyard met l'accent sur l'infinie distance entre l'entendement humain et la stature de Dieu. 'Voilà, dit-il, ce que nous representerons en nos entendemens, pour description de ce qui nous est incomprehensible.'[8]

En germe, la notion de cette infinie distance existait déjà chez les néo-platoniciens et elle est implicite chez Léon l'Hébreu comme point de départ du dynamisme universel au moyen du quel l'intelligence divine, par amour, se porte vers le multiple, à commencer par ses propres émanations, puis vers l'autre. Mais, en assumant à son tour cette dynamique, Pontus de Tyard devenu évêque de la Contre-Réforme n'oubliera pas que la distance ontologique entre Dieu et l'homme provient de la cassure produite par le péché originel.

Nous venons de retracer à titre d'exemple le cheminement diachronique d'une idée séminale depuis l'antique syncrétisme jusqu'à Pontus de Tyard, afin de montrer l'interdépendance des courants platoniciens. Celle-ci résulte de la richesse et de la complexité du colloque humaniste dont Platon est un des enjeux les plus fréquents. Dans les *Disputationes camaldulenses* où Ficin apparaît pour la première fois comme maître à penser de la Florence contemporaine (— 'virum nostra tempestate inter Platonicos facile principem' —) Landino lance néamoins le débat sur l'aristotélisme et sa doctrine du souverain bien, exposée dans le dialogue par Alberti; et attire l'attention sur les affinités péripatéticiennes de Ficin: 'Verum illud admiror, dit Donato, cur dum nominatim nos artistotelicis annumeras, Ficinium silentio praeterieris.' ('Je me demande bien pourquoi tu nous énumères nommément les Aristotéliciens, et passes sous silence Ficin.')[9] Qu'est-ce à dire sinon que Ficin était perçu comme un de ceux sur qui l'on comptait pour concilier en une synthèse supérieure Aristote et Platon? Tout ce qu'a fait Ficin, comme d'ailleurs un Pic et un Reuchlin, dans le but d'établir que la vérité est progressivement révélée aux hommes et qu'elle est une, sera reçu par Tyard comme partie intégrante de son premier platonisme dans l'esprit d'un savoir unifié, très fidèle à la tradition ficinienne, y intégrant toutefois les éléments d'observation, d'expérimentation et de synthèse scientifique qui compléteront plutôt que de la contredire sa vision du processus universel. Platon et Aristote y ont part d'une manière symbiotique; et c'est seulement quand s'approfondit sa conscience théologique, qu'une scission semble s'opérer chez Tyard entre ce savoir intégré qu'il avait recherché toute sa vie, et le statut ultime de celui-ci. Dans le deuxième livre d'homélies, consacré à la Passion de Christ, Tyard expose à propos de Ponce Pilate sa pensée sur la vérité:

Les diligens chercheurs de vérité (qui est en nous un accordé consentement de notre entendement avec l'essence de la chose) l'ont disposee en quatre sortes. A sçavoir l'une des choses qui sont naturelles, & propres à nostre usage, & lesquelles Dieu souffre estre reçeües en nostre cognoissance, combien qu'elles n'attouchent aucunement les points de la religion. La seconde est de certaines choses indifférentes, et desquelles le doute, si elles appartiennent à la religion ou non, n'est encore résolu. La tierce est de celles, desquelles Dieu ne veut que les mortels s'enquièrent, parce que sa Majesté ne veut pas qu'ils en ayent aucune cognoissance. Et de ces trois premières sortes de vérité, la recherche n'est pas nécessaire à nostre salut. Aussi n'est-il besoin d'appuyer ou fonder la fermeté de nostre foy, en la consideration de telles verités: desquelles au contraire il se faut quelquesfois donner garde: d'autant que véritez naturelles ou imaginees ne sont qu'ombres, qui peuvent tromper souvent nos espritz et les détourner de la purité de la vérité divine. Qui est la quatrième sorte: c'est à dire des choses perpétuelles, lesquelles nous recognoissons estre révélées, par permission de la divine volonté: ou de celles qui evidemment, probablement & necessairement apparaissent tirées ou escoulées de celles qui nous sont revelées ainsi divinement.[10]

C'est cette quatrième vérité qui est incarnée en Christ, selon Tyard; d'où nécessité pour le lecteur — et à plus forte raison pour l'auditeur du prédicateur de Chalon — de remettre en perspective les trois premières sortes de vérité d'une manière plus sévère que celle du thomisme: au-delà du vaste domaine de la vérité naturelle il y a des domaines *interdits*. Le fidéisme a remplacé la confiante construction néo-platonicienne et l'héritage humaniste — celui de Ficin comme celui de Léon — demeure à l'état de tentation, sinon de nostalgie. Nous voyons ici, en prenant la longue vie de Tyard comme exemple, les limites auxquelles se heurte en France, au cours du dernier tiers du XVIe siècle, la philosophie néo-platonicienne et intégrative: ce sont les limites chronologiques de la Renaissance elle-même.

Si l'on recherche, au contraire, le modèle néo-platonicien et ses variations dans la production poétique et philosophique des années 1550, on constate chez Tyard une ferveur quasi fabriste pour Platon. Bien qu'il n'y ait aucune preuve concrète de la présence de Pontus de Tyard au collège Cardinal-Lemoine où Lefèvre d'Etaples avait enseigné peu avant les années étudiantes de Pontus,[11] j'incline à penser que Tyard a fréquenté ce milieu collégial. Le Collège royal fut dépourvu, pendant plusieurs décennies après sa fondation en 1530, d'un bâtiment qui lui appartînt en propre et c'est donc dans les collèges existants, et notamment à Cardinal Lemoine, que se répandait la pensée et la méthodologie de Lefèvre d'Etaples. Celui-ci pratiquait, on le sait, une pédagogie qui réconciliait idées antiques et chrétiennes, s'élevant graduellement 'de la sagesse hellénique à la sagesse des apôtres' (Boisset). La réaction de Lefèvre contre les méthodes scolastiques passe primordialement par sa traduction d'Aristote qui cherche à compléter et corriger les traductions italiennes. Pourquoi le rapprocher ici de Tyard? C'est que Lefèvre est aussi l'auteur des *Hecatonomiarum libri* où sont énoncées 700 propositions de Platon extraites de la *République* et des *Lois*, ouvrage réédité en 1511, 1526 et 1543. Or, Ficin avait déjà traduit Platon, et il est possible — et cela a même été réalisé par le regretté Jean Boisset[12] — de mettre face à face les propositions fabristes et le texte platonicien de Ficin relatif à ces propositions. La corrélation est remarquable. Il est à noter, en outre, que ce qui a poussé Lefèvre d'Etaples à faire ce travail en Platon, ce furent les fréquentes allusions faites à Aristote par les néo-platoniciens; d'ailleurs, les *Hecatonomiarum libri* sont joints aux commentaires du *Politique* et de l'*Economique*. L'ordre des fiches ne suit ni Platon ni Ficin, mais les idées de Lefèvre d'Etaples lui-même — indépendance jusque dans la volonté de synthèse qui caractérisera aussi Tyard. L'exemple de Lefèvre nous montre qu'avant la grande vague de traductions platoniciennes vers le français qu'encouragera Marguerite de Navarre au cours des années 1530 et 1540, il y eut en France une présence ficinienne, attentive non seulement aux aspects ontologiques et cosmologiques du platonisme mais aussi aux bases morales de sa construction.

C'est évidemment auprès de Maurice Scève et non des théologiens parisiens que Pontus de Tyard apprend à traduire en poésie la vision platonicienne et ses accents dit pétrarquistes. Loin de s'exclure mutuellement d'ailleurs, ces modèles tendent à notre avis à se recombiner en une synthèse nouvelle dans l'imaginaire tyardien. Il est hors de doute toutefois, et des passages entiers du *Solitaire premier* en témoignent, qu'au cours des années '50 Tyard considère Ficin comme le plus grand médiateur platonicien de son époque, et épouse à bien des égards sa vision tout en la transformant. (La conciliation de Ficin avec Léon l'Hébreu, dans ce même *Solitaire premier*, constitue un exemple majeur de cette transformation.)

Tyard est loin d'être seul à opérer de telles conciliations. Dans la génération précédente déjà, selon Gilmore, 'in his general optimism, in his emphasis upon the freedom of the will and possibly the glory of man, and in the development of a theory of love Ficino has been regarded as the formulator of a Renaissance philosophy'[13] — philosophie qui avait en outre le mérite, on le comprend de mieux en mieux, de véhiculer aussi dans son interprétation de Platon les intuitions des Pères de l'Eglise, des mystiques allemands, de Nicolas de Cuse et, nous l'avons déjà montré, de la tradition aristotélicienne. C'est ainsi également que Ficin était perçu en Angleterre: Cassirer le considère, par exemple, comme l'ancêtre lointain, mais essentiel, des Cambridge Platonists et note à ce propos cette mobilité du ficinianisme qui est aujourd'hui notre sujet. Chez ces penseurs, comme chez Tyard, les lignes de démarcation sont extrêmement difficiles à fixer entre divers éléments néo-platoniciens.

In these writers the teachings of Plato always appear as it were transformed through a refracting medium. It is especially that picture of the Platonic philosophy drawn by Marsilio Ficino and the Florentine Academy

that seemed authentic and exemplary ... They added no essential new
feature to this picture ... Hence all stable historical demarcations vanish:
the primary and the derived, the original and the traditional are never differentiated ... [Plato] is the ancestor and patron of the *pia philosophia*,
which existed even before the Christian revelation.[14]

Tyard poète et philosophe sera longtemps tenté par l'optimisme religieux de l'Académie florentine. S'il limite la connaissance humaine,
comme le Cusain, à un statut symbolique, ce statut est valorisé par le
fait que le symbole correspond à l'essence divine inconnaissable. Noms
et concepts ne sauraient épuiser la réalité ni le sens du divin; mais ils
possèdent vis-à-vis du divin un rôle médiateur, donc une relation avec
lui dont ils vivent, et qui leur confère leur réalité. C'est cela qui
garantit et libère à la fois le savoir des hommes et permet ainsi à la
science de se constituer: 'cognoscitur inattingibilis veritatis unitas in
alteritate conjoncturali.' ('C'est dans l'altérité conjecturale que nous
connaissons l'inatteignable unité de la verité').[15]

Si nous devions considérer Pontus de Tyard uniquement sur le plan
poétique, il faudrait reconnaître en Platon, ou plutôt dans l'intertexte
platonicien, le substrat majeur de son imaginaire. Le difficile est de dis-
cerner (ainsi que le montre Cassirer) les éléments issus directement de
Platon, et ceux issus des différents néo-platoniciens. En tout état de
cause, les trois livres des *Erreurs amoureuses* sont des *canzonieri* selon le
modèle pétrarquien, et comme tels, en apparence du moins, univo-
ques. Le *Troisième livre* prend une certain distance vis-à-vis de la dame
impitoyable, et se situe surtout dans l'intemporel. Il est accompagné,
lors de sa publication, d'un *Livre de vers liriques* dont les sujets sont, au
contraire, très diversifiés et qui pourtant se rattache ostensiblement au
platonisme par une 'Ode du Socratique' alors que, dans l'ensemble, les
Erreurs amoureuses incarnent le platonisme indirectement, au niveau
des thèmes et de l'expression. L'analyse de l'"Ode du Socratique' révèle
cependant que la doctrine platonicienne n'y est nullement traitée pour
elle même, mais comme fait historique, voire biographique; il s'avère
que le Socratique, c'est-à-dire le disciple de Socrate, n'est autre que le
poète lui-même; que la doctrine de Platon est invoquée dans le con-
texte d'une opposition idéologique, et peut-être personnelle, entre
ceux qui choisissent la spiritualité et la contemplation, et leurs détrac-
teurs. Une seule strophe, enchâssée dans le poème à la manière d'un
médaillon, prend pour object la pensée platonicienne elle-même en
une formulation si dense qu'on la sent emblématique pour le reste de
l'oeuvre:

O centre, où sied la bonté

En non mobile asseurance,
Fais qu'en ta circonference,
La vagabonde beauté
Des saints raiz de la clarté
De ta lumiere feconde
Incorpore sa couleur,
Rendant la Sphere du Monde
En sa parfaite rondeur.[16]

Rien ici ne contredit Léon l'Hébreu, et Ficin encore moins, puisque la notion d'un centre d'où émane toute lumière, c'est-à-dire dont tout être est tributaire, est proche surtout de Platon lui même (sans oublier Plotin). Tout au plus pourrait-on penser qu'aux yeux de Ficin la beauté, tout en émanant du centre, est forcément centrifuge et vagabonde, d'où le désir du poète qu'elle reste en tout temps totalement éclairée par la lumière qui provient du centre; alors que dans la perspective de Léon l'Hébreu l'accent serait sur l'altérité du beau par rapport au centre; ce qui à son tour suggérerait que Ficin est plus proche d'Avicenne (doctrine du reflet), et Léon l'Hébreu d'Averroès (doctrine de la réfraction). Au sein du poème cependant, bien que ces variations soient suggérées, elles le sont dans l'unité de la symbolique platonicienne.

Et c'est cette unité, plutôt qu'un certain style pétrarquiste, qui caractérise les *Erreurs amoureuses*, où elle est implicite. Il est vrai qu'au niveau épisodique, l'amour humain avec toutes ses vicissitudes psychologiques est au premier plan, alors que chez Ficin et même chez Léon l'Hébreu — qui toutefois à travers Philon assume parfois le masque de l'amoureux angoissé — cet amour ne constitue qu'un premier niveau de réalité. Certes, l'existence de l'amour principe universel n'invalide en rien le simple amour humain; pourtant, l'amant se détachera de l'objet temporel de son amour pour le remplacer par des symboles ou des aspects de l'être aimé, de plus en plus spirituels.

Ficin, différent en cela de Léon l'Hébreu, met en opposition amour charnel et beauté:

Motus igitur huiusmodi, qui ad ea rapiunt, inter se videntur esse contrarii. Quapropter libido conitus, id est, coeundi, et amor, non modo non iidem motus sed et contrarii esse monstrantur . . . Hinc efficitur ut omnis amor honestus sit, et omnis amator iustus. Pulcher enim est omnis atque decorus, et decorum proprie diligit.
('Les mouvements qui nous portent vers l'une ou l'autre doivent, par conséquent, être contraires. Voilà pourquoi le désir de l'union charnelle et l'Amour apparaissent comme des mouvements non seulement différents, mais contraires . . . Voilà pourquoi tout amour est honnête et tout amant

juste, car tout amour est beau et décent, et aime avant tout ce qui est décent.)[17]

Tous les percepts alimentant l'imagerie des *Erreurs amoureuses* sont de nature visuelle ou auditive, banissant toute impression tactile car selon Ficin la contemplation de la Beauté est en soi une suprême satisfaction; qui aime vraiment connaît 'mente, visuque et auditu' et non autrement.[18] Ce qui tombe sous les autres sens n'a aucun lien avec la Beauté; on peut aimer un corps pour sa beauté corporelle, mais ce que l'on aime est une image fragile, une ombre. Inversement, donc, l'amour le plus fervent vit de contemplation.

Un des premiers poèmes du *Premier livre des Erreurs amoureuses* traduit ce sens quasi religieux de la contemplation; en interprétant ce poème, le sonnet V, on peut évidemment considérer — mais c'est là une réduction indue — toutes ses expressions et connotations ficiniennes à autant de traits stylistiques issus des *Rime sparse* de Pétrarque et des Quattrocentistes qui furent ses imitateurs. Il reste que ce sonnet tire son unité de son sens du sacré qui s'attache au visage de la dame, exacte expression de *l'attitude* ficinienne:

> Quand je m'eslieve en contemplation,
> M'esmerveillant de ce divin visage,
> Saint et divin, contre mortel usage,
> Fait au pourtrait de la perfection,
> . . .
> Alors j'adore en telle humilité
> Ce saint seul Dieu de ma félicité
> Lequel toujours devotement je prie.[19]

L'amour de la dame mobilise des images qui dans la vision ficinienne appartiennent à la Beauté, laquelle à travers elle-même attire son adorateur vers Dieu: philosophiquement (ainsi que nous l'avons dit à propos de l'"Ode du Socratique') la beauté est à la circonférence d'une réalité dont le centre est en Dieu. Il y a donc entre Pontus de Tyard poète et Ficin un certain renversement, non pas des valeurs ultimes, puisque celles de Ficin existent dans le poème tyardien à l'état de connotations, mais de thèmes dominants et de traits narratifs.[20] C'est que chez Tyard, du moins celui des *Erreurs amoureuses*, tout part de l'aimée et aboutit à l'aimée tout en se chargeant de connotations cosmiques, ontologiques, religieuses; tandis que chez Ficin tout part de Dieu pour aboutir en Dieu, en passant par des zônes de l'être de plus en plus éloignées de Lui. On pourrait dire que si chez l'un l'amour humain est source des symboles de l'amour divin, chez l'autre, c'est-à-dire le Tyard des *Erreurs amoureuses*, l'amour divin prête ses symboles à 1 humain.

Semblablement, dans le domaine des relations cosmiques, un poème comme 'Disgrâce' — un des rares poèmes de Tyard en terze rime — montre l'univers désharmonisé à l'image de la désunion des amants; alors que le poème 'Favorite' suggère, utilisant la même forme, le retour à l'harmonie. De nouveau le symbolisme ficinien sous-tend la vision poétique, lui prêtant sa stabilité dans un monde déstabilisé. Non que ce symbolisme soit ici un simple prétexte: comme dans le cas précédent Tyard assume les valeurs et symboles ficiniens, mais syntagmatiquement son propos est autre:

La haute idée à mon univers mere
Si hautement de nul jamais comprise
M'est à présent tenébreuse Chimere.

Le Ciel, qui fut mon haut Ciel Empyrée
Fixe moteur de ma force premiere
Pour m'affaiblir rend sa force empirée.

La harmonie, aux doux concens nourrie
Des sept accords, contre l'ordre spherique
Horriblement entour mon ouïe crie . . .[21]

Vision ficinienne à rebours, pour ainsi dire; car dans la philosophie de l'amour, à condition qu'un être, à travers l'autre, recherche Dieu, tout est harmonie; et dans la théologie platonicienne la hiérarchie des êtres et des intermédiaires, et l'ordonnance de l'univers, fondent également une harmonie de toute réalité, où l'homme aussi est impliqué. Dieu domine la matière, qui n'est sujette à la multiplicité et à la modification qu'à des niveaux inférieurs: l'unité est plus puissante que la multiplicité. Dieu possède unité et stabilité. 'Dans toute nature effectivement on qualifie de stable ce qui possède une seule manière d'être d'une façon si constante qu'il ne s'écarte pas de l'unité de sa nature.'[22] Le poème 'Disgrâce' inverse donc, par imagination, l'harmonie ficinienne par la privation de tout ce qui la constitue. On peut d'ailleurs penser que les symboles de désordre cosmique y connotent aussi un niveau religieux où l'âme se sentirait séparée de Dieu. Niveau amoureux et niveau religieux se correspondent dans cette désharmonie, comme aussi dans l'harmonie du sonnet V analysé plus haut; car chez Tyard comme chez Ficin toute expérience active ou contemplative a pour but l'harmonie avec Dieu.

A cet égard, harmonie avec Dieu, harmonie de ses amants entre eux, harmonie au sein de l'âme et de l'âme avec le cosmos, et harmonie du cosmos sous-tendue par la stabilité de Dieu sont des aspects d'une seule et même harmonie au sein du Tout. En morale, l'homme apprend à se gouverner, de même que dans l'ordre universel Dieu domine les mouvements du ciel. De l'ordre universel Ficin dit que 'ni le corps mobile du ciel, ni le moteur qui se meut d'après le mouvement du ciel ne sont principes premiers . . . Toujours, en effet, le mouvement s'effectue et est guidé vers ce qui est stable et autour de ce qui est stable.'[23] Au nom de ce même principe, l'amant doit désirer en l'aimée le plus stable, c'est-à-dire le plus spirituel. A cet égard, la doctrine de 'l'honneste amour', adoptée par du Bellay dans les *Treize sonnets* à la suite des *Erreurs amoureuses* de 1549, s'insère dans une longue tradition occidentale qui vient de s'exprimer, entre autres, dans *L'Heptaméron* de Marguerite de Navarre, plus spécialement à travers le personnage de Dagoucin. Telle chanson de Tyard enchâsse avec rigueur cette éthique amoureuse inséparable de son esthétique, et toute orientée vers l'immortel en l'être aimé:

> Je suis constraint d'estimer
>   Et aimer
> Ce qu'en vous j'ay peu comprendre
> Tant excellent et parfait
>
> Chacun jugeant de dehors
>   Et le corps
> Et la belle face estime:
> Bien prisé-je en vous ces deux:
>   Mais je veux
> Vous avoir en plus d'estime.[24]

L'amour repose donc sur la connaissance; mais celle-ci, loin d'être un état abstrait, procède, psychologiquement, de l'illumination qu'est la fureur amoureuse. Dans la vie de l'homme qui cherche, à travers l'amour du beau, la connaissance du bien, il y a concordance de toutes les puissances de l'âme, successivement mises en oeuvre par les quatre fureurs; et ces quatre états exaltés, mouvements extraordinaires de l'âme, correspondent à la hiérarchie des quatre cercles qui, dans le monde, entourent la bonté divine.

Pourquoi ne pas remonter, demande Raymond Marcel en expliquant cette doctrine ficinienne, vers Dieu, par le même chemin que celui qu'Il a tracé pour venir jusqu'à nous?[25] Telle est la fonction des fureurs dans la vie humaine: elles sont mouvements vers Dieu, hors de

la multiplicité — et il faudrait ici parler des résonances plotiniennes —
de la division, de la discorde. L'homme qui tombe dans le royaume
sensuel doit, pour revenir à lui-même et à Dieu franchir, dans son
ascension, quatre degrés dont chacun libérera davantage son âme
grâce aux fureurs respectives: la fureur poétique soutenue par les
Muses, la fureur religieuse par Dionysos, la fureur prophétique par
Apollon et la fureur amoureuse par Vénus. L'amour tel que le conçoit
Ficin, et Tyard à sa suite, est donc spirituel et salvateur, d'autant plus
que la progression éthique, par suite des liens ontologiques et cosmologiques de la Beauté, implique une intégration de plus en plus parfaite
de l'âme individuelle avec le dessein universel.

Dans le *Solitaire premier* Ficin est englobé parmi les 'philosophes pla-
toniques' lesquels

tiennent que l'ame descendant en ce corps distribuée en diverses opérations perd l'unité tant estimée, qui la rendoit cognoissante, et jouissant du
souverain *un*, qui est Dieu: tellement qu'en ceste division, et separation de
son unité, ses parties superieures endormies, et ensevelies en une lente
paresse, cedent l'entier gouvernement aux inferieures touchées sans cesse
des perturbations: et ainsi demeure toute l'ame remplie de discordes . . .
Aussi c'est là, où gist . . . le labeur à tirer l'ame embourbée hors de la fange
terrestre, et l'eslever en la conjonction du souverain *un*, afin qu'elle mesme
soit remise en sa premiere unité. Or, pource que l'ame en descendant, et
s'abismant dans le corps, passe par quatre degrez, il est pareillement neces-
saire, que par quatre degrez son elevation de ça bas en haut, soit faite.
Quant aux quatre degrez de la descente, le premier, et plus haut, est l'An-
gelique entendement, le second la Raison intellectuelle, le tiers Opinion, et
le quart la Nature.[26]

Fortement inspirée de la *Theologia platonica*, cette description de la
chute et de la remontée de l'âme illustre d'une manière dramatique le
dualisme ultime de Ficin, et celui de Tyard qui, à cet égard, le suit.
C'est en fréquentant Léon l'Hébreu que Tyard nuancera graduellement son dualisme, dans la mesure où la matière apparaît chez celui-ci
comme le support nécessaire de la beauté, donc de l'intelligible. Certes,
c'est la forme d'un corps qui est le principe de sa beauté; mais la
beauté habite et transfigure les éléments matériels du corps. De plus,
sans admettre que cette notion établisse une différence absolue entre
Platon et Aristote, Léon l'Hébreu reconnaît que chez ce dernier 'la
materia e il corpo entri ne l'essenzia e sustanzia de le cose corporeo.'[27]
Au bout d'une longue démonstration, même si Aristote perd, dans la

réconciliation des deux systèmes de pensée, quelque chose de sa concentration sur le monde des effets, il n'en reste pas moins qu'il a valorisé celui-ci aux yeux de Léon l'Hébreu. Selon le premier dialogue, s'il y a des amours et des désirs correspondant à des objets illusoires et décevants, d'autre objets sont doués de réalité ontologique et fondent des amours réels; et cette réalité humaine se répercute à l'échelle universelle toutes les fois qu'il y a interaction du principe mâle et du principe féminin.

Par ailleurs, la structure littéraire des *Dialoghi d'amore*, qui réapparaît transformée au goût de la haute société française du XVIe siècle, dans le *Solitaire premier*, souligne la valeur ontologique de l'expérience amoureuse en soi; même si le psychisme de l'homme et de la femme ne sont qu'images des principes qu'ils incarnent, et qui renvoient à l'activité créatrice de Dieu vis à-vis de lui-même d'abord, puis du monde, ce sont des images réelles: en effet, tout dans l'univers appartient à son unité organique, laquelle surmonte multiplicité et diversité par le processus cyclique partant de Dieu et retournant à lui.

Ainsi, la familiarité de Léon l'Hébreu, et la réalité qu'il confère aux comportements humains, enrichissent par leurs connotations l'énumération ainsi que le rôle des quatre fureurs au sein du *Solitaire premier*. Le fait que les quatre puissances de l'âme soient hiérarchisées n'empêche pas leur unité. Le 'souverain *un*' dont l'âme procède 'non seulement unit toutes les parties de l'Ame, en l'Ame: mais encore unit par conjonction l'Ame à soy mesmes.'[28] Dans le texte tyardien, avant sa différenciation en quatre états différents, la fureur, on l'oublie trop souvent, est une:

Ainsi que la descente se faisoit par quatre degrez . . . aussi pour remonter estoient necessaires quatre degrez, lesquels se peuvent comprendre en celle illustration d'Ame ou elevation d'Entendement, que je vous ay dit estre nommée fureur divine. Car la fureur divine, Pasithée, est l'unique escalier, par lequel l'Ame peut trouver le chemin qui la conduise à la source de son souverain bien, et félicité dernière.[29]

Donc, ce qui est souvent décrit comme quatre états spécifiques procède d'une seule et même réalité diversement manifestée.

En quatre sortes . . . peut l'homme estre espris de divine fureur. La premiere est par la fureur Poëtique procedant du don des Muses. La seconde est par l'intelligence des mysteres, et secrets des religions sous Bacchus. La troisiesme par ravissement de prophetie, vaticination ou divination souz Apollon; et la quatrieme par la violence de l'amoureuse affection souz Amour et Venus.[30]

Le fait que 'souz ces quatre especes sont cachées toutes les plus abs-traites et sacrées choses, ausquelles l'humain Entendement puisse aspirer'[31] réfère donc au centre nerveux de la pensée de Tyard, où Ficin, de qui provient la description des fureurs, et Léon l'Hébreu avec ses bases à la fois plotiniennes et bibliques reliant tout être à l'Être et donnant à l'âme un dynamique rôle intermédiaire, fondent ensemble la justification de toute activité humaine placée sous le signe de l'intelli-gible. Il est à noter que 'l'honneste amour' y appartient tout comme la poésie et que dans cette perspective l'oeuvre poétique de Tyard, en majorité contemporaine des deux *Solitaires*, est nourrie comme eux du double intertexte néo-platonicien dominé par Ficin et Léon l'Hébreu.

L'amour humain ainsi conçu est non-rationnel en ce sens qu'il est supra-rationnel. Du point de vue ficinien en effet, la raison intellec-tuelle vient après 'l'angélique entendement' dans la hiérarchie des puis-sances; et du point de vue de Léon l'Hébreu, il existe une 'raison extraordinaire' incitant l'homme, et en particulier l'amant, à outre-passer les bornes de la raison 'ordinaire' afin de conquérir plus sûre-ment l'objet aimé. Une fois de plus, l'idéal éthique d'un penseur de la Renaissance se trouve ainsi sous-tendu par une psychologie tournée vers l'ontologie en laquelle toute impulsion trouve son explication der-nière.

Admettre ceci, c'est aussi reconnaître que la structure littéraire des deux *Solitaires*, à la suite de celle des *Dialoghi d'amore*, vaut non seule-ment par la dialogicité que nous avons plusieurs fois analysée ail-leurs,[32] mais par son iconicité sur le plan philosophique. Au niveau épisodique, Sophie et Pasithée représentent bien la femme aristocra-tique cultivée, héroïne de maint *canzoniere*. Mais au niveau du signifié elles sont comme leurs partenaires masculins respectifs, Philon et le Solitaire, en première instance projections d'un débat intérieur. Il est significatif que la différenciation des personnages, chez l'Hébreu comme chez Tyard, soit sexuelle. L'accession de la femme au statut de person-nage du dialogue est en soi un nouvel indice de dialogicité pour l'époque. Mais surtout, au sens le plus général, la division sexuelle est profondément gravée non seulement en l'être humain mais en toute réalité telle que la perçoit Léon l'Hébreu, et qui dans le prolongement de la doctrine platonicienne de l'Eros consiste en un incessant pro-cessus d'engendrement dans le temps corrélatif de l'universelle organi-cité.

Au troisième des *Dialoghi d'amore*, particulièrement, la dualité, à tous les niveaux de l'être, donne naissance à la multiplicité, mais n'en figure pas moins en elle-même l'unité qui lui a donné naissance. Ici, il fau-drait considérer plus en détail la différence entre la dualité ainsi

conçue chez Léon l'Hébreu, et le dualisme ficinien issu de Platon. Le
Dieu de Léon l'Hébreu nécessite l'Autre. Comme l'explique A. Perry

the first love is God's love for himself and is therefore eternal. Though
God is perfectly one and simple, there occurs a mysterious multiplication
within Him: just as Eve is mythologically said to have sprung from the
body of Adam, in an analogous way the original active entity (God's beauty
or simply essence) produces a feminine entity … Beyond this original,
intrinsic love, God also loves extrinsically. In loving himself, God also
desires to reproduce his beauty. Thus, God has two loves: the first toward
himself, the second toward His images or creatures. The crucial role here
is played by the divine intellect, which in addition to loving God in perfect
contemplation, also contains the ideas or patterns of creation.[33]

Or, si l'intellect, en son premier amour, est féminin, il est masculin, car
actif, lorsqu'il se tourne vers les idées, ses créatures. A ce stade, l'Intellect ne contemple plus Dieu mais se contemple lui-même, et de cette
contemplation naît une entité féminine, qui est chaos ou matière origi-
nelle. Ainsi, forme première et matière première, intellect et chaos,
apparaissent alternativement comme principe mâle et principe femelle,
parents premiers de la création dont l'amour donne lieu, dorénavant, à
tout autre génération.

L'originalité de cette conception consiste en ce que principe masculin
et féminin, inférieur et supérieur perdent leurs connotations hiérarchisées; il ne reste qu'un passage graduel de l'intelligible au sensible; il
y a séquence plutôt que chute. C'est là une des principales contributions de Léon à Pontus de Tyard. Dans le *Solitaire premier* il est encore
question de chute au sujet de ceux qui s'endurcissant dans leur maté-
rialisme doivent remonter de très bas. Au tournant du *Discours du
temps*, l'acceptation du processus temporel, et l'exploration scientifique
qui s'ensuit dans l'*Univers* manifestent respectivement l'influence de
l'aspect judaïque et de l'aspect aristotélicien reçu de Léon l'Hébreu.

Il est vrai que Ficin avait ouvert la voie à cette exploration, dans la
mesure où chez lui l'objet de la connaissance demeure aligné avec l'intellect divin: 'Tout ce qui est présenté clairement, l'intellect le reconnaît
naturellement. Tout ce qui se présente sous la raison de bien, la
volonté le désire naturellement.'[34] Mais à l'extérieur de cette zone de
continuité avec le divin il se constitue, selon la tendance platonicienne,
un résidu encore chaotique, insoumis; et c'est cela que Tyard peut sur-
monter grâce à la notion d'un univers totalement organique rendue
possible par la synthèse de Léon l'Hébreu. C'est ce dont fait foi
l'oeuvre philosophique de Tyard: comme Ficin il part de l'âme immor-
telle et raisonnable, issue de Dieu et aspirant à travers toute l'expé-

rience terrestre à retourner vers lui. Léon l'Hébreu lui apprend à s'attarder sur l'univers dans et par lequel se découvre l'harmonie divine.

McGill University

Notes

1 Ce terme est employé ici par *analogie* avec le syncrétisme de l'ère hellénistique, uniquement.

2 Suzanne Damiens, *Amour et intellect chez Léon l'Hébreu* (Toulouse: Privat, 1971), p. 23.

3 Jean Daniélou, *Philon d'Alexandrie: Platonisme et Théologie mystique* (Paris: A. Fayard, 1958), p. 163, cité par S. Damiens, *Amour et intellect*, p. 24.

4 Cité par Gaston Boissier, *Fin du paganisme antique* (Paris: Hachette, 1891), t. IV, 327-42.

5 Grégoire de Nysse, *Sur l'âme et la résurrection*, p. 196 et ss., cité par S. Damiens, *Amour et intellect*, p. 26.

6 Léon l'Hébreu, *Dialogues d'amour*, trad. Pontus de Tyard, edited with an introduction and notes, by T. Anthony Perry (Chapel Hill: The University of North Carolina Press, 1974), p. 166.

7 Pontus de Tyard, *Trois livres d'homilies* (Paris: Mamert Patisson, 1586), pp. 44-45.

8 Tyard, *Trois livres d'homilies*, p. 45.

9 Cristoforo Landino, *Disputationes camaldulenses* II, 19; cité par R. Marcel, *Marsile Ficin* (Paris: Belles Lettres, 1958), p. 319.

10 Tyard, *Trois livres d'homilies*, p. 162.

11 Lefèvre d'Etaples meurt en 1536, c'est-à-dire un an seulement avant l'arrivée de Pontus de Tyard à Paris; son enseignement à Cardinal-Lemoine se situe toutefois dans les décennies précédentes. Dès 1520 il est appelé à Meaux par Briçonnet; en 1523 paraît sa version française du Nouveau Testament et on le voit bibliothécaire royal à Blois 1526 et réfugié à Nérac auprès de la reine de Navarre à partir de 1531. Nous parlons donc qu'une tradition qui lui survit à Cardinal-Lemoine, plutôt que d'un impact direct sur Pontus de Tyard et ses contemporains, Peletier du Mans et Guillaume des Autelz.

12 Lefèvre d'Etaples, *Hecatonomiarum libri*, éd. Jean Boisset et R. Combes (Paris: Vrin, 1979).

13 Myron Gilmore, *The World of Humanism* (New York: Harper, 1962), p. 193.

14 Ernst Cassirer, *The Platonic Renaissance in England*, trans. James Pettegrove ([Edinburgh]: Nelson, 1953), p. 8.

15 Nicolas de Cuse cité par Ernst Cassirer, *The Platonic Renaissance in England*, p.14.

16 Pontus de Tyard, *Oeuvres poétiques complètes*, éd. critique John Lapp (Paris: Didier, 1966), p. 174.

17 Marsilio Ficino, *Commentarium Marsilii Ficini Florentini in Convivium Platonis, de amore*, éd. et trad. Raymond Marcel (Paris: Les Belles Lettres, 1956), p. 143.

18 Ficino, *Commentarium*, p. 144.

19 Tyard, *Oeuvres poétiques*, p. 12.

20 C'est bien la beauté divine qui engendre l'amour, c'est-à-dire le désir de Dieu même, au travers de l'expérience de l'amour d'un objet humain. Tout en faisant de celui-ci son objet principal Tyard entoure l'expérience humaine de l'amour d'un réseau de connotations ramenant l'attention du lecteur à la beauté divine, son objet ultime. Son poème dit indirectement ce que Ficin affirme directement:

'C'est là, par conséquent, que notre désir s'allume, là que l'ardeur des amants se repose, non parce qu'elle s'éteint, mais parce qu'elle est comblée.' Ficin, *Commentaire sur le Banquet de Platon*, trad. R. Marcel, p. 145.

21 Tyard, *Oeuvres poétiques*, pp. 19-20.

22 Marsilio Ficino, *Theologia platonica*, ed. Raymond Marcel (Paris: Les Belles Lettres, 1964), I, p. 121.

23 Ficino, *Theologia platonica*, p. 178.

24 Tyard, *Oeuvres poétiques*, p. 44.

25 Voir Raymond Marcel, Introduction à Marsile Ficin, *Commentaire sur le Banquet de Platon*, notamment p. 64.

26 Tyard, *Solitaire premier*, éd. S. Baridon (Genève: Droz, 1950), pp. 12-14.

27 Leone Ebreo, *Dialoghi d'amore*, ed. Santino Caramella (Bari: Laterza, 1929), p. 338.

28 Tyard, *Solitaire premier*, p. 15.

29 Tyard, *Solitaire premier*, p. 16.

30 Tyard, *Solitaire premier*, p. 17.

31 Tyard, *Solitaire premier*, p. 17.

32 Cf. notamment Eva Kushner, 'Le Dialogue en France à la Renaissance: quelques critères génologiques', *Revue canadienne de littérature comparée*, 5 (1978), pp. 142-53; 'Vers une poétique du dialogue de la Renaissance', *Essays presented to G.M. Vajda on his seventieth birthday* (Szeged: Jçozsef Attila Tudományegetem, 1983), 131-36; 'Le dialogue en France de 1550 à 1560', *Le Dialogue au temps de la Renaissance*, éd. M.-T. Jones Davies (Paris: Touzot, 1984), pp. 151-67.

33 T. Anthony Perry, 'Leone Ebreo's *Dialoghi d'amore*: the argument', in *Erotic spirituality: The Integrative Tradition from Leone Ebreo to John Donne* (University, Alab.: University of Alabama Press, 1980), p. 24.

34 Ficino, *Theologia platonica*, éd. Raymond Marcel, vol. II, p. 264.

Arthur M. Lesley

The Place of the *Dialoghi d'amore* in Contemporaneous Jewish Thought*

Study of the *Dialoghi d'amore* has naturally concentrated on its contribution to Renaissance Platonism in philosophy, poetry, and the visual arts, but enough remains unexplained in the peculiar syncretism of the work to justify an attempt to reconstruct its original setting and meaning.[1] The posthumous success of the work with a wide audience, in Italian, Latin, Spanish, and French, tends to obscure the question of why it was written in Hebrew, for a Jewish audience, over thirty years before its publication in Italian. The success of the work in addressing a European audience has led analysis of it to focus on remote, classical sources — Aristotle, Plato, and Plotinus — rather than on the topics of discussion among Jews in Italy during the 1490s. Until the original setting of the *Dialoghi* can be reconstructed, it will be appropriate to say of its author, Yehuda Abravanel (Leone Ebreo), what his character Philo says to Sophia about Aristotle: 'i libri suoi erano editi e non editi: editi solamente a quegli che gli hanno intesi da esso'. ('his books, though published, were not public, but public only to those who heard him interpret them').[2]

The general neglect of the origins of the *Dialoghi d'amore* has been broken only by examination of the sparse evidence for the biography of the author and by speculation on which language was 'lingua sua,' the one in which he composed the work.[3] By taking as axiomatic the conclusion of Carlo Dionisotti and Isaiah Sonne, that the *Dialoghi* were written in Hebrew, around 1502, the original significance of the work, the reaction of its original audience, and the reasons for its neglect until the 1535 printing all begin to be tractable questions.

As will be seen, both the date and the language of Dionisotti's conclusion conform to the contents of the work and to a reasonable reconstruction of its purpose. Neither a Latin, Italian, Spanish, or French work would have been addressed to a Jewish community at that time and, at a later time, this kind of Hebrew work would not have been attempted. The hostile response to the *Dialoghi* that is found in a Hebrew letter of 1506, as will be seen, indicates the lively, albeit antagonistic, interest that it aroused among Jews at that time. Only a work written in Hebrew would have raised a challenge to Jewish thought sufficient to provoke such opposition; a vernacular work, one addressed to Christians, could have been ignored. And if a vernacular *Dialoghi* had been written at this early date, its thirty years of obscurity would be even more difficult to explain than the oblivion of the Hebrew one.

It is worth recalling the function of Hebrew for Jewish communities. Although Hebrew was not the exclusive spoken language of any Jewish community between the time of the Mishnah (200 C.E.) and twentieth-century Israel, it continued to be the learned language, parallel to Latin, as well as the language of Bible study and prayer, for all European Jewish communities. The extent of the use of Hebrew for scholarship is indicated by the fact that translations of Averroes, Avicenna, and other philosophers were being made for Giovanni Pico della Mirandola, Domenico Grimani, and others, from Hebrew translations.[4]

Original works, of course, continued to be written in Hebrew. Abraham Farissol records having participated in a series of religious debates with a Dominican and a Franciscan at the Este court in Ferrara in 1487. In response to their requests, he supplied them with a copy of his arguments 'in their language,' but only after writing them in Hebrew.[5] In contrast, Jewish works in the vernacular were rare at this time. Later, in 1550, Samuel Usque wrote a major work, *Consolation for the Tribulations of Israel*, in Portuguese, but this, like other Portuguese writings of that time for Jews, was addressed to those who had been Christians, entirely out of touch with Hebrew for two or three generations. Also, by that time the vernacular languages had greatly increased their capacity to deal with subjects that previously had been treated only in Latin.

In addition to these arguments for a Hebrew original of the *Dialoghi d'amore*, there may also be cited the five Italian manuscripts of the third dialogue that have recently been discovered. One, discussed by Dionisotti, and the other four, which so far have not been described, are apparently all different from each other and from the printed text, but differ only stylistically, as would different translations, rather than in content.[6] With greater probability on the side of a Hebrew original than of any other, most of our attention may be concentrated on the circumstances that confirm the date of 1502, found in the text, as accurate for the composition of the work.

Recent study of the several currents of Jewish intellectual life in late fifteenth-century Italy makes it possible to situate the *Dialoghi d'amore* within the particular circumstances of Jewish thought of the time; to recover, in Hebrew terms, the generic identification of the work; and, with the evidence of a Hebrew letter from 1506, to reconstruct some of the reasons for the oblivion into which the work fell until Christians in Rome published it and gave it a place in European literature.

The place of the *Dialoghi* in Hebrew discourse obviously is connected with the social and political circumstances of the Jews in Italy, the major features of which ought to be kept in mind. At the end of the fifteenth century, Jews were scattered along the northern half of the Italian peninsula, in a wide variety of jurisdictions. Except for the old Jewish settlements in Sicily, Naples, and Rome, Jews were, north of Rome, in new, impermanent settlements of dozens of persons, rather than larger numbers. During the fourteenth century, local authorities in those regions had begun to allow Jews to resettle for short periods, which could be renewed or discontinued, for the purpose of carrying on loan-banking. The household of each loan-banker could include a miniature Jewish community of teachers, servants, butcher and physician, along with the extended family of the banker. During the sixteenth century some of these new settlements established more formal communal institutions, as they became more permanent. A further complication for these Jewish communities was the heterogeneity of their population. Although some were composed mainly of southern Italian Jews, and others, of German Jews, there was an increasing mixture of migrants, notably those who had been expelled from France, Provence, and Spain. The sudden expulsion of 150,000 Jews from Spain in 1492 led to a considerable period of Jewish migration, and thousands passed through Italy and settled there. They were culturally distinct and had to be integrated into the communities in which they settled.

The differences between all these groups included such things as the language of daily speech, customs, educational traditions, and methods of applying Jewish law. All Jewish communities would share study of the Bible and rabbinic literature, as well as preaching and the practice of making legal decisions, but beyond these fundamentals there was great variety. Several 'national' groups of Jews had philosophical traditions, which continued the Arabic transmission of the Aristotelian canon, commentaries, and methods. Maimonides was the central Jewish philosopher, Averroes the most important commentator on Aristotle, and the Christian scholastics were increasingly studied.[7] Other communities ignored or suppressed philosophy. Some had one or several schools of Cabala practised among them. In addition to these divergences among Jews from different regions outside Italy, there were distinctive Italian practices. One distinctive Italian Jewish development was a humanist movement, based upon the adaptation of Latin rhetoric to the Hebrew Bible. Unlike both philosophers and Cabalists, the

Hebrew rhetoricians discussed all topics before any audience, instead of restricting their teaching to the initiated.

The political situation which these demographic, economic, and cultural circumstances created was dominated by four critical necessities. The existence of each Jewish community in Italy, and indeed of all of them together, in the era of total expulsion from Spain, France, Provence, and Portugal, depended on the ability of representatives of the Jews in conducting relations with the Italian authorities. Equally fundamental was the need to establish legitimate leadership in communities where there could be no traditional leadership. Closely related to this was the necessity of conciliating, if not integrating, diverse populations within particular communities. Finally, these scattered and weak Jewish communities needed to communicate with others and to establish means for coordinating intercommunal relations, both for dealing with Italian authorities and for establishing lines of authority and obligation in such matters as religious law. These political considerations were a factor in intellectual life as well. Appropriate learning was a characteristic of an authoritative figure in what was, in a way, a society of tiny courts in the shadow of the neighbouring Italian courts. Wealth, ancestry, learning, and influence with the authorities gained ascendancy among Jewish communities. Any literary composition by a member of the élite was, then, a political as well as an erudite gesture.

This factor must be considered in understanding the reaction to the *Dialoghi d'amore*. Yehuda Abravanel, as a learned physician with eminent clients, as a member of a wealthy, well placed family, as an exile from Portugal and Spain, and as the son of the outstanding Biblical commentator and leader of the Spanish Jews, was a candidate for influence among Jews in Italy. Precisely where the intellectual tendency of the *Dialoghi* would place him among the various communities and schools of thought will be apparent after these have been represented by their self-characterizations and by descriptions of them provided by their rivals.

Polemical occasions, on which spokesmen for each group define themselves and their opponents, are generally revealing. It is important to note whom they are criticizing and excluding from conciliation, as well as what they consider to be the core of their own teachings. The dispute which provided the basis for the following survey of Jewish intellectual life occurred in 1490-91, just before Yehuda Abravanel and his father arrived in Naples in 1492. This dispute is particularly interesting because it may well have been provoked by the appearance of the Hebrew work that bears the closest resemblance to the *Dialoghi*.

Elijah del Medigo (c. 1460-1493), a rabbi and physician from Candia, Crete, was Giovanni Pico's first Hebrew consultant, beginning in Padua in 1481.[8] In his *Examination of Religion*, written in December 1490, del Medigo identifies himself as a Maimonidean of the Averroist school, whose major interests are metaphysics, natural science, and logic. As he wrote to Pico, 'I have no stronger desire than to leave behind a student who is truly knowledgeable and understands the teachings of the peripatetics; and I believe that this desire will be realized by you.'[9] Del Medigo explains frequently that this professional interest does not lead to conflicts with Jewish study of the Bible and rabbinic writings, because the topics of discussion and the methods of each discipline are distinct:

I do not think that the words of the Torah are explained through the method of philosophy, nor does the former [Torah] need the latter [philosophy]. No one thinks this way, according to my point of view, except for someone who is neither an adherent of Torah nor a philosopher. . . . Moreover, no one would think me in error because in my philosophic works I deal with the philosophers according to their methodology.[10]

Del Medigo's 'modified version of the double-truth theory' asserts that reason and revelation do not contradict each other on basic principles, but that if there is an apparent contradiction, reason must concede the point to revelation. Del Medigo respects the distinct methods of both rabbinic legal reasoning and the demonstrative, syllogistic proofs of physics. The way to avoid apparent conflicts between the two is to employ only the proper method of each field for studying its canonical texts and subject matter.

Therefore my way differs from that of many self-styled philosophers of our people, who teach the meanings of the Torah and science and mix together the two disciplines, the religious and the speculative methods, the general and the specific, as if to be mediators between the religionists and the philosophers . . . with the result that these men are neither Torah scholars nor scientists. I think that they were brought to this by hatred of the other sects and their explanations. They are, nevertheless, worthy to be given the benefit of the doubt, since they seem only to want to magnify the Torah . . . and since their statements are much closer to rational study, and thus they leave a place for reason, and do not reject it, as do some from the other sects.[11]

Del Medigo's insistence on the appropriateness of the method of study to its particular subject directly opposes, it should be noted, the specific virtue of rhetoric, namely its applicability to all topics.

Del Medigo attacks the Cabalists most forcefully, especially in a letter
to Pico, where he is trying to dissuade his student from pursuing his
interest in 'isto benedicto Chabala,' a phrase in which more than one
scholar has found the word 'benedicto' to be sarcastic.[12] He also criti-
cizes '"a few people, [who] from their love of Plato's method" use the
demonstrations of Aristotle to explain the riddles of Plato, . . . because
they think that there is truth in every type of wisdom.'[13] To emphasize
the philosophic calm that his beliefs allow him, del Medigo caricatures
the other sects as brawlers:

The people of this sect [Cabalists] call the other sect [mediators] heretics
and raise their confused alarums among the masses; and the sect of the
self-styled philosophers say that the Cabalists are stupid fools, who extin-
guish the light of the Torah. And hatred has been great . . . especially
among the ignorant of the two sects, so that the Torah has almost been
made into many Torahs.[14]

At the end of *The Examination of Religion*, del Medigo recommends
that the authorities of the Jewish community condemn to death, apparently as equivalent to false prophets, 'those who reveal the secret of
God to those who are unfit to know it,'[15] that is, those who publicize
and perhaps print syncretistic or Cabalistic teachings, especially explanations for divine commandments. It is worth noting that del Medigo's
offence is also a defence: he appears to have been subjected to criticism
for having printed scientific works in Latin.[16]
    Spokesmen for del Medigo's opponents, either explicitly or by impli-
cation, were also each defending a valuable principle, against his principle of *Lehrfreiheit*. In 1491 the Cabalist Rabbi Isaac Mar Ḥayyim
wrote to Isaac da Pisa, a member of the outstanding Jewish banking
family in Florence, on a disputed fine point of Cabala, to advocate
subjugating rational investigation to the presumed revelation of Cabala:

I do not admonish you, my lord, who are wise as an angel, but remind,
that since you are investigating these things, you must not follow those
scholars who make reason the root and interpret the words of Cabala in a
manner conforming to speculation; rather, you must make Cabala the
root, and try to make reason conform to it.[17]

These remarks can be understood as referring to those whom del
Medigo called 'mediators,' and a recent investigator has identified the

culprit in question as a scholar in da Pisa's household, Yohanan Alemanno, who will be discussed shortly.

In addition to dedicated Averroists and uncompromising Cabalists, there were moralists who traced the troubles of the Jews to philosophy. Yosef Yavets, an exile from Spain who was among those associated with Isaac Abravanel in Naples, developed the argument in his *Or ha-Hayyim* (*The Light of Life*). He particularly attacks the philosophers for their double truth:

They, 'the blind,' interpret David's admonition to Solomon, 'And thou, Solomon my son, know thou the God of thy father' (I Chronicles 28:9) as if addressed only to Solomon, distinct from the whole mass of Israelites. This is supposedly knowledge of God gained by demonstration, which the mass cannot attain. Why did these fools not look at the end of the same verse, 'and serve [*la'avod*] Him [with a whole heart and a willing mind]'? Perhaps they misread it as, 'and destroy [*le'abed*] Him' — God forbid![18]

Yavets continues in the next chapter:

We were commanded not to go after the reasonings of opinion. Know, my son, that just as we were commanded not to pursue the appetites of our instincts, but rather to do the commandments of our blessed God, so were we commanded not to go along the paths of syllogisms, as our reason is inclined to do. For just as the evil impulse naturally loves to commit transgressions and despises commandments of prohibition, . . . just so, human reason misleads man naturally and loves the concepts that it understands, meanwhile despising the veracious opinions of the Torah, the beliefs in reward and punishment, divine revelation, resurrection of the dead, and a great day of judgment, which are contrary to rational proof. Therefore a person must accustom himself to being mindful of the commandments, which are divine concepts, in order to be rescued from the ambush of the human reason, which lurks in wait for man at all times.[19]

A political angle is revealed in Yavets's contrast between simple, faithful Jews, who will be rewarded with eternal bliss, and the élite, who aspire to conjunction with the active intellect:

If there be by chance, God forbid, some ignorant woman who, barren of wisdom and understanding, is unable to conceive of God but in material terms, but on the other hand scrupulously keeps all the commandments and, never transgressing, longs in her heart for her Creator, being ready to sacrifice her very life for God's Law — and indeed, she did suffer greatly on its account — such a woman is kept in much higher regard by the Lord than all those self-styled, wise intellectuals.[20]

Whether or not this populist model of piety is as accurate a description of events in Spain as some historians credit it to be, its bitterness towards the Spanish élite's intellectuality leaves no room for compromise with rationalists.

These three tendencies — Averroism, Cabalism, and moralism — of which other examples could be given, attempt to avoid a conflict between reason and revelation either by suppressing claimants for the other side, or by isolating reason and revelation from each other. As voices of polarization, they appear difficult to conciliate. It is interesting, however, to note that they agree on blaming the 'mediators,' those described as trying to reconcile reason with revelation, evidently through recourse to rhetorical and Platonic discourse, and through rational examination of the Cabala. These are exactly the qualities that would characterize Yehuda Abravanel's *Dialoghi d'amore*, so whoever was the target for this condemnation in 1491 would be a forerunner of the author of the *Dialoghi*.

In the decade before the composition of the *Dialoghi d'amore*, apparently the most notable violator of the borders between reason and revelation, and the precise target of both del Medigo and Mar Ḥayyim' was Yohanan Alemanno. Alemanno (1433/4 — c. 1504), a physician, rabbi, Biblical commentator, teacher, Cabalist, and philosopher, was Pico's other long-time Jewish collaborator. Apparently descended from the last Rabbi of Paris before the expulsion in 1394, Alemanno was active in Padua, Mantua, Florence, and possibly Bologna. He was acquainted with Agostino Nifo, Alberto Pio, and the Mantuan humanist magician, Paride da Ceresara; and Alemanno's son, Isaac, was Gianfrancesco Pico's Hebrew teacher.[21] Alemanno's own statements candidly identify him as one of the 'mediators' whom del Medigo blamed:

How well I know that they will say, 'This one explicitly leaves the paradise of scientific philosophy, without arriving at the speech of a mystic. Where, then, is he?' Necessity has forced me, in explaining this Song of Songs, to leave the ways of philosophy, for it belongs to a different world and to a different science. For the hearts of the ancients are like the gate to a hall, and if they are like mystic angels, we are like human scientists. It is therefore inescapably necessary to rise to the ways of mysticism and Cabala, because this Song is of this genre, as Moses of Narbonne, the first among the latter-day scientists said . . . [On the meaning of the sacrifices in the Bible, we must follow the explations of the Cabalists.] . . . Necessity has brought me to speak of these ways in a middle manner, between mysticism and science. This I have done by citing proof as far as possible from science, to elucidate mysticism. But on some subjects, this is impossible. I shall therefore do as Averroes did in *The Incoherence of the Incoherence* and Ibn Tufayl, in *The Quality of Attachment*. They say numerous times, 'We refer this matter to prophecy.' For of course the giver of the Torah understood its way, and he and the prophets knew its source. Therefore, our words shall be as if neither scientific nor mystical, but as if on the mean between them.[22]

Alemanno recognizes that this choice of crossing disciplinary boundaries, in the manner of rhetoricians, will make him vulnerable to criticism. He makes it, nevertheless, because he considers the double-truth strategy and the obscurity of technical philosophical discussion to be open to abuse by those who mean to be obscurantists. He equally opposes those philosophers' disregard for kinds of knowledge that are not included in Aristotle's canon:

For all kinds of wisdom are worthy of study, because they all support each other and are mutually connected . . . for there is no kind of knowledge that has not its hour, and no science that has not its place. . . . who attains felicity will intend to rise in order, through each science to what is above it . . . I shall tell others just what I say to myself: 'Wisdom is one and inclusive.'[23]

He announces his intention of teaching the unified truth to all audiences:

Everything that I see in the clouds will they, the many, also see, unlike their fathers. *They* took the way of the Lord in one manner on earth, but in another manner they went and spoke to the whole people. . . . This in one of two ways: either they deliberately hid the light from their neighbors, to rise through obscurity upon their backs, and to subjugate them beneath the soles of their feet; or they imagined to themselves that the great lights would wound the eyes of those here with us today, so that evening shadows and faint images would be better for their health, and to themselves alone they would give the perfect light.[24]

Alemanno's interpretive versatility enables him to recover ancient wisdom. Drawing upon an argument used since Hellenistic times, he asserts that the ancient Israelites possessed all learning from revelation, so that, in his time, it is permissible for Jews to investigate or practise a field that was previously cultivated only by the nations. Alemanno uses the argument, more plausibly than justifiers of philosophy, to justify magic, astrology, alchemy, and the equivalent of what was known among the Christians as the ancient theology. He writes, in a notebook entry that lists his central teachings:

Ancient opinions. They appear new, although they are old and are very useful. . . . Clearly a person cannot acquire wisdom unless he rises . . . from the wisdom of the moderns to the wisdom of the ancients. . . . Not only the doctrines of Aristotle and Plato and their predecessors among the nations; but also the most ancient, such as the teachers of the Talmud and the Mishnah, the prophets and Moses, as well as the patriarchs of the world, such as Abraham, Enoch, Methuselah, Seth and Adam, as far as is possible. The wisdom of the ancients, especially of the ancient Hebrews, is not like the wisdom of modern men. For the ancient wisdom is about matters that are certain, is expressed in a few decisive words about the essence of beings, principles and particulars of the sciences, without leaving the slightest doubt in the mind. . . . The knowledge of the modern nations is derived from examples, syllogisms and proofs that remain dubious to people, because of the many arguments that support contrary interpretations.[25]

By rendering permissible for Jews any kind of learning, method, or item of information, the invocation of the ancients opposes Jewish scholastic philosophy to teachings, such as Cabala, which can claim great antiquity and the certainty of revelation. The reaction to such a claim by someone like del Medigo is easy to imagine, especially when Alemanno goes on to teach all this to any audience. Instead of excluding any dubious kind of learning from legitimate study, as del Medigo, Yavets, and Mar Ḥayyim do, Alemanno applies a strategy of inclusiveness, which rhetoric makes possible. Just as Moses and the other prophets knew everything through revelation, and taught it through figurative language to all the Israelites and, in theory, to all humanity, Alemanno could do the same through the use of rhetoric.

Aristotle provides the basis for this strategy. In the *Rhetoric* he distinguishes rhetoric from all other arts, each of which

can instruct or persuade about its own particular subject matter. . . . But rhetoric we look upon as the power of observing the means of persuasion on almost any subject presented to us; and that is why we say that, in its technical character, it is not concerned with any special or definite class of subjects. The duty of rhetoric is to deal with such matters as we deliberate upon without arts or systems to guide us, in the hearing of persons who cannot take in at a glance a complicated argument, or follow a long chain of reasoning.[26]

What Alemanno considers the central virtue of rhetoric is what del Medigo considers its greatest danger. It transgresses disciplinary boundaries and then discusses the topics of each discipline for an untrained audience. When the subject is philosophy, the absence of disciplinary terminology, methods, and preparation makes disciplined argument impossible. Del Medigo would respond by saying that what can be understood only in the technical discussion of a distinct discipline must be concealed from general knowledge. The intellectual, political, and 'national' differences between these two distinguished, Padua-educated physicians and rabbis could not be clearer: Alemanno, the philosopher-Cabalist rhetorician, intends to combine wisdom with eloquence to demonstrate the unity of truth to a general audience, whereas del Medigo, the logician, natural scientist, and metaphysician is willing to appeal to the Jewish authorities to suppress those who would contravene the truce of the 'double truth,' and expose his arcane activity to the ignorant scrutiny of the crowd. The Florentine, descended from French and German Jewish 'nobility,' is opposed by the Venetian subject from Crete. This opposition, which would be generally duplicated by the successors of each — Alemanno by Yehuda Abravanel, and del Medigo by Saul Cohen Ashkenazi — obviously makes facile generalizations about 'Mediaeval' and 'Renaissance' thinkers inapplicable.

Alemanno employed rhetoric to integrate conclusions from such disparate disciplines as philosophy and Cabala in order, it appears, to unify the diverse Jewish communities of central and northern Italy. Composed of Italian, French, German, and Spanish Jews, whose wide divergences could not be eliminated by suppressing certain tendencies, these communities might be harmoniously unified through an application of the model of Florence under Lorenzo de' Medici. Proud of living in Florence, Alemanno makes an effort to show that he has acquired the virtues of the city, which he actually calls 'the just state,' the goal of mediaeval political thought in the Jewish philosophical tradition: 'From them [the Florentines] I have learned the art of gathering all the opinions scattered in Israel, separated by opposition, and how to unify them in a harmony conducive to the true and the just.'[27] Isaac Abravanel similarly preferred republican governments, preeminently Venice, the city in which he spent the last years of his life.[28]

It is Alemanno's commentary on the Song of Songs, *Ḥesheq Shlomo* (*The Desire of Solomon*), that provides the best precedent in Hebrew for Yehuda Abravanel's *Dialoghi d'amore*. Alemanno interprets the Song of Songs to be an allegorical dialogue that teaches how to achieve attachment (*Devekut*) to God. The highest means of attaining this attachment is through the *sefira Tiferet*, or Beauty, the seventh of ten divine aspects or emanations, according to one major system of Cabala. Alemanno's commentary on the Song, like the *Dialoghi*, addresses a general Hebrew audience on a wide variety of topics, and in non-technical language proposes solutions from Biblical study and Cabala for complex

problems of Averroism. Indeed, it could be said that Alemanno's volu-
minous commentary on the Song of Songs stands in the same relation
to the *Dialoghi* as Marsilio Ficino's commentary on the *Symposium* to his
Platonic Theology: the commentary on a classical text prepares for systematic study of some of the same questions.

But why should Alemanno's effort have required the development
that Abravanel gave it? The answer is that, whereas Alemanno was
content to provide, from Jewish sources such as the Song of Songs, an
equivalent of the Platonism that Ficino and his colleagues derived from
Plato, notably from the *Symposium*, Abravanel had to take up the apologetic task on the basis of the same Platonic texts. The most that
Alemanno actually discusses Plato is in invoking his authority from
apocryphal statements, such as Plato's concession that he could not understand the Jewish conception of God because it surpassed human capacity.[29] Abravanel, in contrast, must argue with sufficient effectiveness
to justify Sofia's remark, 'Mi piace vederti fare Platone mosaico e del
numero de 'cabalisti' ('I am content that you are able to reconcile
Plato's opinion with that of Moses and the Cabbalists').[30] Ficino and
Pico made Plato into a support for Christianity; Abravanel had to show
that Plato was no less a Jew. And if the Florentines could turn pagan
myths into secret avowals of Christian truth, if they christened pagan
myths, Abravanel would circumcise them.

It will be necessary to trace the response to Platonism and ancient
theology in Alemanno and Abravanel, to show their advancement
along the same course. The challenge of Pico's platonizing Cabalism
for the sake of Christianity provoked Alemanno to make an analogous
combination of Cabala and philosophy, but on the basis of traditional
Jewish sources that would yield similar doctrines. Where Pico referred
to the *Symposium*, Alemanno referred to the Song of Songs. The correspondence of the biblical to the Platonic book has been explained best
in Chaim Wirszubski's studies of Pico's Christian Cabalism:

. . . From this may be derived the conclusion that the divinely inspired Solomon and the divine Plato intended the same meaning. It goes without
saying that *mors osculi*, or more precisely, the allegorical interpretation
given to death by the kiss, is the connecting link between Plato's *Symposium*
and the Song of Songs.[31]

The challenge of Pico's discussion of divine and human love, and
Alemanno's response, may be compared with Abravanel's discussion of
the topic in the *Dialoghi*.[32] Pico concludes a major part of the argument
of the *Heptaplus*:

If what we say is true, that the extremes can be joined together only through the mean; and if that is truly to be called a mean which has already united the extremes in itself; and if that ineffable dispensation by which the Word is made flesh occurs only in Christ; then it is through Christ alone that the flesh can ascend to the Word.[33]

This Christian explanation of the attainment of immortal bliss is, of course, not satisfactory to Alemanno, who, in his various books, finds different solutions to the problems that he shares with Pico. To this justification of the doctrine of Incarnation, Alemanno responds:

We cannot evade the question by asserting that there is no connection of desire [*hesheq*] between God and us, because the prophets have amply asserted that there is one, from each side. Moses wrote, 'Yet it was to your fathers that the Lord was drawn in his passion [*hesheq*] for them' (Deuteronomy 10:15). And David wrote, 'Because he hath set his love [*hesheq*] upon Me, therefore will I deliver him' (Psalm 91:14). Therefore we cannot deny the existence of this mutual desire, even though we cannot understand its essence, because of the extreme contrast between our nature and the uniqueness of God. This is like what Aristotle says about affection between the beautiful and the ugly; although the ugly one may love the beautiful one only for his beauty, the beautiful one will not love the ugly one, because of his ugliness. Similarly, although we desire God because of His perfection, He will not desire us, because of our imperfection.

If, however, we can show that there is some connection between the separate intellect and the material intellect, we can dispel this perplexity.

Between the extremes of difference between God and us there is a middle term. . . . Let us say, then, that the common or median quality in the desire between God and us, his opposites, is the Good. The good for man is not to become absolutely separated from matter, but only this way to a degree; and the good for God is not — God forbid! — that He become material, but only that His overflow become attached to matter in an attachment that perfects the flaws in everything outside Him.

Alemanno goes on to explain seven means of ascent to the attachment to the good that is common to men and God, and then illustrates them from the life of King Solomon, the presumed author of the Song of Songs, and, by Alemanno's account, the supreme ancient theologian.[34]

Such reformulation for the sake of his own religious community of what Alemanno finds in Pico is adequate as long as each side is content to address only its own community. When, however, the conversionary, polemical address to the other community becomes important, that other community will defend itself. Platonism, especially combined with Christian Cabalism, could be a potent challenge to weak, vulnera-

ble Jewish communities, which were not intellectually unified or for-
tified for the challenges of the times. Plato could become important for
Jewish thinkers to discuss once Christians began using his thought
against the Jews. In a letter, Ficino reminds Domenico Benivieni of an
occasion on which the two of them and Pico were among the participants in debates between Flavius Mithridates, the apostate from Judaism, and two Jewish physicians, likely to have been Elijah del Medigo
and Abraham Farissol.

They insist that the divine words of the prophets do not refer at all to Jesus
but were intended in another sense. They turn them all in a different direction, so far as they are able, wresting them from our hands, nor does it
seem that they will be easy to refute unless the divine Plato enters the debate, the invincible defender of the holy religion.[35]

Jews could respond to the challenge of Christianity that was reinforced
by Plato and Cabala in two ways: by rejecting Plato and Cabala, and
consequently Christianity; or by making Plato and Cabala serve Judaism instead. The first response, of course, is characteristic of Elijah del
Medigo, and the second, of Yehuda Abravanel, in the *Dialoghi d'amore*.
    From a somewhat cryptic, but definitely sarcastic letter of 1506, we
have what could be the first reaction of Jewish readers to the Hebrew
original of the *Dialoghi*. Saul Cohen Ashkenazi (1496-1523), a peripatetic, student of Elijah del Medigo, and also a Candian, who had been
the original addressee of the *Examination of Religion*, presented a dozen
technical philosophical questions to Isaac Abravanel. Claiming not to
be acquainted with those of Isaac's works that a double-truth Averroist
would have to condemn, Ashkenazi pointedly asks both Isaac and
Yehuda key questions about philosophy that seem to be aimed at
undercutting the method and conclusions of their writings. Ashkenazi
appears to be trying either to stump the two Abravanels, to point out
the philosophical flaws in their 'mediating' writings, to catch them dis-
agreeing, or to force them to disagree explicitly with the authority of
Maimonides or Averroes. Any of the results on these questions would
discredit what Ashkenazi must have considered their frivolous, rhetorical arguments and conclusions. His socratic irony is particularly cut-
ting in reference to Yehuda:

Please bring these obscure questions of mine to the attention of your dear
son, my brother, the exalted, most elevated and sublime universal sage,
Rabbi Yehuda, may God preserve him, if he happens to be there [in
Venice]. He will restore my soul and provide for my old age if he answers
my inquiries. For I have heard it said that Yehuda rises laudibly from study

to study along the ascending path to the wisdom of philosophy and its roots, in whatever language and writing, and in exposition of the greatness of the Commentator [Averroes], his statements, his arguments and his demonstrations. And after these things he draws himself along a marvelous path, precious with learning, and utters primeval riddles, to understand fable and eloquence, both divine and of the Torah, that are available to every man.[36]

By the values of Ashkenazi and his late teacher, del Medigo, the Abravanels have violated the disciplinary integrity of Maimonidean philosophy by rhetorically teaching the masses topics that can only be discussed in specialized, philosophic discourse, and have taught things that cannot be demonstrated in such discourse. Yehuda has directly contradicted the proper course of intellectual development outlined by Maimonides in *The Guide of the Perplexed*, by squandering his supposedly philosophical attention on riddles, fables, and eloquence.[37] In peripatetic terms, the *Dialoghi* add up to just this, and no more. The letter does not further specify the character of the work, but the suppressed violence of the reaction, which is indicated by the seriousness of the dozen inquiries, suggests that a substantial, powerful work, which could not be ignored, has drawn the questioner's attention. In addressing such respected communal figures, Ashkenazi cannot openly attack them, so he hopes to embarrass them, to silence such performances in the future. A more precise account of the criticisms that the dozen questions imply will require detailed comparison of the *Dialoghi* with the questions.

The reaction of Saul Cohen Ashkenazi to the *Dialoghi* reflects a polarization of the reactions of Jewish readers that would more or less duplicate the range of reactions to Alemanno's work in 1490. Peripatetics, like Elijah del Medigo and his student, Saul Cohen Ashkenazi, would not consider rhetorical discourse, pagan myths, and Plato to be a fit means of proving anything. Cabalists would not need, and so would not welcome, confirmation of their opinions by syncretists. The inclusive, harmonizing strategy for conciliating diverse communities and scholarly tendencies would seem to have failed again.

Still, why did Jewish syncretists, or 'mediators', not preserve the Hebrew text that became, thirty years later, popular in translation, so that one Jewish writer translated it into Spanish, and several others translated excerpts back into Hebrew? These are questions that certainly cannot be answered now. All that can be said is that it would be even more astonishing for an Italian original to have remained in oblivion for so long, before being published and meeting with such great success.

Shlomo Pines, the outstanding historian of mediaeval Jewish philosophy notes in a recent article that the *Dialoghi d'amore* 'though written in Italian is in many passages a typical product of the Judaeo-Arabic philosophical tradition in its final phase'; he goes on to give an elegiac account of what specialists in Renaissance literature and Platonism instead would celebrate, namely the popularity of the *Dialoghi* and their influence in that literature:

The *Dialoghi*, a treatise that is perhaps, chronologically speaking, the last important work that was produced by the Jewish mediaeval philosophical tradition, had become a favorite topic for polite conversation and literary composition. It is a bizarre fact that the long history of that tradition may, in a meaningful sense, be regarded as ending upon this note.[38]

Elijah del Medigo and Saul Cohen Ashkenazi would altogether agree. What renders one kind of discourse memorable consigns the other to oblivion.

Baltimore Hebrew College

Notes

* Research for this paper was supported by a stipend from the Social Sciences and Humanities Research Council of Canada, for which I express my gratitude.
1 T. Anthony Perry, *Erotic Spirituality: The Integrative Tradition from Leone Ebreo to John Donne* (University, Alabama: Alabama University Press, 1980); Isaiah Sonne, "Traces of the *Dialogues of Love* in Hebrew Literature," [Hebrew] *Tarbiz*. 3, No. 3 (1932), pp. 287-313; John Charles Nelson, *Renaissance Theory of Love: The Context of Giordano Bruno's "Eroici Furori"* (New York and London: Columbia University Press, 1958).
2 Leone Ebreo (Giuda Abarbanel), *Dialoghi d'amore*, ed. Santino Caramella (Bari: Laterza, 1929), p. 102; Leone Ebreo, *The Philosophy of Love (Dialoghi d'amore)*, trans. F. Friedeberg-Seeley and Jean H. Barnes (London: The Soncino Press, 1937), p. 115.
3 Carlo Dionisotti, "Appunti su Leone Ebreo," *Italia medioevale e umanistica* 2 (1959), pp. 407-28; Isaiah Sonne, "On the Question of the Original Language of Yehuda Abravanel's *Dialoghi d'amore*' [Hebrew], in *Tsiyyunim: Kovets le-Zikhrono shel Y. N. Simhoni* (Berlin: Eshkol, 1929), pp. 142-48.
4 David Geffen, "Insight into the Life and Thought of Elijah del Medigo Based on his Published and Unpublished Works," *Proceedings of the American Academy for Jewish Research* 41-42 (1973-74), pp. 72 n.13, 85-86.
5 David B. Ruderman, *The World of a Renaissance Jew: The Life and Thought of Abraham ben Mordecai Farissol*, Monographs of the Hebrew Union College, No. 6 (Cincinnati: Hebrew Union College Press, 1981), p. 58 n. 9.
6 I thank Paul Oskar Kristeller for this information, from a conversation in August 1976.

7 Shlomo Pines, "Scholasticism after Thomas Aquinas and the Teachings of Hasdai Crescas and his Predecessors," *Proceedings of the Israel Academy of Sciences and Humanities* 1, No. 10 (1967).
8 M. David Geffen, "Faith and Reason in Elijah del Medigo's *Beḥinat Ha-Dat* and the Philosophic Backgrounds of the Work," (Doctoral dissertation, Columbia University, 1970); Alfred L. Ivry, "Remnants of Jewish Averroism in the Renaissance," in *Jewish Thought in the Sixteenth Century*, ed. Bernard Dov Cooperman (Cambridge, Mass.: Harvard University Press, 1983), pp. 243-65.
9 '... nullum enim desiderium ita intensum habeo sicut dimittere post me hominem meum vere scientem et in doctrina peripatetica intelligentem, quod desiderium per te erit completum.' Cited in Jules Dukas, *Recherches sur l'histoire littéraire du quinzième siècle* (Paris: Léon Techener, 1876), p. 65.
10 Geffen, "Insights into Elijah Del Medigo," p. 82 n. 46. My translation.
11 Eliyahu del Medigo, *Sefer Beḥinat ha-Dat*, ed. I.S. Reggio (Vienna: A.E. Von Schmid, 1833), pp. 52-53. My translation.
12 Dukas, *Recherches*, p. 62. Cf. Bohdan Kieszkowski, "Les rapports entre Elie del Medigo et Pic de la Mirandole," *Rinascimento* 4 (1964), p. 52 n. 1.
13 Geffen, "Faith and Reason," pp. 19-20.
14 Del Medigo, *Beḥinat ha-Dat*, p. 51. My translation.
15 Del Medigo, *Beḥinat ha-Dat*, p. 78. My translation.
16 Moritz Steinschneider, "Miscellen," *Monatsschrift für Geschichte und Wissenschaft des Judenthums* 37 (1893), pp. 185-88.
17 Moshe Idel, "Between the Concept of Essences and the Concept of 'Instruments' in Kabbalah during the Renaissance," [Hebrew] *Italiah* 3, Nos. 1-2 (1983), p. 90. My translation.
18 Yosef Yavets, *Sefer Or ha-Ḥayyim* (Lublin: N. Hershenhorn, 1910), p. 74. My translation.
19 Yavets, *Sefer Or ha-Ḥayyim*, pp. 75-76. My translation.
20 Cited from Isaac E. Barzilay, *Between Reason and Faith: Anti-Rationalism in Italian Jewish Thought, 1250-1650*, Publications in Near and Middle East Studies, Columbia University, Series A, vol. 10 (The Hague: Mouton, 1967), p. 139.
21 Arthur Lesley, *"The Song of Solomon's Ascents*, by Yohanan Alemanno: Love and Human Perfection According to a Jewish Associate of Giovanni Pico della Mirandola," (Doctoral dissertation, University of California, Berkeley, 1976), pp. 4-50.
22 Yohanan Alemanno, *Sefer Ḥesheq Shlomo*, British Museum, MS. Or. 2854, fol. 162r-v; Berlin, Preussisches Staatsbibliothek, MS. Steinschneider 8, fols. 119v-120r.
23 Yohanan Alemanno, *Sefer 'Ene ha-'Edah*, New York, Jewish Theological Seminary, MS. 888, fol. 6v.
24 Yohanan Alemanno, *Sefer Ḥai ha-'Olamim*, Mantua, MS. Ebr. 21, fols. 1r-2r.
25 Oxford, Bodleian MS. Reggio 23, fols. 141v-142v.
26 Aristotle, *Rhetoric* I, 2 1355b-1357a. Cited from *The Basic Works of Aristotle*, ed. Richard McKeon (New York: Random House, 1941), pp. 1328-32.
27 Lesley, *"The Song of Solomon's Ascents*," pp. 77, 331-32.
28 *Medieval Political Philosophy*, ed. Ralph Lerner and Muhsin Mahdi (Ithaca, N.Y.: Cornell University Press, 1963), pp. 265-67.
29 Alemanno' *Sefer Ḥesheq Shlomo*, Oxford, Bodleian MS. Laud. or. 103, fol. 133r.
30 Leone Ebreo, *Dialoghi*, p. 251; *Philosophy of Love*, p. 296.
31 Chaim Wirszubski, *Three Chapters in the History of Christian Kabbala* [Hebrew] (Jerusalem: Mossad Bialik, 1975), p. 15. My translation.

32 Leone Ebreo, *Dialoghi*, esp. pp. 251 ff., 298 ff. *The Philosophy of Love*, pp. 298 ff., 327 ff.

33 Pico della Mirandola, *On the Dignity of Man*, . . . *Heptaplus*, trans. Douglas Carmichael (Indianapolis: Bobbs-Merrill, 1965), pp. 145-46.

34 Lesley, "*The Song of Solomon's Ascents*," pp. 174-80, 534-40.

35 "Interfuisti et tu disputationibus quae in aedibus Ioannis Pici Mirandulensis ante alios admirandi saepe tractatae sunt atque tractantur, ubi Helia et Abraam hebrei medici atque peripatetici adversus Guilielmum siculum disserunt. Oracula prophetarum ad Iesum minime pertinere, sed alio quodam sensu dicta contendunt, convertentes aliorsumomnia e manibusque nostris pro viribus extorquentes, neque facile convinci posse videntur nisi divinus Platoprodeat in iudicium, invictus religionis sanctae patronus . . ." Marsilio Ficino, *Opera* I (Basel, 1576) p. 873; Cited from Ruderman, *Farissol*, pp. 40-41.

36 *She'elot . . . ha-Rav Shaul Kohen* (Venice, 1574), fol. 2v. My translation.

37 Moses Maimonides, *The Guide of the Perplexed*, trans. Shlomo Pines (Chicago and London: University of Chicago Press, 1969), part I, ch. 34, pp. 72-79.

38 Shlomo Pines, "Medieval Doctrines in Renaissance Garb? Some Jewish and Arabic Sources of Leone Ebreo's Doctrines," in *Jewish Thought in the Sixteenth Century*, ed. Cooperman, p. 391.

Peter V. Marinelli

The Flight of Ariosto's Hippogriff: Genesis, Elaboration, and Function

i

In a famous admonition against excessive poetic license at the beginning of the *Ars Poetica*, Horace advised against the fantastic mixing of breeds, the joining of horses' heads to human necks, spreading of limbs with feathers of birds, and so on.[1] Nevertheless, by creating the hippogriff, a winged courser with the body of a horse and the breast, plumage, and head of a griffin, Ariosto, himself one of the foremost Renaissance Horatians, seems very consciously to have contravened his master's injunction. And — to descend a bit — this paper deliberately yokes the names of Ariosto, Ficino, and Bembo, thus inevitably creating (at least in the eyes of Croce-dominated criticism) another kind of monster, a critical one, formed from the unlikely conjunction of Neoplatonism and Carolingian chivalric poetry, 'non-poesia' contaminating 'poesia' with a vengeance.

Here then we need particularly to recall the Ariosto who first conceived the *Furioso*, an Ariosto who rarely if ever finds his way into criticism, having long been elbowed out of the way by an Ariosto who (supposedly) lived in total detachment from the personages and events of his time, a figure intoxicated by his own purely fantastic art. For this neglected Ariosto, social and exuberant, we must go to the year 1494, when the accolades of the future were far from being a given, and when the poet, aged twenty, grew disgusted with the study of law and persuaded his father to allow him to take up the humanities at the Studio di Ferrara. In the years 1496-7, with an enthusiasm and sense of release he afterwards recorded in his *Satires*,[2] Ariosto underwent instruction by some of the most prominent humanists of his day: by the Augustinian monk, Gregorio da Spoleto, who also taught Giovanni de' Medici, the future pope Leo X; and by the physician and lecturer in medicine and Platonic philosophy, Serafino dell'Aquila. This Ariosto is the personality we sense immediately in the very first recorded document in the epistolary, which is nothing less than a Latin missive from 'Ludovicus Areostus' to no less a personage than 'Aldo Manucio.' The young student writes at the behest of a group of young Ferrarese lite-

rati, and, after noting that his teacher Serafino has been lecturing on
Plato's *Timaeus* to a large concourse of auditors, he becomes the
spokesman for a special request. He hopes the Venetian publisher will
spare the scholars the trouble of sailing up to Venice for such books as
they require and send them some writings of Marsilio Ficino ('libros
Marsilii') and other Latin translations of the Greek Platonists ('aliorum
qui aliquid de hac secta a Graecis scriptum latine transtulerunt'), works
for which they all have, he declares, a 'non mediocre desiderium.'[3]
Ariosto learned litotes early.

Several related facts need recalling at this point. The years 1497-9
and 1502-3 were years when Pietro Bembo, then among the foremost
popularizers of Ficinian Neoplatonism, lived in Ferrara and began to
exercise an influence on Ariosto that lasted till his death. Bembo's
chief work of Neoplatonism, *Gli Asolani*, was composed in Ferrara between 1497 and 1502, and the manscript was entrusted to 'nostro
Ludovico' for delivery to the dedicatee, Lurcrezia Borgia d'Este.[4]
Around the same time, by 1505, the court knew that Ariosto was engaged in resuming the interrupted masterpiece, *Orlando Innamorato*, by
the Count of Scandiano, Matteomaria Boiardo, the cousin, no less, of
Pico della Mirandola. And Ariosto was in Urbino in 1507, when the
conversations recorded in the *Cortegiano* were supposed to have taken
place.[5] In the poet's early education and in his first encounters with literature, the influence of a prevalent and intoxicating literary Neoplatonism should not be too magisterially dismissed, least of all when it becomes superseded by the doctrines of 'arte pura.'

In the following paragraphs I should like to limit my discussion of
the manifold ways in which Ariosto utilizes some basic images, concepts, and hierarchical structures characteristic of Neoplatonism to an
analysis of one of his most suggestive icons, the vehicle of transport for
two of his major heroes, the aerial horse or hippogriff. Here, if anywhere, is a paradigm of the artistic method Ariosto customarily employs to infiltrate and reorganize poetic materials he inherits from
Boiardo, at once paying tribute to his predecessor and firmly marking
the distance between them.

In any discussion of the *Furioso*, it is imperative to recognize that the
poem is a 'continuation' (a term badly in need of qualification) of the
Innamorato, a torso of sixty-nine cantos. In adopting the entire body of
the *Innamorato* as its poetic *materia*, the *Furioso* provides a particular
opportunity to match Ariosto's own text against Boiardo's and to sort
out clearly what is the foundation and what is the new overlay, and
thus to isolate and evaluate the specific Ariostan contribution. A constant set of comparisons between the two texts reveals that Ariosto
makes more radical gestures in the direction of the learned tradition

and to the society at large than does Boiardo, that he more openly
displays his ability to absorb and concentrate the art and learning of
his contemporaries. In a word, the *Furioso* is more radically societal
than the *Innamorato*, which, indeed, prescinds from actuality with remarkable intensity; and it also gives evidence of being more schemati-
cally structured than has been hitherto acknowledged. Because Ariosto
works with a variety of sources at any given time, no one text is likely
to provide a key to his art, and there is no need to fear, therefore, that
Ficino or Bembo wil provide the one wholly systematic, essential answer to the poem, or that the poem will tolerate being revealed as the
poetic embodiment of all the abstruse doctrine to be found in Ficino's
Commentary on the Symposium.[6] An image like that of the hippogriff ac-
quires its iconic value only when seen as a cluster of associated images
and ideas common in the love-literature of Italy up to and including
Ariosto; and it is the result of an extraordinarly complex artistic process. In that process authors as various as Ovid, Boethius, Petrarch,
Boccaccio, Salutati, and Frezzi have a share, while Ficino and Bembo
provide the most proximate resources in time. A work like Pio Rajna's
Le fonti dell'Orlando Furioso[7] ransacks a vast range of literature, classical
and vernacular, for the sources of Ariosto's art, yet it never even
broaches the subject of Ariosto's relationship to his Platonizing contemporaries. This is an oddity that needs readjusting. Nevertheless, since
Ariosto always and everywhere begins with the poetic father he never
names or acknowledges, it is with Boiardo, who always provides the
foundation for Ariosto's overpainting, that we need now to begin.

ii

It must be said at once that the *Innamorato* provides little or nothing
in the way of an equivalent to the detailed image of the hippogriff in
the *Furioso*. Our search for something like it takes us to the concluding
four cantos of Boiardo's truncated poem, where the *Innamorato* throws
out, showeringly, a host of symbolic, allusive inventions that Ariosto
found powerfully rich in poetic suggestiveness and by which his eye
was caught as he began to compose. Here the reader needs to be reminded of the narrative situation in Boiardo's Book III: one of his heroes, the pagan Ruggiero, an Achilles-like youth lured across the seas
to France from his home in North Africa, is engaged in fighting
Charlemagne's forces as they battle the Saracen invaders. The youth's
old tutor, the magician Atlante, foreseeing his eventual baptism and
early death (though, Aeneas-like, he will become the dynastic founder
of the Estean line) appears to be behind a series of enchantments con-
trived to keep the youth from fulfilling his heroic destiny. Magical
forces begin to envelop the heroes, though none of them is directly at-

tributable to Atlante's charms, and the scene shifts constantly from the battlefield to enchanted woods, fountains of laughter, underwater realms of leisure and pleasure. The *locus classicus* for this set of traps and delays is the 'Fonte del Riso,' set in the middle of the Magic Wood, predecessor of Tasso's more famous one. Various heroes are allured into its precincts, two of them worthy of special scrutiny. In the heart of the Wood, Ruggiero, fresh from his first meeting with his destined wife, Bradamante, a meeting in which he has been stricken by the sight of the Christian maiden's overwhelming physical beauty, strikes at a menacing tree-root, thereby significantly releasing the phantom of a beautiful girl whom he pursues into the Fountain; into its depths he plunges with glee, and he remains a prisoner there, charmed by water-nymphs and beguiled by an endless succession of dancing, singing, and feasting. A second victim of enchantment is Gradasso, a pagan who lusts, not after a maiden, but a famous steed, Bayard. In an assault similar to Ruggiero's upon the forest, he also strikes a tree and *he* releases (appropriately enough) a horse that bounds upward from the earth (III.vii.24-8). Leaping onto its back, he is conveyed to the Fonte del Riso and dropped into its depths, whereupon the steed returns to its home in the Wood, never to reappear in the two remaining cantos of the truncated poem.[8] The Wood, then, is a place where warriors are beguiled with phantoms of their own desires — a damsel, a courser — and the romance-motifs verge constantly on allegory.

Here is the germ of Ariosto's hippogriff, and the most minimal comparison assures us of his notable originality in creating an image and impregnating it with meaning of his own, independent of his chief source. The appearance of the horse in Boiardo is a single brief one, and it is most definitely not winged: it moves 'sì ratto come avesse a piè le penne' ('as swiftly as if it had wings on its feet'); nor does it have — as it has in Ariosto's revivified and re-imagined Atlante — a master who rides it through the heavens and directs its flight. In summation, then: what the *Innamorato* gives us is a complex of forests, horses, enchanted pools, in which age-old images of desire mingle with equally ancient images of sensual pleasure, but nothing like a winged courser capable of extended flight, either above or close to the earth, or to the upper and lower levels of the universe.

iii

So much for genesis. We are only four cantos into the *Furioso* when Ariosto begins a long, far-reaching elaboration of the *Innamorato* ending. Basically, it involves the magician Atlante and his magical winged courser, and it proves to be one of the most complicated of the poem's strategies for re-introducing Boiardo's personages and events, but in a new and more carefully structured light. The strategy takes the form of extraordinarily careful narrative preparation for the magician's first appearance in a wholly new, unprecedented role as creator and rider of the hippogriff. There is nothing in all the *Furioso* more heavily marked by this kind of authorial insistence, repeatedly, and with what at first glance appears to be superfluous emphasis, calling attention to the poet's radical rewriting of his source. Here again a narrative situation needs to be recalled: when the *Furioso* begins, Bradamante is represented as wandering sadly around the battlefield, having been separated by accident from Ruggiero, her fated husband, whom she had dazzled with her beauty by lifting her helmet from her head, thus propelling him into the first steps of a love which at this point is more appetitive than cognitive. That, apparently, is the explanation for Ruggiero's having been so easily seduced into Boiardo's Fountain of Laughter by the phantom-maiden released from the smitten tree-trunk. Now, beset by love-longing and derelict in her duty to Charlemagne, Bradamante is in quest of the lover she has no sooner met than lost. Soon, coming upon a similarly love-stricken knight, Pinabello, she hears important news: her lover has been spirited away from France by magical means, transported by a winged horse. No longer wantoning his time away in geographically undefinable fountains of laughter, Ruggiero is now represented as having been whirled away to a steel castle pinnacled high among the crags of the Pyrenees, where, amid a troop of high-born knights and ladies, all young and handsome, he is safe from the world of warfare and arms.[9] All in all, this already represents a forceful Ariostan remanagement of the Boiardan original.

At this point in Pinabello's narrative, Bradamante and the reader are apprised of a number of significant things about Ruggiero's raptor: first, he is armed head to foot like a warrior; second, he rides a winged steed with great oddly-colored wings; third, he is in search of youths and maidens; fourth, his chief weapon is a magic shield whose light stuns the eye with its power and causes those who look on it to fall down in a trance; fifth, he transports his victims to his castle in the midst of a wild, savage, inhospitable landscape. It takes a full twenty octaves, one-hundred and sixty lines of inset narrative to introduce this phenomenon, during which Ariosto, with the utmost care and with insidious artistic purpose, avoids giving him a name. In other words, he allows a complex of familiar iconographic attributes to create the allegorical figure in the reader's mind and defers clinching the identification till two cantos have elapsed, and we hear, at IV.30, the magician identify himself as Atlante, long after he has been invested with the attributes of Amor.

Pinabello's long speech (II.37-57) represents the poet's weightiest and most portentous rewriting of Boiardo, but it represents only the first and longest of several quickly ensuing descriptions that call attention to themselves as intensification of the details Pinabello provides. Melissa, the enchantress who presides over the fates of the Este dynasty and is anxious to see the dynastic pair united and married, instructs Bradamante in the means to conquer the raptor and liberate his captives (II.66-8), a passage that recapitulates and reinforces what Bradamante has learned already from Pinabello. Soon thereafter there follows a sudden, startling epiphany of the horse and its rider as it breaks out of the heavens like an eclipse or a comet (IV.3-5). There next ensues a third, briefer description of the magician's awesome powers by the host of the tavern where Bradamante first glimpses the apparition (IV.5-7); and, finally, the enchanter astride his beast reveals himself fully, descends in slow circles to the earth, and begins to act out his tyrannous strategems in her very sight, hoping to entrap the chaste damsel as well (IV.16-21). There are thus no less than five separate stages in the complex evolution of this wholly new portrait of Atlante and the hippogriff — three narratives and two epiphanies. As the magician and the maiden confront each other in battle, a complex of repeatedly asserted motifs about the magician clearly emerges. They are: sorcery and magic, whereby the enchanter continually produces illusions; militancy, whereby his posture is seen as one of military aggression directed against highborn youths and maidens; flight, in his capacity to move like lightning through the air on his 'quadrupedal bird'; hunting, for he is engaged in a perpetual quest for youths and maidens to stock his pleasure-palaces; light and blinding, for he can unloose a blaze of light from his magic shield that dazzles and confuses the visual sense; primitivism and savagery, for he inhabits wild, solitary, desert places, uncultivated and uninhabited; and, finally, ease and retirement from the world of quotidian, practical activity, for all his questing terminates in a world of pleasurable indolence. This complex of details constitutes a major, indeed an almost total, overpainting of Boiardo's sentimental 'negromante' and of a magic horse capable of merely bounding, though wingless, into the air.

Because his death terminated the *Innamorato* at its most crucial point, we shall never know what Boiardo intended to make of his own Atlante, but anyone with even slight acquaintance with the classical and mediaeval traditions of love-lore in European poetry will find the nexus Ariosto attaches to his own Atlante suggestive, to say the least. The earliest commentators of the *Furioso* were unanimous in declaring him to be cast in the role of Amor, the god of cupidinous love who interferes between the future dynasts at a crucial time in their lives, right after their very first meeting, when the activity of their eyes, playing over the attractive surfaces of their bodies, might prove — as it does repeatedly in the literature of which we have been speaking — especially dangerous to the future course of their love. Long regarded with contempt, though often rightly so, the early critics may on this occasion have been wiser than has been thought. Readers accustomed to a familiar figure like the Greek Eros or the Alexandrian Cupid as the customary representation of Amor will scarcely be in a benign mood to accept the magician Atlante in place of either. But this is a most carefully remanipulated Atlante, and a wholly reimagined aerial horse. Here we can see Ariosto most clearly in his role of maker of icons, infiltrating Boiardo's images and creating a composite of multiple sources for his own individual creation.

Time enforces a swift overleaping of these components, to which we might well at another time give detailed attention. This means merely preparing the ground for the introduction of Ficino and Bembo as probable sources for Ariosto by pointing out the common features in the mythography of Amor that he has employed to characterize Atlante. A swift survey means, in essence, a very rapid glance at the emphasis on Ovidian *otium* in the portrait, as well as at the Ovidian militancy of Amor; another equally rapid glance could be turned on Boccaccio's portrait of Amor with griffin's talons, figuring the tenacity of the amorous passion he inspires, a detail Ariosto seems to have recalled in his joining the griffin to the horse, long the primary Platonic symbol for bodily passion.[10] A swift survey means only nodding in passing, first, at Petrarch's *Trionfo d'Amore* where one of Amor's appellations is not only 'mansueto fanciullo' ('gentle child') but 'fiero veglio' ('fierce old man'), and where the appearance of the tyrant-conqueror is accompanied, as in Ariosto, by a great burst of light ('vidi una gran luce');[11] it means bearing in mind the *Rime* as well, where the god repeatedly leads the erring poet into 'i più deserti campi,' the scenic equivalent of the uncultivated places of the human heart, where Amor, the figure for the sensitive appetite, habitually resides.[12] And it means having on the edge of our consciousness as we read that Federigo Frezzi, in the 'Regno d'Amore' section of his *Quadriregio*, had written that Amor leads the narrator-lover 'tra duri scogli dell'aspro deserto / con tanti inganni' ('among the hard rocks of the bitter desert, by numberless deceptions').[13]

At base, then, Atlante incarnates the cupidinous appetite, and his mount both the horsey and avian aspects of human nature that love habitually bestrides and dominates. That is why the hippogriff is twice and with a certain ironic emphasis declared to be not at all a fiction created by enchantment but 'vero e natural' (IV.18-19). Nothing more

real, Ariosto might have found his audience agreeing, than human nature and the desires and instincts by which it is propelled and transported.

iv

What now remains to be shown is the way in which Ariosto connects
this older tradition to a more up-to-the-minute tradition of love-
theory, Ficinian at base, Bembistic in its most proximate and most
glamorous appearance, that permeated Italian literature at the beginning of the first decade of the sixteenth century and was soon to envelop the literature of Europe, to the point that Pierre de Ronsard
could, in his *Amours de Cassandre*, concentrate a whole set of meanings
in a phrase like 'Amour-oiseau' and signal the volatility of love by the
briefest possible means.

The new Atlante of Ariosto is a sorcerer and sophist who flies and
who hunts. This particular nexus of characteristics seems, inexplicably,
never to have been referred to the *Commentary on the Symposium*, where
it appears in the Sixth and Seventh speeches. Several times at least
Ariosto seems to be working clearly with reminiscences of Ficino in
mind: once when the sophistical Atlante is said to be capable of making red seem yellow (IV.20); and twice more when Atlante's flight is
described as alternately soaring to the stars and descending to graze
the earth:

> Sin alle stelle il volator trascorse;
> indi girossi e tornò in fretta al basso; (II.52)
> (The flyer flew up as high as the stars,
> then wheeled about and returned in haste to the ground.)

> Volando, talor s'alza ne le stelle
> e poi quasi talor la terra rade (IV.6)
> (Flying, sometimes he rises to the stars,
> and at another time he almost skims the earth).

Surely it is not unreasonable to hear twice over the voice of Ficino:
'These two eternal loves in us are daemons which Plato predicts will always be present in our souls, one of which raises us to things above;
the other presses us down to things below.'[14] To students of the English Renaissance, moreover, the lines of Ariosto, no less than the prose
of Ficino, will awaken memories of Sidney's version of the two loves in
a famous sonnet of renunciation, opening with the line 'Leave me, O

love, which reachest but to dust,' and closing with 'Eternal Love, maintain thy life in me.'

The crucial passage about the two loves in Ficino gives us generative and cognitive loves. This is especially interesting in an Ariostan context since the only two fully human fliers aboard the hippogriff (and very different ones they prove to be indeed) are Ruggiero, the soldier and future dynast, and Astolfo, almost alone in not possessing a female love-object, who ultimately, from the perspective of the moon, sees the vanity of terrestrial pursuits; this is an act of cognition that forms one of the limits of the poem's wisdom and, more importantly, links him to the perspective from which the poet himself views his own creation. There is most definitely a distinguishing of loves in the *Furioso*, but to assess the ways in which it operates poetically in the comic Carolingian epic requires a breadth of treatment that can scarcely be suggested in so brief a paper as this.

v

Here, finally, we move beyond the genesis and elaboration of images to their function in the poem at large. Flight is the element that most crucially differentiates the *Furioso* from the *Innamorato* — flight figuring the motion and level of love, which is itself an index of whether the life by which that love is informed is either erratic and human (as in Ruggiero's case) or aspires to something higher (as in the case of the breezy but curiously steady Astolfo). A crucial point to note in passing is that while both these heroes are linked and differentiated by their riding of the hippogriff, both are at the same time severely marked off from Orlando, the third and lowest of the poem's major lovers, who is merely bestial and flies not at all. For Ficino, one recalls, a purely animal lust is not love in any way, but a medical condition, *insania*. So Orlando, 'paccio' in Boiardo at the first sight of Angelica (I.i.30), and 'furioso' in Ariosto in remembrance of the *Hercules Furens* of Seneca, is by Ficinian standards 'insanus.'[15]

The introduction of flight into the landscape of the chivalric poem as a metaphor for the capacity of the sensitive appetite, bridled or unbridled, to rise and fall on a vertical scale, integrates the landscape, and causes things to fall into place in a hierarchical scheme that is not diagramatically fixed and rigid but dynamic and ever-changing as the heroes pursue their different lives to different ends. How the hippogriff-vehicle behaves in its motion is an indication of how the human who rides it is faring morally, according to whether he is at the mercy of his passions or has applied the bridle to his horsey nature and restrained its capacity to run away with him and take to the heavens of delight in transport and rapture. Where the characters put down is an indication of where they are morally: Ruggiero allows the unbridled hippogriff to wing off to Alcina's gardens, and he knows the pleasures of physical consummation in her arms. He is a flier in precisely the sense that Bembo wrote about in the *Asolani*. Poets have equipped Amor with wings, he says,

non per altro rispetto se non perciò che gli amanti, dalle penne de' loro stolti disideri sostentati, volan per l'aere della loro speranza, sì comme essi si fanno a credere leggiermente, infino al cielo.
(because lovers, who are lifted up on the pinions of their mad desires, flit lightly through the empty air, even, their hopes make them believe, right up to heaven.)[16]

Not only that: when he is not seeing delightful visions of naked maidens chained vulnerably to rocks in the ocean, Ruggiero sees, from the back of the hippogriff, what is appropriate for him to see as an embodiment of the practical, active existence awaiting him at the end of the poem. Flying over England he sees the English army being assembled, and describes the stir and bustle of men-at-arms quite clearly. In studied contrast, Astolfo, flying at a much higher level, looks down on the earth and sees all its glories diminished to a mere speck in the heavens: for him, involved in a humorous meditation on human aspiration, the perspective of Macrobius and Lucian is amusingly combined. This is Ariosto's highly individual variant on the second kind of flying, the one figured, for instance, in one of Pietro Bembo's own medals, which has, on its reverse, a winged horse rearing on its hind feet, ready to take flight to the heavens: a familiar image, deriving its meaning ultimately from Plato's *Phaedrus*, though with the possible influence also of Donatello's 'Bust of a Young Man' in the Bargello in Florence.[17]

Astolfo is not a Dante, there is no question whatever of his flying up to the 'la divina bellezza,' which is strictly off-limits to human observation in the *Furioso*; as well, his flight is only to the lower heavens, as befits the decorum of a Carolingian romance with popular origins, and a character whose grosser past history the poet is at pains to redeem and purge. Nevertheless, Astolfo does achieve a level identified with the author's in his contemplation of human madness in the sublunary theatre. Modern readers are certain to find something hilariously comic in Astolfo's being greeted by Enoch and Elias in the Terrestrial Paradise: the saints, says Ariosto, gave the knight a fine welcome and allotted him a room; and in another, his steed, comfortably stabled, was furnished plenty of forage (XXXIV.60). Would Ariosto, we may well wonder, have written that passage without the knowledge of the tradition that the saints and prophets operate the Mystic Mill and grind the corn that provides nourishment for the spirit by separating the wheat from the chaff?[18] And may the bizarre comic wit not signal us to what modern sensibility undoubtedly finds equally bizarre in its imagery, a passage in Ficino's *Commentary* (VII,14) where the four madnesses are under discussion:

And so the first madness distinguishes the *good horse*, that is, reason and opinion, from the *evil horse*, that is, from confused fancy and the appetite of the senses. The second madness subjects the evil horse to the good, and the good to the charioteer, that is, the intellect. The third directs the charioteer to *his own head*, that is, to his unity, the apex of the intellect. The last turns the head of the charioteer toward the head of all things. Here the charioteer is *blessed*, and *stopping his horses*, that is, accommodating all parts of the soul subject to himself *at the stable*, that is, at the divine beauty, *he puts before them ambrosia and, more than that, nectar to drink*, that is, the vision of beauty, and from that vision happiness.[19]

Possibly *Orlando Furioso* is the story of more than one madness, and possibly the light-witted Astolfo is the cracked vessel at the heart of that conception. In the course of his move from Boiardo's pages to those of Ariosto, the paladin Astolfo is even more radically metamorphosed than Atlante or the hippogriff. That, however, is another very complex story. For the moment, a 'debita pausa' and a deferral 'all'altro canto.'

University of Toronto

Notes

1 See 11.1-13 of *Ars Poetica* in *Satires, Epistles and Ars Poetics*, tr. H. Rushton Fairclough (Cambridge, Mass.: Harvard University Press, 1961), pp. 450-1.
2 See *Satire VI* in the excellent bilingual edition and translation by Peter DeSa Wiggins, *The Satires of Ludovico Ariosto* (Athens, OH: Ohio University Press, 1976), pp. 147-65.
3 See Angelo Stella, *Lettere di Ludovico Ariosto* (Verona: Arnoldo Mondadori, 1965), p. 3 (for the original Latin) and p. 419 (for an Italian translation). The letter is dated 5 January, 1498, when the poet was twenty-three, and adds to this interesting constellation of names (Ariosto, Manutius, Ficino, Serafino) yet another, that of Alberto Pio, Lord of Carpi, Ariosto's fellow-scholar, who is said to have recently had from Manutius a volume, translated by Ficino, containing a gathering of writings by Academic philosophers, a book identifiable (see Stella, p. 419) as an 'Iamblichus de mysteriis Aegyptiorum . . .' In the brochure *Marsilio Ficino: An Exhibition in honour of the publication of Ficino's translation of the Platonic dialogues at Florence, 1484* prepared by William R. Bowen for the Victoria University's Centre for Reformation and Renaissance Studies to describe the volumes dis-

played during the conference at which this paper was given, the title of the volume Ariosto refers to is given as: *Jamblichus of Chalcis. De Mysteriis Aegyptiorum, Chaldeaorum, Assyriorum. Proclus in Platonicum Alcibiadem de Anima, atque Daemone. Idem de Sacrificio & Magia. Porphyrius de Divinis atque Daemonib. Psellus de Daemonibus. Mercurii Trismegisti Pimander. Eiusdem Asclepius.* The brochure notes (p. 5) that this collection of Neoplatonic authors was first published at Venice in 1497, eleven years before Ariosto mentioned it in his very first letter.

For all this evidence of Ariosto's early interest in, and close contact with, Neoplatonic philosophy, the notion that his poetry might have been touched in some way by his early intellectual interests has generally remained a fairly risible one. One exception to the tradition is to be found in Eduardo Saccone's *Il 'soggetto' del 'Furioso' e altri saggi tra Quattro e Cinquecento* (Naples: Liguori Editore, 1974), in his 'Third Appendix' (pp. 157-60), where the author adduces evidence of Ariosto's continuing interest in Neoplatonism, earliest revealed in his Latin work, composed in 1495, during his student days, 'De Laudibus Sophiae ad Herculem Ferrariae ducem II.'

4 Wiggins, p. 148.

5 Wiggins, p. 52.

6 See, for criticism of an especially egregious example by M. Chini, no. 3136 of Giuseppe Fatini's *Bibliografia della critica ariostea, 1510-1956* (Florence: Felice Le Monnier, 1958), p. 575.

7 (Florence: Sansoni, 1900: rpt. Sansoni, 1975): a work remarkable for its total indifference to the writings of any of Ariosto's major contemporaries, specifically Ficino, Bembo, and Castiglione. Rajna's aesthetic presuppositions, roughly those of Italian romantic criticism as developed by De Sanctis, militate against his finding any point of contact between Ariosto's poetry and what we might call a 'prose of thought.'

8 All references to Boiardo's poem are taken from the edition by Aldo Scaglione, *Orlando Innamorato, sonetti e canzoni*, 2 vols. (Turin: UTET, 1951), reprinted as *Orlando Innamorato, Amorum Libri* (Turin: UTET, 1963).

9 All references to Ariosto's poem are taken from *Orlando Furioso*, ed. Santorre Debenedetti and Cesare Segre (Bologna: Commissione per i testi di lingua, 1960).

10 See Boccaccio's *Genealogiae* (Venice, 1494), Bk. IX, ch.iv: 'De Cupidine primo Martis filio: qui genuit Voluptatem,' in which Boccaccio asserts that Francesco Barberino, in a vernacular poem, had attributed 'griphis pedes' to the figure of Amor. For an analysis of this misreading, see the essay by Erwin Panofsky, 'Blind Cupid,' in his *Studies in Iconology: Humanistic Themes in the Art of the Renaissance* (rpt. New York: Harper Torchbooks, 1972); and see illustrations 88, 89, 90, and 91.

11 See the *Triumphus Cupidinis* (I.11) in *Rime e Trionfi di Francesco Petrarca*, ed. Ferdinando Neri (Turin: UTET, 1960), p. 515.

12 See the sonnet, 'Solo e pensoso i più deserti campi,' (No. XXXV), in *Rime e Trionfi*, p. 80.

13 For this remarkable allegorical poem of the fifteenth century by the Bishop of Foligno, see *Il Quadriregio*, ed. Enrico Filippini (Bari: G. Laterza, 1914). The lines quoted occur in 'Capitolo XII' of the *Regno d'Amore*, p. 60.

14 See Marsilio Ficino, *Commentary on Plato's 'Symposium' on Love*, trans., introd., & notes by Sears Jayne (Dallas, TX: Spring Publications, 1985), p. 119. For the Latin original see the *Commentariorvm Marsilii Ficini Florentini in Convivium Platonis, De Amore* in Marsilio Ficino, *Divini Platonis Opera Omnia* (Frankfurt, 1602), p. 1159, col. A: "Hi duo amores in nobis perpetui, duo sunt daemones

illi, quos Plato nostris animis semper adesse vaticinatur: quorum alter ad superna erigat, alter deprimat ad inferna." (Sixth Speech, ch. viii).

15 For a discussion of the lowest form of human on a triadic scale of loves as a kind of madness (*hereos*), see the essay by Panofsky, 'The Neoplatonic Movement in Florence and North Italy' in *Studies in Iconology*, pp. 129-70. The chart of loves (p. 145) by which Panofsky illustrates, in diagrammatic form, the hierarchy of loves according to Ficino and Pico, reveals 'amor ferinus' or 'amore bestiale' as a mere insanity, not even worthy of the name of love.

16 For the Italian text of the *Asolani*, see *Prose e Rime di Pietro Bembo*, ed. Carlo Dionisotti (Turin: UTET, 1966), pp. 313-504. For the English translation, see *Pietro Bembo's 'Gli Asolani'*, tr. Rudolf B. Gottfried (Bloomington, Ind.: Indiana University Press, 1954). The quotations occur on pp. 347 and 39 respectively.

17 For the Bembo medal, see Edmund G. Gardner, *Ariosto, the King of Court Poets* (rpt. New York: Greenwood Press, 1968), illustration facing p. 134. The larger of the two medals illustrated (both in the British Museum) shows on its verso a winged horse rearing on its hind feet, ready to take flight into the heavens. For the Donatello bust, see the monumental art-book *Donatello, Prophet of Modern Vision* (New York: Abrams, 1975), photographs by David Finn, text by Frederick Hartt. As the third of the three photographs of the bust reveals in remarkable detail, the young aristocrat wears a medallion around his neck on which a Platonic *biga* or chariot, guided by a charioteer, is drawn by two horses, one obedient, one refractory, in exact representation of the nature of the wilful and passionate parts of the soul as represented by Plato in the *Phaedrus*. Needless to say, Michael J.B. Allen's *Marsilio Ficino and the Phaedran Charioteer* (Berkeley: University of California Press, 1981) is especially relevant here and throughout this paper.

18 For a discussion of the symbolic nature of milling and grain in mediaeval art, see D.W. Robertson, Jr., *A Preface to Chaucer: Studies in Medieval Perspective* (Princeton: Princeton University Press, 1962), p. 290, and Bernard F. Huppe and D.W. Robertson, Jr., *Fruyt and Chaff: Studies in Chaucer's Allegories* (rpt. Port Washington, N.Y.: Kennikat Press, 1972), p. 104, n. 3. For a relevant illustration, see François Souchal, *Arts of the Early Middles Ages* (New York: Abrams, 1968), p. 35, which shows a capital, entitled 'The Mystic Mill,' in the abbey church of the Madeleine at Vezelay. As the text notes of the two bearded male figures engaged in the process of milling, 'The connection between the Old and New Testaments is presented symbolically on this capital: the grain of the Old Testament passes throught the Mystic Mill to become the flour of the Gospels.'

19 See the *Commentary on Plato's Symposium on Love*, p. 171. Ficino's Latin original reads: "Primus itaque furor bonum equum, id est rationem opinionemque, a malo equo, id est, a phantasia confusa & sensuum appetitu distinguit. Secundus malum equum bono, bonum aurigae, id est, menti subiicit. Tertius aurigam in caput suum, id est, in unitatem mentis apicem dirigit. Postremus caput aurigae in caput rerum omnium vertit. Vbi auriga beatus est, & ad praesepe, id est, ad diuinam pulchritudinem sistens equos, id est, accomodans, omnes sibi subiectas animae partes, obiicit illis ambrosiam, & super ipsam nectar potandum, id est, visionem pulchritudinis, & ex visione laetitiam": see the *Opera Omnia*, p. 1172, col. B (Seventh Speech, ch. xiv).

Dennis J. McAuliffe

Neoplatonism in Vittoria Colonna's Poetry: From the Secular to the Divine

In this discussion of Neoplatonism in Vittoria Colonna's poetry I describe, first of all, the cultural, intellectual, and emotional circumstances in which these influences first manifest themselves. I then discuss some of the sonnets from her early *Canzoniere*[1] (I prefer this designation, taken in its strict sense, to the more commonly used one, 'secular sonnets'), along with an example from a contemporary (1540s) commentary which makes explicit reference to Vittoria's Neoplatonism. Finally, I discuss the change that takes place later in Vittoria's life and in her writing as well as in her Neoplatonism, a change so radical that one must talk of a second *canzoniere*. The terms secular and spiritual must be used with caution since they are likely to give, as they have done in the past, a false impression of what Vittoria Colonna's poetry is about. It is an intensely spiritual poetry from the earliest sonnets and the 'secular' elements of the earlier *canzoniere* are finely filtered through a Neoplatonic screen.

Paolo Giovio tells the story of how the Marchese of Pescara, Ferrante Francesco d'Avalos, summoned his wife, Vittoria, to his side when he realized his death was near in November, 1525.[2] The wounds he had received in the battle of Pavia the previous February were proving fatal. He was in Milan and Vittoria was on Ischia. As soon as she received his summons she set out in all haste, travelling day and night; but when she was only as far as Viterbo she was met by a second messenger bringing news of Ferrante's death on November 25th. Giovio says that when Vittoria heard the news, she fell from her horse as if struck dead; and she had to be nursed for several days in a nearby monastery. When she was well enough to travel she returned to Rome and immediately petitioned to be allowed to enter the convent of the Poor Clares, San Silvestro in Capite, which had been founded in the thirteenth century in honour of her ancestor, Margherita Colonna. But Vittoria's brother, Ascanio, probably in hopes that she could be convinced to marry again, sought the aid of Jacopo Sadoleto, Bishop of Carpentras and papal secretary, to persuade Clement VII to forbid Vittoria to become a nun.[3] A papal brief which was written and signed

by Sadoleto on December 7, 1525 allowed Vittoria to enter San
Silvestro as a guest in order to receive spiritual and temporal consolation for her loss ('omnibus spiritualibus et temporalibus consolatio-
nibus'), but forbade the sisters to allow Vittoria, driven rather by her
sorrow than by mature judgement ('impetu potius sui doloris quam
maturo consilio'), to take the veil without specific papal authorization.[4]

The sonnets written in memory of Ferrante are the product of the
grief that the poet felt during those first years of her widowhood. Ferrante's death caused profound changes in Vittoria's way of life. She
withdrew from the pleasure-seeking activities of secular life and passed
most of her time behind convent walls. We know both from reading
her poetry and from the testimony of those who knew her that she
spent long hours in prayer and in contemplation of the state in which
Ferrante's death had left her. On the other hand, the fact that she no
longer was obliged to carry out the Neapolitan court duties of an Imperial Commander's wife left her free to spend more time in Rome
and consequently brought her in close touch with important events of
her time. She witnessed the ruinous and demoralizing attack on Rome
in 1526 carried out by her own family, led by Prospero Colonna, the
warrior-cardinal, who allowed his mercenaries to imprison the Pope in
Castel Sant'Angelo and wreak havoc on the city's wealthy citizenry. She
witnessed the even more terrible Sack of Rome in 1527, when the Imperial troops raped the city with unprecedented savagery. And she re-
sponded with tireless acts of charity to the need to rehabilitate the dev-
astated Roman populace.

The apparent contradiction between these two lifestyles to which she
was drawn after her husband's death was to preoccupy her for the rest
of her life. It is the conflict, to which she refers repeatedly in her
poetry, between the contemplative life of prayer and the active life of
good works. It is the same conflict that the Protestant reform movement of Northern Europe was turning into an intellectual and spiritual
debate which would touch the lives of all educated society. Vittoria
Colonna was perceived by everyone around her as the person who was
best able to reconcile these opposing attitudes. She showed this ability
not only through her poetry, but also through her conversation, as we
know from contemporary sources,[5] and through her participation in
the burgeoning Catholic reform movement which involved many of the
principal intellectual figures of pre-tridentine Roman society. When
Pietro Carnesecchi was asked by his inquisitors, during the trial of
1566 that led to his condemnation as a heretic, to explain Vittoria
Colonna's stand on the question *de sola fide*, he replied that she followed the advice of Cardinal Pole who told her during the early 1540s
to believe as if it were faith alone that brought salvation but to act as if

that salvation had to be achieved by good works. We may take it on Carnesecchi's word that Vittoria suffered a crisis of doubt on this issue, as did so many of her spiritually active friends; but the advice she received from Pole was, in essence, to act no differently than she had been doing since she first retired to convent life.

The first sign of the poetic talent for which the Marchesa di Pescara was so enthusiastically and sincerely praised by her contemporaries (Ariosto and Bembo among others) was the *Epistola a Ferrante Francesco d'Avalos, Suo Consorte, nella Rotta di Ravenna* in which the author describes her pitiful state of abandonment after Ferrante left her, a bride of only two years, to join the Aragonese forces fighting in the north of Italy against the French. Benedetto Croce describes this *Epistola* as 'tender, sorrowful, trembling, and impassioned' and he likes it best of all of her compositions because of its spontaneity and freshness of sentiment.[6]

Despite this appearance of spontaneity, however, the young poet betrays her dependence on the scholastic models studied during her humanistic education, especially Ovid from the Latin and Dante and Petrarch from the Tuscan classics. The *Epistola* provides the background for the Neoplatonic influences which characterize her later poetry. It shows the beginning of the process of mythicizing her husband as hero and also — ironically, since she could not have foretold his premature death in 1525 — it determines her choice of literary mode, the colloquy with the absent lover.

Whether Vittoria began writing sonnets in Marino soon after Ferrante's death or whether she began them later in the, perhaps, calmer environment of Ischia, we have no way of knowing. There is no direct testimony concerning these sonnets until Bembo praises them in a letter to her in 1532.[7] The poet must have kept them mostly to herself in the beginning because only her most intimate friends remark on her ability as a poet before that time.

In the sonnet 'Scrivo sol per sfogar l'interna doglia' (A1:1) which appears to have been written as an introduction to her earlier *canzoniere*, Vittoria sets forth her reasons for writing. We can immediately sense the sincerity of commitment both intellectual and emotional which sets her poetry apart from the slavish imitators of Petrarch who abounded in Italy throughout the sixteenth century and who are so roundly condemned by modern critics of the aesthetic schools.[8] Vittoria is not writing about her real or imagined past-life's experience filtered through her literary models but rather about one all-important, devastating event which determined the course of her emotional deveopment: the death of Ferrante. She does not ask for pity, pardon, and understanding or brag about her 'vario stile,' nor does she invoke the muses with prayers for lasting fame, as Petrarch and Bembo do in their introductory sonnets. She is writing for the intensely personal reason of relieving the terrible grief that Ferrante's death has caused her. The sincere humility of her poetic stance and her profound feelings of pain and sorrow are manifest in the sonnets of her earlier *canzoniere*, in her lifestyle, and in her constant refusal either to have her poems published or to show them to any but her closest friends. The fact that they became widely known in the 1530s and were eventually published against her will in 1538 reminds us of the custom of the day for friends to pass on to other friends even the most intimate forms of private correspondence.

Platonism and its Christian development, Neoplatonism, were at the basis of Vittoria Colonna's humanistic education. Many examples of Neoplatonic language occur in both her earlier and her later *canzonieri*. There are continual oppositions of body and spirit, light and dark, fire and ice, fervour and aridity. From her earliest poetry Vittoria showed her acceptance of one of the basic tenets of Platonism, that poetry is intended as a propaedeutic device to create admiration and subsequent emulation of supernatural beings and noble heroes. The heroization of Ferrante in the *Epistola* and in the early *canzoniere* reveals the poet's desire to take part in this traditional exercise of the literary profession. For Vittoria and her contemporaries poetry is also imitation and its mimetic effort is, in Platonic terms, to bypass the imperfect, created world and imitate the divine archetype.

Vittoria's adoption of both these Platonic tenets is based on her inner conviction, following the Platonic world-view, that it is the soul's desire and necessary end to break away from the prison of this present life. Her soul longs to attain the true world of the spirit where she can live in happy harmony with her beloved, whether it be Ferrante (as in these early sonnets) or Christ (as in the later ones). The sonnet 'Se per salire a l'alta e vera luce' (A2:34) explains Vittoria's Neoplatonic conception of reality. Vittoria's ascent from a world of false impressions and shadows toward the true light by means of love shows her adherence to the traditional Platonic concept. The key word in the second quatrain is 'chiostri,' which may be understood to mean an enclosed space (as a convent): the prison of life on earth. Vittoria uses the word 'carcere' ('prison') many times in these sonnets, more often and in a more firmly dualistic sense than Petrarch does. Love has captured her in his 'carcer soave' (A1:45); this life is a 'carcere' in which living becomes a 'viva morte' (A1:54); she has tried in vain to leave the 'carcer cieco' of this life (A1:64); her soul is trying to free itself from the 'carcer tetro' (her body) which keeps her bound to this shadowy, bitter, and base reality (A1:56).

It is left to those with special grace, the 'cari eletti' of line 10 in the above-cited sonnet (A2:34), among whom Ferrante is numbered, to find everlasting glory. This appellative which echoes the Neoplatonic notion of the elite is repeated several times. Vittoria speaks of 'anime gloriose e i spirti eletti' (A1:16); 'anima eletta, ch'anzi tempo spinta' (A1:50); and so forth. Of particular significance are the following lines where the use of 'eletti' in rhyme with 'concetti' demonstrates the poet's intentional use of Neoplatonic vocabulary.

> . . . voi, spirti eletti,
> ch'adornate sì rari alti concetti,
> onorate di lui le vostre carte. (A2:23)

The most common Neoplatonic theme found in the early sonnets is that of the winged soul which longs to return to the source of its joy. This theme is present in twenty-six out of the total of one hundred and forty sonnets.[9] In 'Mentr'io qui vissi in voi, lume beato' (A2:44) it joins the motifs of prayer, mysticism, and death to form a revealing statement of Vittoria's intellectual, spiritual, and emotional state of being. In the first quatrain Vittoria echoes the Platonic definition of love whereby the lover dies a voluntary death in order to relive in the beloved.[10] In the second quatrain she prays that her beloved will come to her aid against the world which is their enemy. In the first tercet she envisions her soul as having wings with which to fly to her beloved. And in the final tercet she repeats her belief that the mortal world and its pleasures are but a false reflection of the true and eternal world that awaits her after death.

The poet's imagination turns to the image of the winged flight from this world for herself (A1:52, 76, 79; A2:14, 15, 17), and for her beloved (A1:10, 45, 50, 57; A2:18, 43; E25).

> Anima eletta, ch'anzi tempo spinta
> dal proprio merto lieta al Ciel volasti,
> se conforme al valor luce portasti
> ogn'altra stella fu adombrata e vinta. (A1:50)

And it is not only her soul, but also her spirit, her reason, her thought, her desire, that must take flight from this darkness and be reunited with her 'Bel Sole'.

> Ristretta in loco oscuro, orrido e solo,
> ascosa, e cinta dal proprio martire,

> legati i sensi tutti al bel pensero,
>   con veloce expedito altero volo
> unir la mente al mio sommo desire
> oggi è quanto di ben nel mondo spero. (A1:13)

Yet she despairs of realizing her desire.

> L'alma rinchiusa in questo carcer rio
> come nimico l'odia, onde smarrita
> né vive qua né vola ov'io desio. (A1:29)

Thus, torn between hope and despair, the poet rejects the possibility of ending her torment by suicide ('por fine al duol per vie più corte?' A1:64) and resolves her internal struggle with an act of pure Neoplatonic faith in 'Pensier, ne l'alto volo ove tu stendi' (S2:35). The first quatrain of this sonnet sets forth the proposition that her 'valor' is unable to measure up to the heights which her thoughts reach and that because of this she must put an end to the endeavour even before it progresses beyond its beginning. There are a number of levels at which this sonnet may be interpreted. At least two of these are pertinent to the present discussion. First, the lover constantly imagines herself as able to join her beloved in a better world, but her physical attachment to this world will not allow her to reach him. She is, therefore, immediately defeated. At another level Vittoria is talking about her poetic inspiration which is so far beyond her technical ability to do it justice that the attempt itself (this very sonnet) is evidence of its failure. The word 'penne' is to be understood literally (pens) as well as figuratively (wings). The word 'intendi' is to be taken literally in both cases. In the second quatrain the poet elaborates these ideas by stressing such Neoplatonic vocabulary as the 'bel lume immortale' and the use of the inner eye which must focus on the higher world both of forms (to which Ferrante has been graduated) and of inspiration.

At least one third of Vittoria's early sonnets contain mention of, or allusion to, death. Out of her sorrow over losing Ferrante come references to her own death.

> Come non deposi io la mortal salma
> al miglior tempo? Da chi fu impedita,
> per non volar in quella eterna vita,
> l'alma, al partir de l'altra mia vera alma? (A1:44)

Her thoughts of death are always intimately connected with her Neoplatonist belief, as expressed in the last line, that Ferrante had captured and taken with him her 'true soul.' And she crowns this contemplation with the prayer that she be delivered of her sorrow through death.

> ma, non trovando alfin ragion che giove
> a l'alma nel suo duol sempre proterva,
> prego che 'l pianto mio finisca morte. (A1:51)

Vittoria sees death not only as the end of her sorrow, and of the gnawing necessity of lamenting her separation from Ferrante through poetry, but also as her salvation.

Along with her contemplation of death goes Vittoria's need to renounce the world, its pleasures, and its attractions. Because Love gave her Ferrante, even though he was afterward taken from her, she has renounced all other earthly love.

> Di così nobil fiamma Amor mi cinse
> ch'essendo morta in me vive l'ardore;
> né temo novo caldo, ché 'l vigore
> del primo foco mio tutt'altri estinse. (A1:7)

This renunciation, coupled with that of other worldly pleasures, is reflected in Vittoria's life as well as in her poetry. Her request to enter a religious order, denied by Pope Clement VII, her constant refusal, in opposition to her brother Ascanio's insistence, to consider remarrying, and her withdrawal to the contemplative life of the convent speak eloquently of the sincerity of the content of her poetry.

> Così lo spirto mio s'asconde e copre
> qui dal piacer uman; non già per fama,
> o van grido, o prezzar troppo se stesso;
>   ma sente il lume suo ch'ognor lo chiama,
> e vede il volto ovunque mira impresso
> che li misura i passi e scorge l'opre. (A1:72)

Her various attitudes toward death lend it the same predominance in her poetry that it had for her in daily life.

She is afraid of death:

> Ma se timor del crudo pianto eterno

tronca l'audaci penne al bel desire . . . (A1:56)

She is envious of the dead:

> Quant'invidia al mio cor, felici e rare
> anime, porge il vostro ardente e forte
> nodo . . . (A1:88)

Death took away her hope:

> Nudriva il cor d'una speranza viva
> fondata e colta in sì nobil terreno
> che 'l frutto promettea giocondo e ameno;
> morte la svelse alor ch'ella fioriva. (A1:3)

But by far the dominant attitude is her strong desire to die in order to become free and be reunited with Ferrante. This desire is voiced again and again in various ways throughout the early *canzoniere*. In A1:26 Vittoria complains that death took Ferrante but refused her who would happily die. In A1:66 she prays to be made free, body and soul, from this life. In A2:8 she says that she seeks death as a tiger seeks her young. In A1:53 she says that she is afraid lest she live too long. For Vittoria life without Ferrante is a living death and the only true life is to close her eyes forever to this world and bask for eternity in the light of the sun.

> Oh viver mio noioso, oh aversa sorte!
> cerco l'oscurità, fuggo la luce,
> odio la vita, ognor bramo la morte.
> Quel ch'agli altri occhi offende ai miei riluce,
> perché chiudendo lor s'apron le porte
> a la cagion ch'al mio Sol mi conduce. (A1:68)

It is her contemplation of renunciation and death as she continually reworks the myth of Ferrante that leads Vittoria to the mysticism which eventually replaces her Neoplatonic view of reality in her later sonnets. An outstanding example of this mysticism is found in the imagery of 'Qual ricca oblazion, qual voler pio' (A1:55). This sacrificial offering of the naked, burning heart, described in patently sensual imagery, is a commonplace which has been called the epitome of baroque conceits. It was destined to become an icon of the Counter-Reformation through the efforts of Teresa of Avila, Ignatius Loyola, and others. As Robert

J. Clements points out it was also a commonplace in the poetry of Michelangelo.[11] This image finds itself unforgettably enshrined in Bernini's 'Saint Teresa in Ecstasy' in Rome's church of Santa Maria della Vittoria.

Up to this point the verses cited from the earlier *canzoniere* show the heavy charge of emotion lying behind the intellectualization of the poet's suffering, fear, and hope. Examples such as these clearly refute the accusation made by a great number of critics that Vittoria Colonna's poetry lacks warmth or depth of feeling. It is with this *caveat* in mind that the reader should peruse commentaries on Vittoria Colonna's *Rime*, such as that printed by G.B. and M. Sessa in Venice in 1558. In it Rinaldo Corso, Vittoria's contemporary, explores, among other things, the Neoplatonic content of one of Vittoria's verses. A good example is his commentary on 'D'ogni sua gloria fu largo al mio Sole' (Bullock's edition, A2:20, has 'grazia' for 'gloria'), which is one of Vittoria's more detached statements of her situation. This sonnet is a frank self-assessment in which the poet declares that she has always lived in the world detached from sensual pleasures, having learned to accept in her personal life the Neoplatonic dualism which portrays pleasure of the senses as something to be avoided and intellectual pleasures through and beyond the senses as the only kind to be sought. It is evident from Corso's commentary that what her contemporaries admired in Vittoria was that she lived as she wrote. There was no dichotomy between the self-image she presented in her poetry and that which she presented in everyday social intercourse. It seems ironic that it is this very fact which causes many modern readers to reject her poetry as artificial and lacking in depth of sincerity and personal inspiration.

Vittoria's Neoplatonism underwent dramatic change from the earlier to the later *canzoniere* as a result of a personal spiritual conversion which she experienced at about the time that Juan de Valdés, the Spanish evangelical leader, established himself in Naples in 1534. Neoplatonic vocabulary is still evident in her later poetry — the dichotomies of light and dark, the despised false world of the senses and the real world of the spirit, the winged soul taking flight upward, away from the body — but Vittoria's acceptance of the evangelical message meant accepting the immanence of the Son along with the transcendence of the Father. The struggle between these two conflicting elements in Vittoria's perception of reality resolves itself in the complete transformation of the lover (Vittoria) into the beloved (Jesus) as she makes the difficult but imminently realizable flight to the Cross in imitation of her Saviour:

Spogliando i gran tiranni a campo aperto
prese di terra in croce un picciol volo;
ivi l'affisse e lo dannò col sangue. (S1:40)

This realizable flight stands in contrast to the impossible flight toward
Ferrante depicted in the earlier *canzoniere*. In recognition of this new
approach to salvation Vittoria goes so far as to build her own ladder of
ascent: in 'Tira su l'alma al Ciel col Suo d'amore' (S1:73) the four steps
of the ladder are constituted by the three cardinal virtues (faith, hope,
and charity), and the Christian virtue of humility. In the first quatrain
Vittoria shows that the knots which bind the soul to the transcendant
Father are tightened by the immanent hand of the Son. The poet feels
an immediate sense of satisfaction in the cry that signifies at once the
separation and the reuniting of the Father and his children — the cry
that Jesus sent out from the Cross; 'Father, Father, why have you for-
saken me.' It is worth noting, also, in the second quatrain that the poet
is foreshadowing the use of the word *onore* which, as Dionisotti states,
is to take the place of *amore* in the second half of the sixteenth century
as the predominant preoccupation of the poets.

It is important to the question of Vittoria Colonna's Neoplatonism to
note that nowhere in the later *canzoniere* does the concept of the beautiful receive attention. It seems that the poet was no longer concerned
with the Neoplatonic perception of the good through the beautiful that
was present in 'D'ogni sua grazia fu largo al mio Sole' (A2:20) now that
she has abandoned her contemplation of Ferrante, her 'Bel Sole', and
'Bell'Oggetto.' Vittoria's theology has changed from the Renaissance
Neoplatonic to the Pauline tradition which distrusts even this symbolic
use of the senses. In 'Felice il cieco nato a cui s'aperse' (S2:28), distrust
of the eyes calls forth the longing to have the inner sight of the blind.
The poet also recants her belief in the reliability of the external sense
of hearing, a belief repeated throughout the earlier *canzoniere*. She
substitutes for it the concept from Neoplatonic mythology of the harmony of sound in the universe signifying Divine order, a concept made
popular by Dante in his *Divine Comedy* as the music of the spheres. In
'Vorrei l'orecchia aver qui chiusa e sorda' (S1:28) Vittoria's distrust of
the senses fits in with the traditional way of perceiving harmonious
sound through an inner capacity, an intuition of the soul.

In conclusion I would like to underscore the insight that a close and
sympathetic reading of the Marchesa di Pescara's poetry gives the
reader. Vittoria Colonna, in the intellectualization of her every emotion, was drawing upon a life experience of total commitment and
unity of vision and it can be demonstrated, as I have tried to do in this
study, that her philosophical and theological preoccupations were the

media through which she filtered those experiences in her poetry. Furthermore, an examination of the small body of evidence concerning Vittoria's intentions for the publication of her verses indicates that she wished them to circulate only among her immediate friends. She was writing for her own edification and that of her circle of *spirituali* (including, for example, Michelangelo), rather than for a general reading public. If modern readers take these considerations into account, they will avoid many of the pitfalls incurred by critics who have placed Vittoria Colonna's poetry in the context of competitive Petrarchism and they will recognize in Vittoria a poet who is bringing a new sincerity of commitment to the salvific properties of literature.

Scarborough College
University of Toronto

Notes

1 All references are to Vittoria Colonna, *Rime*, ed. Alan Bullock (Rome-Bari: Laterza, 1982).

1 *Le vite del Gran Capitano e del Marchese di Pescara* (Bari: Laterza, 1931); written in the 1540s.

3 The Medici pope and the Colonna family, leading military allies of the Emperor, were fighting bitterly over the Imperial presence in Italy, and so an intermediary had to be used in this transaction.

4 This brief is cited in its entirety by Pietro Ercole Visconti in *Le Rime di Vittoria Colonna* (Rome: Salviucci, 1840) pp. cxliv-cxlv.

5 Among the many contemporary references to the formative influence of Vittoria Colonna's conversation are the letters of Reginald Pole; the testimony of Pietro Carnesecchi before the Roman Inquisition; the historical accounts of Paolo Giovio (*La vita del Marchese di Pescara*, 1549), Ascanio Condivi (*La vita di Michelagnolo Buonaroti*, 1553), and the Portuguese artist, Francisco d'Olanda (*Da pintura antiga*, written in 1548 but not adequately edited for publication until the nineteenth century. There is a modern Italian edition by Antonietta Maria Bessone Aurelli: *Dialoghi Michelangioleschi di Francisco d'Olanda*. Rome: Fratelli Palombi, 1953).

6 Benedetto Croce, *Poesia popolare e poesia d'arte* (Bari: Laterza, 1933) p. 430.

7 Vittoria Colonna, *Carteggio* raccolto e pubblicato da Ermanno Ferrero e Giuseppe Müller, seconda edizione . . . da Domenico Tordi (Turin: Loescher, 1892) pp. 79-81.

8 Arturo Pompeati in *Storia della letteratura italiana* (Turin: UTET, 1957), II, 516-18 characterizes these Petrarchists as performing 'scimmiottatura meccanica ed esteriore, velleità di ricreare il segreto di una grande poesia col riprodurne le parole e i suoni; deserto di ispirazione personale; insincerità; . . . uniformità desolante degli infiniti imitatori.'

9 Pietro Ercole Visconti (*Le Rime di Vittoria Colonna*, Rome: Salviucci, 1840) puts 117 sonnets in the first group, adding two sonnets that were left out of preceding editions, and fifteen sonnets and a madrigal that he claims were previously unpublished. Althea Lawley (*Vittoria Colonna*, London: Gilbert and Rivington,

1888), Domenico Tordi (*Sonetti inediti*, Pistoia: G. Flori, 1900), Alan Bullock (in several articles culminating in *Rime*, Rome-Bari: Laterza, 1982), and others increase this number to 140 sonnets.

10 J.C. Nelson in *Renaissance Theory of Love* (New York: Columbia University Press, 1958), p. 51 cites Lorenzo de' Medici on this point.

11 R.J. Clements, *The Poetry of Michelangelo* (New York: New York University Press, 1966), p. 45.

Olga Zorzi Pugliese

Variations on Ficino's *De Amore*: The Hymns to Love by Benivieni and Castiglione

This paper deals with two works containing reformulations of Ficino's love-theory: namely, Girolamo Benivieni's 'Canzona d'amore,' a poem which inspired the well-known commentary from the pen of the philosopher Pico della Mirandola and is believed to have influenced Michelangelo and, possibly, Spenser,[1] and the speech on love delivered by Pietro Bembo in Book IV of Castiglione's *Il libro del cortegiano*, a source book for innumerable European writers. The analysis of these texts, which occupy an important place in the history of literature, is intended to demonstrate how Ficino's seminal treatise was rewritten by two literary theorists of love. It inevitably involves reiterating the essential features of Renaissance Neoplatonism, but it also allows us to single out certain basic expressive structures adopted by these authors of Neoplatonic texts.

As a member of the Neoplatonic circle in Medicean Florence, Girolamo Benivieni (1453-1542) was one of the first to offer a rendition of Ficino's *De Amore*. He wrote his 'Canzona' some time after 1469, the year Ficino produced his commentary on *The Symposium* in Latin, but before the tragic events of 1478, which, according to the poet's own avowal, inspired him to turn to more religious concerns.[2] In the letter to the reader prefacing his 'Canzona,' Benivieni explains that his intention at the time of composition had been to provide a summary of Ficino's treatise: 'io havevo in pochi versi ristrecto quello che Marsilio in molte carte elegantissimamente descrive.'[3] What the eight-stanza poem offers is, in fact, a reduced version of the philosopher's theory of love. Yet the omissions, additions, and stresses all help to elucidate the choices and rejections effected by the poet on Ficino's text.

Like Ficino's *De Amore*, Benivieni's poem is Platonic, first of all in the sense that it is not about love directly, but about the *theory* of love — a distinction made by Thomas Gould in his study on Platonic love.[4] It is not a declaration of love addressed to a specific beloved person, but an attempt to explain, through the apparent elucidation of an earlier text (or pre-text), the Platonic doctrine of love. In his 'Canzona,' Benivieni reaffirms the standard hierarchical world-view and the pervasive role that love plays within that framework. Foregoing the metaphor of concentric circles, he adopts the traditional imagery of light in the delineation of the downward and ever diminishing diffusion of beauty from the divine Sun, through the angelic Mind, to the soul, the body, and eventually matter, although the lowest rung is never named specifically. As the lower beings 'convert,' that is, in an etymological sense, 'turn' toward the light, their innate desire to reach the higher levels is kindled. The types of love which man can thus achieve are of three kinds, as Ficino too had stated in the *De Amore* (VI, 5, 8-9): Benivieni writes how Love 'Questo al ciel volga, et quello ad terra hor pieghi / Hora infra questi due l'inclini & fermi' (st. 2) (turns some persons to heaven, bends others toward earth, and makes still others tend toward a midpoint and stop there).

Following Ficino (VI, 7), Benivieni highlights the polarity between celestial and vulgar love, between the contemplation and generation of beauty. But only the heaven-directed species of love and only the more spiritual parts of man are of interest to him. None of the physiological phenomena involved in vulgar love, as Ficino details them (VI, 9; VII, 3-5), find their way into Benivieni's scheme. The corpus of Platonic myths is reduced too: the birth of Venus, involving the castration of Uranus, is barely hinted at in the reference to Heaven's having created Venus out of itself ('che di sé il ciel facea, chi Cypri honora,' st. 3); the myth of Venus's birth from Plenty and Penury is given similarly short shrift ('Di inopia nato, & di richeza,' st. 3); and the Androgyne tale is excluded completely. Benivieni provides only passing mention of the astrological factors which give rise to love, that is, of the 'valor' which the soul derives from its star (st. 6; cf. Ficino II, 8). What he stresses most, instead, is the process of spiritual elevation, involving the vertical movement of ascent.

Yet the steps on Benivieni's seven-runged ladder of contemplation, precisely numbered with the help of the poet's own marginal notes, reveal a slight, but significant, departure from the Ficinian scheme. The middle phases, following upon external contemplation of an object, involve an inner moulding of an even more beautiful image of the beloved (st. 6-7). This is the key stage of 'reforming' referred to twice, with a Petrarchan phrase, as a 'dolce error.' But whereas Petrarch's 'sweet error' (Canzone 129) consisted of thinking he saw his beloved, in Benivieni it is a philosophical concept which the poet merely couches in traditional poetic language. Even the reformation process Ficino had spoken of (VI, 6) was a negative sort of self-deception, while for Benivieni it is a positive phenomenon allowing the lover to behold the divine light present in the beloved. By reforming the 'spoglie,' or external wrappings (a term Petrarch used for Laura's body and Poliziano repeats in *Stanze*, I, 90), one can then proceed to abstract a universal concept from specific instances of beauty. In earthly 'vestiges' (st. 8) one can detect the divine, and eventually fly upward to the Sun where, filled with its unique living light, man, by loving, experiences the beauty of the mind, the soul, the world, and everything in it ('amando si fa bello / La mente, l'alma, e 'l mondo & cio ch'è in quello,' st. 8).

The procedures involved in this spiritual ascent, though based on Ficino, also conform to the *extra—intra—supra* movement and to the emphasis on vestiges, or footprints, which are central tenets of the *Itinerarium Mentis in Deum* of Saint Bonaventure — a text which Benivieni was to utilize and quote profusely some years later. It would appear that, when he wrote this early 'Canzona,' which he later transformed into a 'Canzone dello amore celeste et divino secondo la verità della religione christiana et della fede catholica,' the poet had already culled, perhaps through Ficino (who uses the term *vestige*, for example, in I, 4; II, 3; VI, 10), the concepts and language which were to become his standard medium for more religious subjects.

Indeed the 'Canzona d'amore' already bears evidence of a more Christianized tendency: God is described as the uncreated good and uncreated sun ('increato ben,' st. 2; 'increato sol,' st. 4, 7), phrases which echo the qualifier commonly found in patristic writings (including Bonaventure, *Itin.* II, 9; IV, 3).[5] In the second stanza, man is implicitly portrayed as being in a bent-over state (only through love is he made to raise his brow from earth) and also in need of guidance on the 'camin cieco,' or blind path. This characterization bears some similarity to Bonaventure's sinner, termed *incurvatus* and *excaecatus* (bent over and blind, I, 7). Religious connotations are also suggested by the embodiment of the spiritual ascent in the 'pio cor' or 'cor pietoso.' This pious heart has nothing in common with the Petrarchan one of sonnet 340, who feels pity for a fellow sufferer in love, but is comparable, perhaps, to the humble and 'pious' persons to whom Bonaventure directs his teachings (Prologue, 4), as well as to the followers of the type of 'pietas' which Ficino says will lead us back to God (VII, 15).

In dealing with this theme of the pious heart's almost mystical flight to the sight of God, Benivieni, like many writers before him, including Dante, faces problems of ineffability. In fact, going beyond mere deference to the topos of modesty, he dedicates a good portion of the first two stanzas and of the envoy of the 'Canzona' to the subject of verbal inadequacy. Although Love is the inspiring and dominant force which moves his tongue and mind to speak of love, and to reveal what is in his burning bosom, his tongue resists at first. In the struggle, the greater force of Love wins and he is forced to express his 'concepto.'

The true protagonist of the 'Canzona,' then, more than the third-person lover or pious heart, is the fictive writer who, using the first-person, theorizes on love-writing. The apostrophes to his work, termed 'Stanche mie rime' and 'languidi & infermi / Versi' at the beginning, along with the lengthy address to his poem in the envoy, show that the 'Canzona' is a highly self-conscious literary act. The whole theme of flight can be read, not only as a spiritual experience, but also as the flow of words.[6] Tired, sluggish, and weak, at first, his verses must be restrained later by Love, who reins in the poet's daring heart which has been spurred beyond its destined course ('el fren raccoglie / Al temerario ardir che 'l cor mio sprona / Forse di là dal destinato corso,' st. 9). Indeed the bit of the bridle, the *freno* and *morso*, also signify the restrictions placed on his freedom to verbalize.

In the *congedo* the fictive poet receives instructions to relay the message of love exclusively to those able to comprehend it; to these — the initiate, reminiscent of the exclusive audiences addressed in much early poetry (cf. Cavalcanti) — he is to convey the foliage and the fruit; to the others, only the externals, denying the essence. The poem ends thus on a negative note, with the imperative 'niega' suggesting almost a denial of the preceding exposition. Silence and reticence prevail here, as at the beginning when the poet's tongue was still reluctant to move. The ambivalence of the text, which reveals and yet does not reveal its secrets, is heightened by the language in which it is encoded. The predominant expressive modes are, in fact, abstract ones. There is in the poem, it is true, a sprinkling of artistic terms, probably of Ficinian derivation, but they are not of the type which later gathered such concrete experiential resonance in Michelangelo's verse. Benivieni's tend to be Latinate and highly conceptualized, as a few verses from stanza 6 on the birth of love illustrate: the poet explains how, if the infused engraving ('stampa') of the sun, which the soul carries sculpted ('sculto') within it, descends into a kindred soul, the latter is enamoured and embellishes it ('Piú bella a' divin rai / Di suo virtù l'effinge'). Intellectualized terminology, often based on etymological roots (e.g. the phrase 'divin culto' in stanza 6, meaning not, as might be expected, 'the worship of God' but, rather, 'the act of polishing carried out by the creator'), and difficult syntax with hard-to-define antecedents, contribute to the creation of an impenetrable construct which, at certain points, defies interpretation on the literal level.

On the other hand, the general structure of the 'Canzona' is readily discernible. Following Ficino, who states at the beginning of the *De Amore* that the proper Platonic method is to praise good and to blame its opposite, Benivieni builds his poem according to a rhetorical pattern. His epideictic hymn of praise contains an *exordium* (dealing with problems of language and inspiration), a narration in the second stanza indicating the topic and its parts (how Love is diffused, when it was born, how it rules the universe, enters human hearts, and elevates them to God), the central stanzas presenting the details of his scheme, all leading up to the climactic vision of God. However the peroration is followed by a conclusion which quickly brings the enraptured heart and the reader down from the heights of divine love to the problems of amatory language.

* * *

Turning now to our second text, *Il libro del cortegiano*, we find that Castiglione too shares, with his Platonic predecessors, a rhetorical approach to the subject of love.[7] The characters in Plato's *Symposium* had contributed discourses on the god of Love, in order to honour a deity who had been neglected. Castiglione's courtiers call upon Pietro Bembo, well-known as a lover and as author of the love-treatise entitled *Gli Asolani*, to respond encomiastically to a vituperation of love uttered at the beginning of the discussion (Ch. 49), and to defend feminine beauty when it is condemned later on by a misogynist (56). Consequently, the distinction between right and wrong love becomes, as it had been in *Gli Asolani*, the epideictic principle governing much of the discussion (the words *biasimo* and *laude* recur frequently in the discussion). In *Il libro del cortegiano*, Bembo offers first a confutation of the erroneous interpretations of love held by some of the objectors, and then the confirmation of his more positive views on a more rewarding kind of amorous experience.

What he outlines, as critics now generally acknowledge, is essentially Ficino's love-theory.[8] He begins with a clear definition of love as the desire to enjoy beauty (51), and he repeats such key ideas as the cohesive force of love, its circular movement (70, 57), and the spiritual nature of beauty, discernible in the 'vestiges' (69) or footsteps of God ('orma di Dio,' 68). Assimilating the views of other thinkers as well, Castiglione makes some modifications in Ficino's theory, though. To the experience of love, he adds, for example, the spiritual kiss (64), viewed by Pico as the union of souls.[9]

Most important, however, is the tone which is established in the text: whereas Benivieni makes Ficino's scheme even more ethereal, Castiglione renders it more earth-directed, faced as he is with the need to adapt Neoplatonic theory to the realities of court life. He omits the myths on the origins of love — the first part of the tripartite arrangement adopted by Ficino — choosing instead to concentrate on the essence of love — heterosexual love, that is — and on its effects. Viewing love in the context of the courtier's human 'conditions' (50), he admits that it acts as an incentive to carry out worthy deeds ('cose virtuose') for the purpose of impressing the ladies (54). Formulating what is a space- and time-related theory, rather than a utopian and absolute one, he accepts sensual love (corresponding to Ficino's vulgar love) for the young (54), while advising the mature courtier to strive for divine love.

Such a human perspective is reflected in the structure of the work, which places the hymn to love within a lively dialogue involving several interlocutors — a structure which contrasts with the series of speeches framed in a flimsy historical and human setting devised by Ficino in the *De Amore*. Castiglione's more realistic approach is reflected in the everyday analogies drawn to illustrate his points: divine goodness illuminates human beauty just as a ray of sunlight strikes a golden and bejewelled vase; people who rest in sensual love are like sick persons who cannot find contentment (52) — similes alien to the stricter philosophical argumentation and metaphysical type of imagery found in Ficino's text, and alien also to the abstract language of Benivieni's poem.

In the treatise, realism often becomes subversion. The validity of the rather generic ladder of love Castiglione proposes in order to lead the lover along the 'path' (60, 62, 68, 69) from an appreciation of particular physical beauty right up to the mind's eye's contemplation of absolute beauty in God, is radically questioned when Cesare Gonzaga, one of the skeptical albeit minor figures, notes that the path outlined is too steep (72). This, along with other objections made by Morello — to the effect that love which excludes the body is just a dream (55), or that it is preferable to produce a fine baby (62) —, tend to negate the message of Bembo's speech, indeed to refute Ficino's theory. It is interesting to note that these negative voices are heard at the beginning and at the end of the discussions, thus forming a contrasting frame for the positive hymn of love itself. A specific illustration of the irony shown Ficino is the interpretation given to the image of the hook. In Ficino's *De Amore* (VI, 2), the *hamus* is a divine enticement which can lead man to God; one of Castiglione's characters, instead, sees it as a form of deceit used by evil persons whose fair appearance is really equivalent to bait on a hook (56).

The major disruption occurs, however, when Bembo reaches the passionate climax of his speech, marked by exclamations and effective images of inebriation, that is, when he is actually rapt in a vision of God and, in essence, is acting out his theory. Right at this point in Chapter 71, when for some time now the spectators have been listening very attentively (they will, in fact, be left feeling a certain spark of divine love), the spell is suddenly broken as signora Emila tugs at the edge of Bembo's robe and pulls him down to earth, warning him that his soul might leave his body. Thus the vertical ascent is rudely interrupted.[10]

Just as an element of irony clearly colours the reception of Bembo's oration, so it also tinges the very character of the speaker himself.[11] An authority on love in his own right, Bembo is made to utter what is essentially someone else's doctrine. As he declaims, though, he demonstrates his oratorical ability convincingly. The *persona* created by the figure of Bembo is, therefore, not just that of the lover, or of the historical author of the *Asolani* text, but more generically that of the speaker on love. Accordingly, he makes frequent use of the verb *dire* (to say or speak) throughout his script ('dirò ciò che vorrete,' 50; 'Dico adunque che,' 51; 'diremo che,' 52, and so on), and he uses the first person singular pronoun almost exclusively to refer to himself as a *speaker* on love. On the other hand, he describes certain love experiences in the third person only or, at most, in the rather generic first person plural. However, in this role as orator, he, like Benivieni, expresses qualms about taking on the heroic task, or 'impresa' (50), of explaining divine love; he expresses reluctance and unworthiness, and must be urged on by the semi-divine Duchess at the outset, just as he must be inspired by the god, who will move his thoughts and his tongue, when he approaches the serious phase of his oration (61). At the end, moreover, he asks helplessly what mortal tongue can praise love adequately (70). Urged to continue, he replies that he has spoken what the holy amorous furor dictated; no longer inspired, he has nothing further to say (71).

These declarations by Bembo arouse the suspicion that perhaps there were more mysteries to be revealed, that something has been suppressed by the abrupt ending brought to his impassioned speech. And, indeed, the topic of women's ability to experience divine love is postponed and therefore is excluded from the text. The ineffability of love was implied in the classic distancing technique — the *oratio ficta* — used by Plato when he had his character Socrates quote the speech of Diotima. Castiglione follows a similar course when he has his speaker, Bembo, refer to the need to seek advice from Lavinello's hermit (50), thus suggesting that what is being composed is a speech within a speech within a speech. Indeed the analogy with Plato is appropriate if we recall that a character in the *Cortegiano* refers to Diotima (72).

* * *

The texts considered here were obviously inspired by Ficino's *De Amore* as both authors took up the challenge of the day to try their hand at formulating their own Neoplatonic doctrines of love — a task to be accomplished through a dialogue with Ficino's ground breaking treatise. Benivieni explains in the letter-preface that he was 'invitato' to write his 'Canzona d'amore' by the pleasurable reading of Ficino's commentary on the *Symposium*. Castiglione too, like the fictive Bembo in his work, may have prayed to be admitted to the *banquet* of angels ('esser ammess[o] al *convivio* degli angeli,' 70 [italics mine]). However, a notable displacement of the exemplary *De Amore* is effected in both cases. In Ficino's treatise, all the ideas were fitted into a neatly constructed system based on unwavering verticality and closed circles. The speakers of all seven orations showed no hesitation, and made no reference to any difficulties encountered in expressing their ideas on love. In fact, in the exclamatory peroration of the last speech, very near the end of the treatise, a prayer of thanks was offered to the Holy Spirit which had allowed them to speak on love (VII, 17). Consequently, *De Amore* ended on a very high note. By contrast, the texts by Benivieni and Castiglione, although they follow what is essentially the same rhetorical structure, are hymns to love which bear ironical frames, as the analysis presented here has aimed to demonstrate. Both the 'Canzona' and *Il libro del cortegiano* begin and end on a note of uncertainty, and both are brought to a close by a sharp fall, which is related to a certain degree of skepticism with respect to the Ficinian doctrine of love itself, as well as to the viability of the Neoplatonic language of love. Nonetheless, these ironies, ambiguities, and displacements are not to be viewed unfavourably. The result, undoubtedly, of serious reflection on the part of the authors — the one becoming ever more steeped in Christian teachings, the other caught in earth- and court-bound concerns — they constitute features which make the 'Canzona' and Book IV of the *Cortegiano* two of the most stimulating variations on the Ficinian model.

University of Toronto

Notes

1 Hieronymo Benivieni, 'Canzona d'amore,' *Opera* (Florence: li heredi di Philippo di Giunta, 1519), fols. 37r-39v. The other basic texts quoted in this paper are the following: Marsile Ficin, *Commentaire sur le Banquet de Platon*, ed. Raymond Marcel (Paris: 'Les Belles Lettres,' 1956) and Baldassarre Castiglione, *Il cortegiano*, ed. Silvano Del Missier (Novara: Ist. Geogr. De Agostini, 1968).

Benivieni's poem had not been translated into English in a completely satisfactory manner, in spite of the versions produced by Thomas Stanley (1651), Jefferson B. Fletcher (1934), and Joseph Tusiani (1971). The translation recently published by Sears Jayne in Giovanni Pico della Mirandola, *Commentary on a Can-*

zone of Benivieni (New York: Peter Lang, 1984), clears up many of the difficulties. Unfortunately, it was not yet available when this paper was prepared.

Criticism on this difficult poem has been rather sketchy. In the sole monograph written on Benivieni, Caterina Re (*Girolamo Benivieni fiorentino: cenni sulla vita e sulle opere*. Città di Castello: Lapi, 1906, p. 96) dismisses the poem as a mere curiosity piece. According to her, it can have no aesthetic value because of its doctrinal content. Eugenio Garin too, in his article 'Marsilio Ficino, Girolamo Benivieni e Giovanni Pico,' *Giornale critico della filosofia italiana*, 23 (1942), 94, labels it an obscure exercise. The most detailed analysis is that of G. Massetani who, in *La dottrina filosofica nella canzone d'amore di Girolamo Benivieni* (Livorno: Debatte, 1904), stresses the Neoplatonic influences, including that of Plotinus. A major pitfall in the interpretation of the poem (see, for example, John Charles Nelson, *Renaissance Theory of Love*. New York and London: Columbia University Press, 1955, pp. 54-63) has been that of forcing Pico's commentary on the poem. In my view, the two texts should remain somewhat more distinct.

On the poem's influence on other writers see Walter Binni, *Michelangelo scrittore* (Turin: Einaudi, 1975), pp. 39-41, 78n, and Veselin Kostić, *Spenser's Sources in Italian Poetry* (Belgrade: Novi Dani, 1969), p. 76.

2 'Argumento in ella quarta egloga,' *Opera*, fols. 87v-88r.

3 'Hieronymus Benivenius civis florentinus ad lectorem,' *Opera*, no signature, but on the recto of the third leaf.

4 Thomas Gould, *Platonic Love* (New York: The Free Press of Glencoe, 1963), p. 2.

5 The term *increatus* was used by early exegetes as a predicate of God, as the *Thesaurus Linguae Latinae*, Vol. 7, Pt. 1, explains.

6 The analogy of poetic writing and inspiration with the flight of birds is found in Dante, *Purgatorio*, XXIV, 58-59. See also Poliziano, *Stanze*, I, 5-6.

7 In his booklet entitled *L'ordine e la persuasione: Pietro Bembo personaggio nel 'Cortegiano'* (Urbino: Quattro Venti, 1983), Guido Arbizzoni analyzes the rhetorical skills, typical of philosophical treatises, which Bembo uses in his speech on love in order to persuade and captivate his audience. Pietro Floriani ('Dall'amore cortese all'amor divino,' *Bembo e Castiglione: studi sul classicismo del Cinquecento* (Rome: Bulzoni, 1976), pp. 169-86) deals with the traditional structure of Bembo's oration.

8 Luigi Baldacci, 'Gli *Asolani* del Bembo e Venere celeste,' *Il petrarchismo italiano nel '500* (Milan-Naples: Ricciardi, 1957), pp. 107-10.

9 Giovanni Pico della Mirandola, *Commento sopra una Canzona de amore composta da Hieronymo Benivieni*, in Benivieni, *Opera*, fols. 53v-54r.

10 My article entitled 'Castiglione's *The Book of the Courtier*: A Matter of Time,' *Res Publica Litterarum*, 5, No. 2 (1982), 175-87 deals with vertical and circular structures in the treatise.

11 Lorenzo Savino, 'Di alcuni trattati e trattatisti d'amore italiani della prima metà del secolo XVI,' in Erasmo Percopo, *Studi di letteratura italiana*, Vol. 9 (Naples: Jovene, 1909), pp. 411-2, 422, deals with the ironical treatment accorded divine love in the *Cortegiano*. The treatise is viewed as a criticism of the Neoplatonic theory of love (see p. 426).

Riccardo Scrivano

Platonic and Cabalistic Elements
in the Hebrew Culture of Renaissance Italy:
Leone Ebreo and his *Dialoghi d'amore*

Although this paper cannot boast sensational new findings, it does aim
at establishing connections between certain facts and at formulating
hypotheses, or at times mere assumptions, by relating, where possible,
data on the Renaissance which have been established in different fields
of knowledge. This introduction is not a *captatio benevolentiae* pursued
for modesty's sake; it is based, rather, on limitations familiar to those
who have studied the Hebrew culture of the Renaissance. These limitations arose and grew not only because people, materials, and libraries
were repeatedly scattered, but also because it is difficult to consult extant documents located in faraway places, sometimes in private collec-
tions, and written in a language — Hebrew — which is not widely
known to Renaissance scholars in all its aspects. As a result, scholars
have found themselves relying on facts and on materials collected by
others and transmitted in such a way as to allow for little checking.
This, alas, is the situation in which I find myself and which I dare to
denounce, trusting that my confessing awareness of it can be taken as a
redeeming factor. A clear assessment of this problem is provided by
Frances Yates:

What seems to be particularly lacking is any sustained attempt, from any
quarter, to define Christian Cabala in relation to genuine, or Jewish, Cabala. As one tries to think about this problem, one is faced with a void. It
requires specialised training by Hebrew experts to tackle such a theme,
and the book, or books, by such experts have not yet appeared.[1]

Dame Yates does, of course, refer to 'François Secret's labours,' which,
she acknowledges, 'are providing materials for such a work,' but without attempting 'any synthesis or definition of the ideas of the Christian
Cabalists.' In the 'Introduction' to her book, she herself energetically
stresses the importance of clearly establishing the differences between
Hebrew Cabala and Christian Cabala 'in its Christian use of Cabalist

techniques and in its amalgamation of Hermeticism and Hermetic magic into the system.'[2]

Some headway in the search for links, correspondences, and mutual influences between Christian and Hebrew culture has been made by William Melczer who, at the conference on Giorgione and Venetian culture held in Rome in 1978, presented a brief but useful register of Hebrew intellectuals operating in the Renaissance.[3] Listed are such well known figures as Elia del Medigo from Crete, a teacher in Padua (also teacher of Giovanni Pico della Mirandola), who was interested in the Cabala but also had a solid base, as Melczer points out, in the classics of Islamic and Hebrew philosophy, especially Maimonides and Averroes.[4] The register also includes individuals who are less well known in Renaissance scholarship nowadays, figures who, in many cases, were familiar with the Hermetic and Cabalistic sources used by Renaissance Neoplatonists and who were able to fit the peculiarities of Cabala, in particular, nicely into the official cultural tradition of Hebraism. From Melczer's study there emerges a picture of the average intellectual, of the Mantuan Azariah Rossi, or de' Rossi, for example, who possessed an extraordinarily broad classical, Hebrew, and Italian culture, and who quoted from the classics, modern Italian authors, the Scriptures, the Talmud, and mediaeval philosophy with the same ease and *sprezzatura* with which he cited the Fathers of the Church.[5]

Azariah de' Rossi lived a generation after Leone Ebreo, but his portrait matches, to a large extent, the one we could sketch of Leone Ebreo against the background of the first decades of the sixteenth century. Azariah had a very high opinion of Leone Ebreo, as has already been pointed out by Josef Klausner, who examined him especially from the point of view of the ill favour Leone received from official Hebraism.[6] This conflict between the rationalist tendencies of the tradition's official thought and the search for the mystical ardour present in the Cabala experienced moments of greater and lesser intensity and is a significant phenomenon in the general framework of intellectual ferment which pervaded the Renaissance. What parallels can be drawn — only for the period in question, of course, that is from the end of the fifteenth to the first decades of the sixteenth century — with the schisms and Reformation in the Church of Rome, as well as with the developments and problems in the Catholic Reformation, cannot and must not be ignored.

Leone Ebreo is to be seen against this intricate and, in many respects, still obscure background, even though little by little some light is being shed on it by recent research on contemporary persons and events. It is advisble to begin discussing Leone with reference to an indisputable fact: the publication of his *Dialoghi d'amore*, printed by

Blado and edited by Mariano Lenzi in 1535. However much one might hope to contribute to the knowledge of the relationship between Cabala and the Renaissance through these *Dialoghi* and through their author, it is precisely from this date and from these facts that the first disturbing doubt arises.

From the time he came to Italy in 1492, Leone Ebreo lived, for varying lengths of time, in several cities: Naples, Genoa, and Venice (where, as the present stage of research shows, he most probably wrote his *Dialoghi*), Barletta, and perhaps Monopoli di Puglia, where his father lived for some time — a most learned man, and an important businessman in charge of finances under King Alfonso V in Portugal and under King Ferdinand II in Naples. Leone may also have been in Florence, and in Rome as well. It is possibly in Rome that he met the future publisher of his *Dialoghi*, Mariano Lenzi, who was not a Roman but a Tuscan, and perhaps more precisely a Sienese, since he was a friend of Claudio Tolomei. Consequently it is necessary to turn our attention to Lenzi to investigate the reasons why he so eagerly undertook publication of the work, and to look beyond the obvious explanation provided by the cultural climate they shared. The *Dialoghi*, which included some of the most typical elements of Roman and especially Florentine culture, which had as its direct inspiration Giovanni Pico della Mirandola, Marsilio Ficino, and other Neoplatonist philosophers, met with immediate success: they went through other editions and were soon translated into Spanish, French, and Latin. One of the most complex problems concerns the language in which the work was originally written, an issue to be touched upon later in this paper.

In the meantime, however, one cannot help wondering whether there were other motivations for this initiative besides a possible acquaintance or friendship between the author and the publisher, and particularly what audience the publisher and printer were expecting to reach in Rome in the year 1535. It is precisely this type of question which cannot be answered today, given the data available on the relation between Hebrew culture and Roman, or even Renaissance Italian, culture. This is so in spite of the fact that the existence of personages like Egidio da Viterbo proves to be so illuminating. A starting point for this inquiry could be provided by the research being done, along the general lines established by Attilio Milano, on the Jewish communities of Rome and of Latium.[7] These communities were caught in the web of contradictory policies pursued by the popes who, at times, lukewarmly tolerated Jews or even favoured them, but at other times persecuted them harshly, especially with the advent of the Counter-Reformation.[8]

From this more general perspective one can examine with greater clarity the fundamental problems relating to the *Dialoghi d'amore*[9]: for instance, the connection between this work and Renaissance humanist culture, with its principal stress on the classics, a culture which the *Dialoghi* undoubtedly reflect; the *Dialoghi*'s relation to both official Hebrew cultural tradition and to the Cabala, which was of such importance to the learned humanists, and which, as a current of Hebrew mysticism, was also very complex, sharing as it did in both profound truth but also heresy. (At the beginning of the sixteenth century certain Western Christian doctrines, like Savonarolism and Neoplatonism, contained similar complexities.) Does Leone's composition establish new systems of relationship between Renaissance and Hebrew culture? If these systems exist, how do they affect, together or individually, the development of Renaissance and Western culture? And, finally, focussing on the text itself, is it an exemplar of the type of syncretism promoted by Pico, the prototypical Renaissance thinker who worked on a synthesis of Platonism, Hermeticism, and Cabala? (Let us not forget that Renaissance syncretism soon moved on, in an orthodox direction, to become a general reconciliation of Platonism and Aristotelianism, the latter including also Averroistic as well as Christian, namely Thomist, interpretations of Aristotle.)

But, continuing with the list of questions, problematic as they are to varying degrees, do the *Dialoghi* constitute the attempt made by a Jewish intellectual, suffering deep trauma for not having achieved integration into Western society, to find an acceptable mode of being, without renouncing the culture of his forefathers, by showing the common origin of the doctrines of both worlds, both societies, and both cultures? Or in contrast to the latter interpretation which, being the most readily arguable, has been most popular, is the treatise the consistent effort made by a believer and intellectual, exceptionally gifted in learning, education, and mind, to show that, beyond the existing divisions, everything stems from a single true and authentic dimension, that is Hebraism?

These are important questions which, in the course of research to be undertaken in the future, will probably be formulated differently. In the meantime, it may be helpful to retrace Leone Ebreo's biography against the background and in the *milieu* of the scholars who populated the cultural landscape of Italy during the years of his lifetime, even if the question of whether he met them or not must remain unanswered.[10]

Leone, together with his father and other family members arrived in Naples in 1492 as a direct result of the edict expelling the Jews from Spain. After leaving Lisbon, where he had studied medicine and where his father had held an important position at the court of King Alfonso

— a position he lost under the next king, John II, after having been accused of taking part in a conspiracy — Leone had lived for ten years in Seville and Toledo. Upon leaving Spain, Leone had sent one of his children, one year old at the time, back to Portugal. He recalls this event in his 'Elegia sopra il destino' (Elegy on Destiny), the first of five poems he composed in Hebrew, and the best of the group for its literary and poetic qualities as well as for the scope and depth of the information it conveys about the doctrine, faith, and customs of high-ranking Jews.[11] Some of his works, which were conceived as forewords or introductions for the books written by his father, who was a commentator and illustrator of sacred texts, conform to the literary and writing codes deriving in all probability directly from the poetic books of the Bible. His 'Elegia', on the other hand, is essentially an autobiographical account, which brings together a network of sparkling images, expressive analogies, and phrases which have a place and a meaning within the Hebrew tradition, along with a series of concrete, historical, and realistic elements which become, very subtly, symbols of the suffering and distress of his body and soul. This description should serve to prove, for now, how crucial this text is not only for the purpose of reconstructing Leone's erudition, but also for the more challenging task of showing the substance, breadth, and the strong personal stamp of his culture.

A sampling of the poet's language (e.g. the metaphor 'marrow of my soul' used to indicate his son) and of certain references to customs concerning names (Gershom Scholem stresses the significance of true names which reveal secrets when he speaks of his friend Walter Benjamin) is to be found in the verses cited below, which evoke a persecution of Portuguese Jews (probably that of 1495)˙which forced his son to convert to Christianity:

Egli forzò tutta la comunità di Giacobbe, e obbligò
a trasgredire la legge tutti i figli del mio nobile popolo.
E molti si uccisero da sé, per non calpestare
le leggi di Dio, mio soccorritore.
E fu preso il midollo dell'anima mia, fu mutato
il suo nome buono, che è come la roccia da cui venni sbozzato.[12]

The last verse, based on the fact that Leone's son had been named after his grandfather Isaac, transforms the familial transmission of names into a symbol of repetition which is part of the act of creation.

The social and economic prestige of the Abravanel family in Naples soon grew, thanks to Ferdinand II of Aragon who granted Isaac his protection and, since he was a financial expert, appointed him king's counsellor. This position must surely have helped Leone enter the learned circles of the kingdom's capital. However, this does not necessarily mean that Leone adopted the new Neoplatonic culture or that he accepted Pico's invitation to write a book *De Coeli Harmonia (On the Harmony of the Heavens)* — the book that the renowned Jewish doctor, Amato Lusitano, a commentator, among other things, of Dioscorides, said he had seen, in manuscript form, at the home of a nephew of Leone in Salonica in 1559. The work, most probably written in Latin, has not survived. Many of Leone's modern biographers maintain that it was during these years in Naples that he began to work on his *Dialoghi*; however, there is no substantial evidence to prove this conjecture. Furthermore, these same biographers unhesitatingly maintain that much progress was made on the *Dialoghi* during Leone's stay in Genoa, from 1495 to 1501, that is, from the time the French army of Charles VIII arrived in Naples until Leone was recalled to that city by King Frederick. It is not certain whether Leone stayed in Naples for the next three years (his father never went back and, after residing in Sicily and Corfù, moved to Puglia and, finally, Venice), but we do know that he went to Venice in 1504, was in Naples again in 1506 and, soon after, in Venice. Nothing is known of his whereabouts during various intervals, though in 1516 we find him in Ferrara where, much later, in 1536, his younger brother Samuele was to take up residence. Samuele too was very learned and followed his father's doctrine closely; he continued in his father's footsteps mainly as financier in the viceregal court in Naples and later at the Este court during the time of Ercole II.[13] Thus Ferrara, like Salonica, became a stable point in the fate of the family and also a privileged locale for possible contacts between Leone and other members of his family.

In 1520 he was in Pesaro for the purpose of publishing a work his father had written; towards the end of 1520 and then in 1521 he is mentioned in documents in Naples as holding the very prestigious post of court physician. His fame was indeed so great that high personages from other areas, like Cardinal Grimani of Venice, spoke of his authority and reputation as a doctor. Later we lose track of him; there are those who favour the theory of a fairly long stay in Rome, basing themselves especially on the testimony of his Spanish translator Carlos Montesa, who states that he was invited repeatedly to assume the office of papal physician.[14] Some, including Melczer, are convinced that Leone stayed in Rome until his death; the exact number of years is unknown, although there is a fifteen-year gap separating the date of the Neapolitan papers referred to above and the next major event in Leone's life, the Rome edition of the *Dialoghi*.

The thesis of a long Roman sojourn could be proven if one could validate Dionisotti's tentative attribution of an epigram to Leone.[15] The epigram, written in Hebrew and signed by one Leone Giudeo, appears at the end of a work published in Rome in 1522 in honour of the *condottiero* Marc' Antonio Colonna who died the same year outside the walls of Milan. The publication in question also contains a Greek epigram by Lelio Massimo, a humanist who was not altogether unknown in Rome during the reign of Leo X, and Latin poems by many renowned authors, among whom Girolamo Vida, Lazzaro Bonamico, and Pierio Valeriano. Dionisotti concludes, therefore, that if our author is the same person as Leone Giudeo, not only his presence in Rome, but also his association with the highest ranking circles of Rome in that period, would be verified. Even if this were not the case, Dionisotti cleverly adds, the fact that a Jewish Leone, whether or not he is our author, is included, with his Hebrew composition, in such erudite company, testifies to the existence of a situation which was extremely favourable to Jewish thought and possibly fruitful in ways still to be discovered. Of course, none of those mentioned above, Dionisotti points out, would have written such an ambitious book, or in any case, a work of such intellectual scope as the *Dialoghi*, in the vernacular, especially if one considers its linguistic and stylistic features. It appears, however, that this is of little importance, since one can legitimately deduce from Dionisotti's study the conviction that the *Dialoghi* were not originally written in the vernacular, but either in Latin, which is most likely, or in Hebrew, that is if Hebrew scholars ever authorize us to believe that such a work could have been written in Hebrew by a Jew who was not only cultured, or should we say erudite, but also, and above all, faithful to the tradition of his forefathers and possibly an orthodox believer as well. This issue has, in principle, a rather simple and even obvious solution: that is, Leone wrote not for the followers of his own faith, but for the Christian intellectual world. It was precisely this world which he wanted to win over to the view that the ancient Biblical matrix was present in all ancient knowledge, that it had influenced and, in certain respects, determined it, and that it represented wisdom itself, that is, ancient, unique, true wisdom. Therefore, he had no need to write in Hebrew, but rather in Latin or, better yet, in the vernacular.

It will be useful to add another item to the collection of documents and evidence we have rapidly surveyed. Starting from a reference given by Kristeller,[16] I tracked down in the Estense Library in Ferrara a collection of copies of letters by a sixteenth-century doctor, Jacopo Tiburzio da Pergola, or more commonly Giacomo Tiburzi, who had studied at Ferrara and who already in July of 1521 had applied for the Chair of Theoretical Medicine at Perugia. Among these letters, there is one addressed to a Leone Ebreo, requesting, among many declarations of esteem, explanations regarding medical books. From this we can deduce that the addressee could not have been a man of little worth. Even given that in this period, in this type of medical chronicle, there is no shortage of Leone Ebreos, there could not have been many deemed worthy of such respect and even veneration. This is precisely the manner in which one addresses a personage like ours, particularly if he was in Rome, in the position of authority which we have outlined above as probable or at least possible. This letter, which indicates the addressee ('Jacobus pergulensis Leoni Hebrejo salutem') but not the place to which it was sent, is clearly dated 'pridie calendas Januarij 1534', that is December 31, 1533. Therefore, if this 'Leone Hebrejo' was our Leone, we have a date of singular importance, uniquely late with respect to the documents to which it has been possible to refer so far; a date falling between 1521 when we left Leone in Naples at the height of his activity and 1535 when the publisher of his *Dialoghi* mourns his death. Certainly it is not advisable to jump to conclusions, at the risk of committing the familiar errors which have been curiously frequent in the study of Leone. Let us recall only the somewhat sensational case of Edmondo Solmi who, in 1903, studied Leone Ebreo as a possible source for the philosophy of Spinoza and, in 1909, believed he had identified in a Leo Judae, who died in Zurich on June 19, 1542, our Leone Ebreo.[17] Based on this, he formulated his theory that Leone must have invented his editor friend, Mariano Lenzi, and passed himself off as dead in order to protect himself from eventual difficulties arising from the publication of his *Dialoghi*. The theory stood on shaky foundations and collapsed pathetically when the Leo from Zurich was identified more accurately as a Swiss Protestant Reformer.

At present, new facts about the life of Leone Ebreo are not forseeable, unless one is willing to accept the information aired here. Certainly not all of the data which his modern biographers have accumulated over time are equally convincing and substantiated, from Pflaum to Gebhardt (who distinguished himself in Leone scholarship as the German editor of his complete works and also the Hebrew editor of his poetry) to Santino Caramella, who, in the 1929 edition in Laterza's *Scrittori d'Italia*, added an important essay in which he methodically reviews all the information available at the time. However, in certain interpretations and evaluations, Caramella exaggerates a little, as Klausner has observed,[18] regarding, for example, the concept of beauty expressed by Filone's interlocutor Sofia, which Caramella sees as entirely spiritual, singularly celestial and divine, and in no way terrestrial, when in fact, many passages in the text point to the opposite.

It is a reminder to use caution and to adhere to the text which should be heeded for its programmatic value, because in effect the *Dialoghi* often seem to offer an opportunity for conclusions which later reveal themselves to be exactly contrary to the ones supposed or are even internally confuted by other elements which could serve equally well as conclusions. The value of Klausner's study lies precisely in his attempt to see what in Leone is original and new, and what is old, that is mediaeval, derived variously from sources of his cultural traditions starting from Avicebron's *Fons Vitae*, an amalgam of complex and contrasting elements, diverse and even remote. It offers suggestions for identifying certain of Leone's Platonizing tendencies, but also for seeing certain gross superstitions, which are surprising in a mature intellectual and especially so in a physician. Whatever one thinks of that, it is clear, however, that the new and the old in Leone are not to be identified according to an abstract and even changing idea of the Renaissance and of its role in the history of civilization. It is not enough to believe that his newness lies in his Platonizing elements, which could, especially through a particular group of sources, be tremendously old, nor in the rationalist method according to which myths, legends, and beliefs were interpreted. This rationalism was no less burdened by the convolutions, slackness, and prejudices with which we are all too familiar in sixteenth-century culture. In any case, what must be done now is to proceed to a detailed commentary which identifies suggestions and sources and considers how they have been developed and interpreted. Using this approach we will focus on some elements of Leone's doctrine which appear, in the present state of research, to be the central issues of his thought. The intent is only to indicate perspectives and to avoid conclusions which might soon prove arbitrary.

The *Dialoghi* is an intricate text; its three parts are uneven not only in length (the second is twice as long as the first, the third four times), but enormously so in the way they introduce new themes and topics, causing a constant expansion of their horizon. It is a feature of the work which might appear casual and even lead the reader initially to hypothesize that the work grew haphazardly, from an aggregation of parts born of open reflection in progress. However one can also argue the opposite, that he is using a model deriving from Hebrew literature such as the *Talmud* or that he invents a more radical structure which repeats, by means of language, the Neoplatonic image of the universe.

The first dialogue, which concentrates on the definition of love and its operations, has the consistency of a *summa* of ideas and current notions, such as the distinction between the external and internal senses, between usefulness and pleasure. The focal point is the crucial relationship between love and virtue, which manifests itself as a concrete manner of living, with particular emphasis on health, concern for one's children, conjugal love, and thus on self-realization and on the pursuit of honour and fame. A higher goal is grasping the concept that one loves God more the more one knows Him. However, the immensity of the divine constitutes an insurmountable limitation on human understanding. The problem of the relationship between God, love, and knowledge is abandoned at this point in order to be resumed in later dialogues as a discussion of the notion of God as beloved and lover and of the idea which results from it, of first love as the intrinsic love of God for Himself. It is likely that the very conception of the origin of the Universe, a conception stemming from the simultaneous presence in God-love of knowledge, being, and creation is connected to this premise. This is obviously a Neoplatonic scheme in which the universe is conceived as a manifestation of the One, the efficient and final cause to which all the created world tends to return. Thus, in this first book — a kind of invitation to meditation and deeper consideration of a subject matter with unpredictable developments — there is not much that is new or personal, nor even any rare sources and references, were it not that the conclusion, in which the concept of love is given a Platonic accent, transforms itself into a *furor*, free of ordinary reason and governed instead by an extraordinary and heroic reason of its own. Another feature to note is a vague aesthetic perspective underlying the discussion, as though Leone were bringing into discussion elements drawn from known treatises of poetics, perhaps even principally from the *Ars Poetica* of Horace. To be absolutely sure, however, it would be necessary to undertake a careful analysis of single words and phrases deriving from the classical contexts.

The second dialogue is an explanation of the concept of love as passion and furor; that is, in its human, sublunar dimension. However, the explanation requires large expansions of the argument, beginning with the relationship between the sublunar and celestial worlds, between man and heavenly bodies and entering, therefore, into astrology. The complexity of these problems in the early phases of the Renaissance is well known. Suffice it to recall the opposing positions taken by Pico and Ficino with respect to astrology in order to be fully aware of this complexity in the pages of Leone Ebreo, who appears, on this subject, to be much closer to Ficino than to Pico. Leone seems not to have been influenced in the slightest by Pico's invocation of man's freedom from the influence of the stars nor by the idea that the error of philosophers, and of man in general, was the belief that human destiny descended from Heaven, while man, in fact, carries it within himself from his very origins. Leone's lack of sympathy for these ideas of Pico was, in any case, inevitable, once he had established the identity of first and final cause in Book I. Therefore, an even greater affinity with Ficino results than the discourse on friendship in the first dialogue would indicate. It is not certain, however, if one can see in this the motivation Cassirer puts forward in *Dall'Umanesimo all'Illuminismo* that Ficino's attitude toward astrology was conditioned by a mediaeval fear of the stars, a fear which he retained in spite of all explicit criticism of mediaeval culture, and therefore that, in Leone too, there persists a condition of acritical subordination to the past.[19] Even though Leone draws abundantly on material from the vast classical and Hebrew Biblical traditions, there is no explicit proof that he maintains a conscious distance from them. Indeed, if anything, the opposite holds true. There is in him an all-encompassing notion of knowledge as a truth which can undergo deviations but which can also be restored to its wholeness, not with philological proof but only through a return to its principles.

This rather difficult problem invites a return to the more circumscribed one, but with regard to the thesis that Leone is closer to Ficino than to Pico, it must be said that their closeness is placed in doubt by the affinities — established albeit without truly definite evidence by scholarly tradition — between Leone and Pico's Hebrew teachers, especially Johanan ben Isaac Alemanno, whom Leone may have known personally. It is certain that Leone, rather than rejecting the problem of astrology, was greatly interested in it and based his thinking on the concept of the repetitive relationship between macrocosm and microcosm, of the universe as living organism, and on that of the human microcosm as simulacrum of the three levels of the universe, earthly, celestial, and divine. Leone adds immediately to the notion of the universe, or macrocosm, as the harmonious relationship of celestial bodies, by embracing the Pythagorean doctrine of the harmony of the spheres. The lost *De Coeli Harmonia* points to Leone's special interest in this topic, one which occupies a prominent place in the *Dialoghi*, as a necessary preamble to the questions of the correspondence between celestial and angelic spheres. It is curious that this special consideration of the ancient Pythagorean doctrine does not receive mention in Leo Spitzer's extensive study on the 'harmony of the world' in which he proposes to single out whole series of the expressions which, even with changes in their sound and meaning, transmit an ancient idea.[20] It is all the more surprising since the analysis of the relationship between macrocosm and microcosm is filtered in Leone through a vast cultural terrain in which the extraordinary and spectacular breadth of his culture is recorded in the form of a theosophic reinterpretation of Greek mythology. In fifty extremely dense pages classical Western culture meets the Hebrew tradition for the first time in the book and the rationalist interpretations given to pagan myths by humanists from Boccaccio on are displaced to varying degrees.

Other clarifications and even new interpretations are introduced in the third dialogue, in which Leone tackles the problem of cosmogony. Here Leone begins by refuting the Aristotelian theory of a world produced *ab aeterno*. He then passes on to an evaluation of the Platonic doctrine of primeval and formless chaos produced by God, and arrives at last at the acceptance and praise of Biblical thought on this subject, with words which should be considered in full for their methodological implications:

We [who believe the sacred law of Moses] allow that in the course of nature nothing can be made from nothing; yet we hold this possible miraculously, through divine omnipotence; not that the material consists of nothing, as statues are made out of wood, but that God can create things anew without the previous existence of any material whatsoever. And we believe that although the heavens and first matter are naturally neither generable nor corruptible, they were originally created out of nothing with the whole of creation, by miraculous and divine agency. For although it is naturally repugnant to the successive generation of opposites, circular motion and time, to have a beginning, none the less they originated at the time of the wondrous creation, depending as they do upon first matter and the heavens which were newly created. With regard to the nature of the Creator, we believe that eternal God acts not of necessity, but of free will and omnipotence; and as He was free to establish the universe as He pleased, the number of orbs and stars, the size of the heavenly spheres, the elements, and the number, measure and quality of all creation — so He was free in His desire to give a beginning in time to creation, even though He could have made it eternal like Himself. With regard to the end of His work, we believe that although His purpose in the Creation was to do good, and according to our reasoning eternal good is better than temporal, yet since we cannot attain to an understanding of His peculiar wisdom, so we cannot attain to a knowledge of its true purpose in His works. And perhaps in His sight the temporal good in the world's creation precedes the eternal: for the omnipotence of God and His free will is sooner recognised in having created all things from nothing than from eternity; for this latter form of creation would seem to be a necessary dependence, like the continual dependence of light upon the sun, and would not prove the formation of the world to proceed from free grace and wondrous kindness, as David says, 'I said that the world is fashioned through the grace and mercy of God'.[21]

The explanations given by Filone to Sofia are based on Biblical passages, with particular preference here for the poetic books and for the Psalms especially, in such a way as to function as commentaries on them, following the models provided by the *Talmud* and *Midrash*. On the one hand, then, it is clear that Leone is not concerned about any disagreements, or outright contradictions, which Filone might eventually fall into. Rather, he exalts in them, and when Sofia marvels that the world can be both temporal and eternal, Filone answers that this is in itself a sign of the greater power of God which the peripatetic philosopher in vain believed he had penetrated. It is, therefore, an act of faith, but one presented in such a manner as to give the impression that it could have affected and influenced, a little later, the thought of natural philosophers from Telesio to Bacon.

There is a section of the work which seems to contain what really concerns Leone most: the commentary on a passage from Genesis dealing with the sixth day of creation, that is the creation of man. Filone underlines the contradictions in the text (which he immediately declares are only apparent) according to which God first creates man, who contains unified within him both male and female, and then separates them into Adam and Eve. It is a passage, he continues, of which 'the ancient Hebrew commentators in their Chaldean commentary' have explained the true meaning without causing the doubts and impression of futility left by 'ordinary commentar[ies].'[22] His adherence to a simpler, more ancient esoteric interpretation, which rationalizers of the Biblical text had dangerously lost sight of, emerges quite clearly. In essence, this esoteric tradition could belong to the Cabalistic doctrine or, at any rate, possess some points in common with it.

The explanation is preceded by another passage of great interest in which Leone recounts the Platonic fable of the Androgyne as it appears in the *Symposium*. The reason for retelling the fable is that the 'story is full of charm and beauty' and 'was handed down by earlier writers than the Greeks — in the sacred writings of Moses, concerning the creation of the first human parents, Adam and Eve.'[23] However, the story does not explain the Mosaic text, as has been hurriedly deduced by most Leone scholars. Rather the story obscures, veils, and confuses the text, as happens every time one attempts to pass on to too many a secret, concealed wisdom accessible to a few elect. Such is the wisdom of the Cabala, confided by God to Moses at the same time that He gave the commandments for all men, but with the order that it be passed on only orally and to a chosen few. This behaviour is not unusual in the history of the transmission of Hebrew culture; Michelini Tocci points out that the *midrashim* was passed on orally and was finally written down much later because, since it consisted of commentaries of the Bible, it was feared that, if they were to be written down, they might contaminate the sacred text.[24]

This great interest in the first books of the Bible leads Leone back to a tradition of Roman Hebrew culture. Suffice it to recall Immanuel

Romano who was and remained famous, notwithstanding a certain negative opinion expressed by his contemporaries and by later scholars. Michelini Tocci exemplifies this criticism by referring to the charge of frivolity and fatuousness laid against him by Moses of Rieti for the *Mahbarot* compositions, the last of which is an imitation of Dante.[25] Romano was also the author, however, of a commentary on the *Pentateuch, Ma'aseh Bere'šit,* from which the same Michelini Tocci published the commentary on Chapter I of Genesis in 1963,[26] bringing to light the way in which themes like those just reviewed and other related ones are approached: the necessity of and the reason for creation, whether creation took place *ab aeterno* or in time, the simultaneity of creation, the intervention of intermediaries, angels or sephiroth — the most difficult and unresolved problem in the whole of Cabalistic history. Perhaps we are dealing with problems that are ever present in the tradition of Hebrew thought and reflection, and therefore there is no reason to assume a link between Immanuel Romano and Leone Ebreo. What remains certain, in any case, is that Leone allied himself solidly to a unified tradition, which was broad and extremely rich.

After outlining various proposals, theses, and doubts, we come, if not to real conclusions, at least to two different considerations.[27] On the one hand, I should like to emphasize, however cautiously, the curious epilogue, certainly of symbolic value, of the *Dialoghi* which, after having dealt with the concept of love as the key to a harmonious universe, record Filone's permanent condition. For Filone, in fact, love does not coincide with delight, but with grief and torment, because Sofia continues to deny herself to him; that is, knowledge will never be totally mastered by the wise man, nor will it remain for long in his possession, even though in the act of searching for it, he is superior to knowledge itself. On the other hand, I should like to stress the unitary concept of knowledge which governs Leone's philosophical thought as it had governed that of another great thinker of the past, Philo of Alexandria. Beyond obvious differences of time and substance, and without Leone knowing the works of Philo directly (as many modern biographers tend to maintain), both, in fact, are convinced that only by going back to the origins can one clear the air of the useless glitter, fables, and lies accumulated by man in the course of the centuries, and live again in truth.

To summarize, we can say that Leone Ebreo put forward the hypothesis of a unique syncretism, fairly advanced with respect to the more simplistic mediaeval versions, and similar, not identical, to the continuously developing syncretisms of humanism. It was, for him, a matter of demonstrating how the classical tradition was deeply rooted in, and even indebted to, the Hebrew tradition seen as a complex whole that included both the official orthodox line and the mystical Cabalistic current. His life and other significant evidence, such as the 'Elegy', prove Leone's persistent loyalty to the creed of his forefathers, to their religion and culture, to the social and historical quality of that culture within the Christian world which, in its revival of the classics, was doing nothing more than retrieving its true, Biblical roots. Within these parameters, it does not seem plausible to repeat for Leone the accusation often made against Philo of Alexandria, that is of a Hellenization of Hebraism, in other words of having made Hebraism part of a universal anthropology. This may be so, but only in the sense that Hebraism, even in its variations, includes all that is necessary to man, who, though he tried to obscure it, did not preclude a new revelation of the truth. Leone Ebreo transmits and expresses an important aspect of the question of Hebrew culture by proclaiming the superiority (that is the continuity and influence) of the Hebrew tradition over the classical, mediaeval, and modern ones. Leone Ebreo, therefore, cannot be understood entirely within the bounds of the recent humanist Hermetic-Neoplatonic tradition, nor within the Platonistic experiences of the circles which he frequented in Italy and with which he probably shared only the common project of undertaking the search for deeper roots, for cultural terrains that may have been lost in the mists of time but were, nonetheless, retrievable.

University of Rome II

(Translated by Kiloran McRae and A. Manuela Scarci)

NOTES

1 Frances A. Yates, *The Occult Philosophy in the Elizabethan Age* (London: Routledge and Kegan Paul, and Boston: Henley, 1979), p. 189.
2 Yates, p. 3.
3 William Melczer, 'Giorgione ed i (possibili) contributi ebrei alla tradizione ermetica,' in *Giorgione e la cultura veneta tra '400 et '500: mito, allegoria, analisi iconologica* (Rome: De Luca, 1981), pp. 213-18.
4 Melczer, p. 215.
5 Melczer, p. 216.
6 Josef Klausner, 'Don Jehudah Abravanel e la sua filosofia dell'amore,' *La rassegna mensile di Israel*, 7 (1932), 39.
7 Attilio Milano, *Storia degli Ebrei in Italia* (Turin: Einaudi, 1963) and *Il ghetto di Roma* (Rome: n.p., 1963).
8 See Ariel Toaff, 'Lotte e fazioni tra gli Ebrei di Roma nel Cinquecento,' *Studi romani*, 27 (1979), 25-32; Nello Pavoncello, 'Gli Ebrei di origine spagnola a Roma,' *Studi romani*, 28 (1980), 214-20 and 'Le comunità ebraiche laziali prima

del bando di Pio V', in *Lunario Romano 1980: Rinascimento nel Lazio* (Rome: Palombi, 1980).

9 The edition consulted for the *Dialoghi* and for the Hebrew works is: Leone Ebreo (Giuda Abarbanel), *Dialoghi d'amore*, ed. Santino Caramella (Bari: Laterza, 1929). The quotations in English are taken from Leone Ebreo, *The Philosophy of Love (Dialoghi d'amore)*, trans. F. Friedeberg-Seeley and Jean H. Barnes, with introd. by Cecil Roth (London: The Soncino Press, 1937).

10 On the life of Leone Ebreo see especially S.H. Margulies, 'La famiglia Abravanel in Italia,' *Rivista israelitica*, 3 (1906), 97-107, 147-54; and also H. Pflaum, *Die Idee der Liebe — Leone Ebreo* (Tübingen: Mohr, 1926).

11 'Elegia', in *Dialoghi*, ed. Caramella, pp. 403, 404, 406.

12 *Dialoghi*, p. 397. The verses read as follows in English prose: He [that is the new king, who is called a foolish and vain man in the preceding verses] violated the whole community of Jacob, and forced all the children of my noble people to disobey the law. And many took their own lives, so as not to trample the laws of God, my helper. And the marrow of my soul was taken away, and his good name, which is like the rock from which I was hewn, was changed.

13 See note 10.

14 *Dialoghi*, p. 423n.

15 Carlo Dionisotti, 'Appunti su Leone Ebreo,' *Italia medievale e umanistica*, 2 (1959), 425-28.

16 Paul O. Kristeller, *Iter italicum* (London: Warburg Insitute, 1965) Vol. I, p. 60, refers to Ferrara, Biblioteca Comunale Ariostea, MS. II 357, fasc. 9, containing sixteenth century 'Epistolae di Jac.Tiburtius'. I wish to thank dottoressa Raffaella Trabalza for the data she collected for me. On Tiburzi, see E. Guarino, *Gente spadaccina: la maccheronea inedita del prefolenghiano perugino Vincenzo Baglioni detto Quadrone* (Assisi: F.A.R.R.I.O., n.d.).

17 Edmondo Solmi, *Benedetto Spinoza e Leone Ebreo: studio su una fonte italiana dimenticata dello spinozismo* (Modena: Vincenzi, 1903), and 'La data della morte di Leone Ebreo,' *Giornale storico della letteratura italiana*, 53 (1909), 446-47.

18 Klausner, pp. 500-01, note 4.

19 Ernst Cassirer, *Dall'Umanesimo all'Illuminismo* (Florence: La Nuova Italia, 1967), p. 114.

20 Leo Spitzer, *Classical and Christian Ideas of World Harmony* (Baltimore: The Johns Hopkins Press, 1963).

21 *Dialoghi*, trans, Friedeberg-Seeley and Barnes, pp. 281-82 (cf. Caramella, pp. 239-40).

22 *Dialoghi*, pp. 348-49 (cf. Caramella, p. 294).

23 *Dialoghi*, p. 345 (cf. Caramella, p. 291).

24 Franco Michelini Tocci, *La letteratura ebraica* (Florence: Sansoni and Milan: Accademia, 1970), p. 128.

25 Tocci, pp. 167-68.

26 Franco Michelini Tocci, *Il commento di Emanuele Romano al capitolo I della Genesi*, Studi semitici 10 (Rome: Centro di Studi Semitici, Università di Roma, 1963).

27 Suggestions for future work on Leone Ebreo have been made recently by Marco Ariani in his book entitled *Imago fabulosa: mito e allegoria nei Dialoghi d'amore di Leone Ebreo* (Rome: Bulzoni, 1984), which contains a vast amount of bibliographical information and interesting observations on the themes of myth and allegory. The scholarly fervour being shown Leone is evident in the thesis by Georg Gelb, defended in 1983 at the University of Innsbruck under the supervision of Prof. Krömer, and about to be published. A background study on the question of Hebrew culture is contained in Fausto Parente, 'Il confronto ideologico tra

l'Ebraismo e la Chiesa in Italia,' in *Italia judaica: atti del I Convegno internazionale* (Rome: Multigrafica Editrice, 1983), pp. 303-81. Finally I should like to point out that the *Dialoghi* have been included among the texts to undergo an exhaustive linguistic analysis, as part of a vast research project, which has been in progress for some time with the aid of the National Research Council of Italy and of the Ministry of Public Education, and which includes the preparation of a dictionary of the arts in the Renaissance.

Charles Trinkaus

Marsilio Ficino and the Ideal of Human Autonomy*

A generation and a half ago no topic aroused a more intense interest among students of early European culture than the thesis of Max Weber deriving what he called *Der Geist der Kapitalismus* from the Protestant ethic. The inculcation of a routinized, goalless mode of behaviour by the Lutheran and Calvinistic injunctions to please God in one's calling and to prove one's election by a strict adherence to the rules of morality gave to the modern world a docile population of spiritless robots.[1] Weber, elaborating on the earlier Marxian notion of alienated labour, repudiated the more ample vision of Jacob Burckhardt. Burckhardt, let us recall, hailed the birth of the self-conscious individualism in the Renaissance as the quality rendering Italians the 'first-born among the sons of modern Europe.'[2] Burckhardt's conception of Renaissance individualism stressed the element of self-conscious search for the understanding of man and the universe and the uninhibited pursuit of the secular goals of power, fame, and wealth. The ideal of human autonomy is a post-Burckhardtian conception, fueled by Nietzsche's amplifications of Burckhardt, and developed, especially in the 1930s and 1940s, as a counter to the gloomy forebodings of Marx, Weber, and others.[3] It is the vision of man commanding his environment with the resources of science, creating his own rules of personal behaviour, free from the restrictions imposed by theologians, and governing his relationships with his fellows in an open, psychically informed, and mutually tolerant discourse.

Certain ingredients of this ideal did indeed exist during the Renaissance. But the ideal was formulated ordinarily with a deep awareness of the limitations that God, the physical universe, and the human polity placed upon it. The theme of the dignity and excellence of man, derived though it was from a patristic and mediaeval Christian tradition, was the principal medium through which the status and powers of man in relation to divinity, cosmos, and polity were treated in a focused way. This occurred in works of this genre by Petrarch, Fazio, Manetti, Brandolini and other humanists, and was usurped by Pico as a fitting introduction and invitation to debate his *Conclusiones*.[4] Other

humanists, in a less formally thematic way, carried the assertion of human self-direction farther and more effectively — certainly Coluccio
Salutati, Lorenzo Valla, Benedetto Morandi,[5] and in political thinking
Leonardo Bruni[6] among them. It will be my claim in this paper that
the philosopher and physician, Marsilio Ficino, developed the fullest
and most far-reaching exposition of the ideal of human autonomy in
the Renaissance, and that this was certainly one of the most important
contributions of his philosophy to the future of human culture, along-
side his great work of textual recovery and dissemination of Platonism
and Neoplatonism.[7]

Ficino attempted in his *Theologia Platonica* to demonstrate the divinity and immortality of man. What better way to do this than by showing how man, created in God's image and likeness, attained remarkable
powers over himself and his natural environment, and in shaping his
relations with his fellow men, provided he did not turn against and re-
pudiate the very divinity within his soul? What better way of demonstrating man's dignity and autonomy than by proving his divinity and
his immortality?

Just as Lorenzo Valla asserted that man was superior to the animals
by his possession of immortality, so Ficino develops this theme of
man's godlikeness in a variety of ways. Since God created the world by
the very act of knowing the world, He does not despise man, one of
whose chief characteristics is intelligence.

Indeed if God does not in any way neglect the least parts of the world, certainly He will not despise mankind, which is such a precious part of the
world that it is the mean between temporal and eternal things, since it receives the eternal and commands the temporal. So close to God is this His
work that, sliding itself into the secrets of the divine mind, it actually
knows the order of the world. Understanding of the world order is more
excellent even than that order, since this kind of order is created and ruled
through intelligence.[8]

Critical for Ficino's conception of human autonomy is man's use of
intelligence for shaping the world of nature. God, whose trinitarian
nature of infinite power, absolute intelligence, and most blessed will is
stressed, is the most perfect author who,

does all things in that kind of action which is most perfect. Thus He is not
led to action by a necessity of nature but rather by a certain purpose of the
will. For what is done by freedom of the will is more excellent than what is
dragged into action by a necessary instinct of nature. That action is

happiest in which the author is in command of his own actions, so that he prescribes the manner, measure, and end of acting.[9]

Such freedom and control of action is certainly the quality of autonomy, here applied to God, but intended to describe man as well, since this statement is followed in his *Disputatio contra Iudicium Astrologorum* by a demonstration that God intended man so to act. 'If God is pleased with Himself, if He loves Himself, certainly He cherishes His own images [men] and His works. The smith loves his own works which he makes from external material.'[10]

In order for man to act freely and to operate on nature, it becomes necessary for Ficino to show two things: that man's freedom is not restricted by divine foreknowledge, and that man's actions are not determinate as are the movements of nature, upon which men act; nor are they determined by nature. Man is distinguished from the divine, but he is not coerced by God in his actions; man is different from and above nature, which cannot act upon or determine man. It is therefore necessary for Ficino to define man as a rational soul, distinct from the body, which is also a part of nature which man can employ as an instrument and which he need not allow to influence or move his soul, though it can if he permits it.

The rational soul is a mean between the eternal and the temporal, the divine and the natural. It cannot be acted upon or compelled by natural things, else it could not rise above them in knowledge or emotion and direct itself toward the divine. Although there is no motion in divine things, there is some in the soul, namely changes in time and variation of the affects. The soul possesses primacy of movement which is supreme and efficacious in causing the movements of the body. Therefore, moving by its own nature and power, it is free and most comprehensive. The soul, thus, can transfer itself into anything, descend into corporeal forms and matter, ascend to the angels and God. It can be moved and not be moved into anything created by God. It can be moved into one thing or equally into another.

It is not compelled by the divine, from whose providence it is free from the start, nor is it coerced by anything natural over which it widely rules, nor is it dependent upon them, for indeed they are moved and judged by it; . . . since it is not acted upon by any natural object, therefore it is not determined by it, thus it moves along freely.[11]

God's foreknowledge does not circumscribe the freedom of man's will because 'just as He foresees *that* you will do this, so He foresees

how you will do it, that is willingly and freely.'[12] Ficino then explains
that the will operates when the intellect presents two opposing alternatives of equal seeming goodness. The will cannot choose neither, or
both, because it would become a mean or a contradiction. Choosing
one, it does so freely. 'Hence when both are equally attractive, if the
will leans toward one, it proceeds spontaneously and is not forced.'
Then he repeats, concerning an act of the human will, exactly what he
had said earlier concerning God's voluntary action: 'Hence a voluntary
action is nobler than acting by necessity of nature because it adds intelligence above nature, is master of its own act, places a measure to the
act, prescribes the end, makes a different act in a different manner.' A
natural action is coerced because the matter is prepared and cannot
happen otherwise. 'For fire unimpeded cannot not burn dry close-by
material, a stone unimpeded cannot not descend to a lower level.' The
property of a voluntary action is to act contingently and freely. 'Therefore when there is a voluntary principle in man, there will also be a
principle of liberty.' There must be the contingency of choosing between two alternatives, otherwise it would not be a mean between the
necessary and the impossible, thought by Ptolemy and others to be the
condition requiring conjecture rather than knowledge. For Ficino it is
also the condition for *consilium*, meaning intention, or deliberate decision. 'If everything happened by necessity, it would be in vain that we
deliberate. We should remember that the proper function of any species cannot be entirely in vain.' No one would say that bees collect
honey, spiders weave webs, ants assemble grain in vain. 'Therefore no
one would dare to confess that the proper office of man, which is to
deliberate and decide, is in vain. I would say, moreover, that this is the
property of man in so far as he is man.' All men, always and everywhere engage in deliberation and choice; those who are above men do
not need deliberation; those who are below are unable to choose.[13]

Ficino continues to analyze the relationship of human, voluntary,
purposive action to the condition of nature in his *Theologia Platonica*
IX,4, a chapter which he inserts in the *Disputatio* at this point. First the
quality of human autonomy is developed on the relationship of the intellect to the will. The intellect deals in conceptions of universal reason
which hold to a common good. The will must apply the universal reason to particular circumstances and locate a choice between particular
goods in order to will one or the other of them. In this range of
choices of particular and contingent courses of action lies man's freedom. Other animate creatures do not have this choice. They make or
eat one thing always. The character of nature is to obey certain innate
laws and to be always the same. Men can err, but nature cannot. Ani-

mal actions are coercive, corporeal, unrepenting or unemending, always the same.

Since the nature of any thing is affixed to one certain form and one certain force is born with it from the beginning, it functions (*opus fit*) in one similar never changing way.[14]. . . But we have a certain common exemplar of the good in our mind, and comparing single things to this, we either reject or more or less approve, not drawn by the things themselves or the body, but dragging the things rather to the exemplar and the body to the mind. . . . For by deliberation and decision (*consultatione*) it happens that we do not subject the soul to things but things to our souls.[15]

Certainly the direct opposite of the Marxian diagnosis of *Verdinglichung* or reification!

It was important for Ficino in this assertion of psychic dominance and human autonomy to protect them from the powers of nature, especially the supposedly fatal ones of the heavens. The entire second half of the *Disputatio* (referred to by Ficino as *On Divine Providence, Free Will, and the Judgment of Astrologers*)[16] is devoted to a refutation of astrology, as are the final sections of this chapter (IX,4). But it should be evident that he clearly accepts the influence of the heavens on human bodies affecting the balance of the humours through irradiations of the four qualities. (In Book XIII of the *Theologia* he also refers to the theory of the spirit, this in 1474, fifteen years earlier than *De Vita Coelitus Comparanda*.[17] The *Disputatio* is dated 1477.)[18] Here in *Theologia Platonica* IX,4 he says:

Since we direct all pursuits of life toward our soul by the beautification of morals, who does not know that the end of our duties is the soul and therefore the soul is their beginning? The humours are not the principles of these actions, since the humours do not invite to something contrary to the body and above bodies; nor are the heavens which move through the humours. Certainly the far-removed body of the heavens does not move our four humours before it moves the four elements, nor does it move the soul unless it is agitated by the humours. Indeed the soul is opposed to the agitation of the humours when it condemns their impetus by the effort of speculation, inhibits them by zeal for morals, conquers them by the activity of the arts.[19]
. . . If we resist the humours, we also oppose the elements and the heavens; . . . Indeed the soul of man is not subject to the heavens.[20]

Neither are man's intellect and will subject to the heavens.

The form of the heavens is corporeal, singular, local, and temporal. The form by which the mind intellects is incorporeal, universal, and absolute. Therefore this is not born from the heavens. . . . Moreover, since the intellect does not receive its own action or the principle of its action from heaven, it is not subject to a heavenly body, especially because our mind according to that power by which it is joined to the things which are said to be above the heavens is not only not subject to the heavens but also is above them.[21]

As far as the will is concerned, since the things of nature are led to an end by determined means, and always get there in the same way, they are predetermined for some one end. 'The elections of man, however, reach an end by diverse ways both in morals and in the arts.'[22] We shall shortly examine Ficino's eulogy of man's dignity through the arts and human customs.

A last word on the rational soul and nature would here refer to his later efforts to control man's humours through a spiritual magic bringing into the phantasy the favorable spirits from the proper planets to counter disagreeable humoural conditions. I believe, as he says in De Vita Coelitus Comparanda, that he regarded this as a form of medical art consistent with what he had written by 1474.[23] However, I would concede that the emphasis is different, and that is important. It should also be pointed out that through torpour or weakness of the rational soul, a man could be enslaved to his humours, or on the other hand could sink into the kind of mental detachment from the sensual world which would permit the influx of celestial clues rendering him capable of prophecy. Ficino discusses these matters especially in chapters 1 and 2 of Book XIII.[24]

Book XIII of the Theologia Platonica is devoted to showing how the human soul dominates matter and the body. Ficino announces in its chapter 2: 'The soul, therefore, is through the mind above fate and in the order of providence alone, as though imitating the supernal and governing along with these. For, as though a participant of providence on the model of divine governance the soul rules itself, the home, the city, the arts, and the animals.'[25] Thus the following third chapter delineates how man, on the model of divine governance, operates in the material world and regulates himself and the animals.

The other animals either live without art or have each one single art to the use of which they do not turn by their own power but are drawn by a law of fate. The sign of this is that they gain nothing from time for the work of making things. Men, on the contrary, are the inventors of innumerable arts which they practise according to their own decision. This is shown by the fact that individuals practise many arts, change, and become more expert by extensive practice, and, what is marvelous, human arts make by themselves whatever nature itself makes, so that we seem to be not the servants of nature but competitors.[26]

Naming the realistic artistic creations of ancient artists, the paintings, flying doves, Hermes's talking idols, Ficino concludes that man imitates the works of divine nature and perfects and corrects those of lower nature.

This leads to what must be viewed as a threnody for *homo faber*, an ecstatic passage which should be repeated here as the most emphatic description of human autonomy.

The power of man, therefore, is very similar to that of the divine nature, seeing that man by himself, that is through his own decision and art, rules himself without being in the least limited by his physical nature, and imitates individual works of the higher nature. And he has as much less need than the beasts for the aid of inferior nature as he is endowed by nature with fewer natural aids to bodily protection than the animals, but he himself provides his own supply of food, clothing, bedding, housing, furnishings, and arms. Hence he supports himself by his own capacity more richly than nature preserves the beasts. In connection with this an indescribable variety of pleasures are developed for delighting the five senses of the body which we invent for ourselves by our own talents.... Our soul is concerned not only with the necessities of the body like the beasts subjected to the rule of nature but with various delights of the senses as though a kind of food for the phantasy. And the soul not only flatters its phantasy with these various pleasures while daily seducing it with various games as if for jest, but meanwhile also the cogitative reason acts seriously, and it comes out eager to propagate its own progeny, and to show how strong its own inventive genius is through various silk and woolen textiles, paintings, sculptures, and buildings. In composing these works it often respects no bodily comforts, no pleasing of the senses, since it sometimes willingly undergoes hardship and trouble, but it also expands and proves its productive power.[27]

Starting with the old *topos* from Pliny of how man equals the natural endowments of animals by his inventiveness, Ficino develops it in a way that clearly reflects the rich artisanal and artistic environment of Florence, exceeding Giannozzo Manetti in his enthusiasm. But he hastens to restate the phenomenon in terms of his ideal of human autonomy:

In these industrial arts it may be observed how man everywhere utilizes all the materials of the universe as though all were subject to man. He makes use, I say, of the elements, the stones, metals, plants, and animals and he transforms them into many shapes and figures, which animals never do. Nor is he content with one element or a few, as animals, but he uses all as though master of all. He tramps the earth, he sails the water, he ascends in the air by the highest towers, as I pass over the feathers of Daedalus or Icarus. He alone lights fire and uses his familial hearth, especially appreciating it. Correctly only a celestial animal is delighted by a celestial element. With celestial virtue he ascends the heavens and measures them. With supercelestial intelligence he transcends the heavens.[28]

Ficino moves from there to man's historical ecological role in transforming the earth and beautifying it by his cultivation and urbanization:

But man not only uses the elements, he adorns them, which no brute does. How marvelous the cultivation of the earth throughout the world! How stupendous the structures of buildings and cities! How ingenious his works of irrigation! He acts as the vicar of God, since he inhabits all the elements and cultivates all; present on earth, he is not absent from the ether.

Indeed, he employs not only the elements but all the animals of the elements, terrestrial, aquatic, and flying, for food, comfort, and pleasure, and the supernal and celestial ones for learning and the miracles of magic. He not only uses the animals but he rules them. . . . He not only rules the animals cruelly, but he governs, fosters, and teaches them. Universal providence is proper to God who is the universal cause. Therefore man who universally provides for all things living and not living is a certain god. He is the god without doubt of the animals, since he uses all of them, rules them, and teaches some of them. He is established also as god of the elements, since he inhabits and cultivates all of them. He is, finally, the god of all materials, since he handles all, and forms and changes them.

Human autonomy in commanding and utilizing and transforming the physical and biological universe leads Ficino to proclaim man's divinity on the model of God's total providence. 'Anybody who dominates the corporeal in so many and such great things and acts as the vicar of immortal God is without doubt immortal.'[29]

But man is not only a consumer, producer, and industrial manager; he is also a governor, a superior office to that of *homo faber*: 'But the arts of this type, although they mould the matter of the universe and command the animals, and thus imitate God, the creator of the universe, are nevertheless inferior to those arts which imitating the heavenly kingdom undertake the responsibility of human government.'[30]

Man rules himself first, then his family, administers the state, and commands the world. He is impatient of servitude, but he will submit to death for the sake of the public good.

Yet beyond both the industrial and civil arts, Ficino places those that are not necessary for physical survival and existence, namely the liberal arts and sciences:

The subtle computation of numbers, the meticulous description of figures, the most obscure movement of lines, the mysterious consonance of music, long observation of the stars, the study of natural causes, the investigation of enduring things, the eloquence of orators, the madness of poets — in all of these the soul of man despises the ministry of the body as though he would one day be able and now already begins to live without the aid of the body.[31]

The ultimate achievement of man, to become God Himself, remains beyond the powers of the human species, so that man's autonomy is not complete. Yet Ficino so yearns for this total fulfillment of human autonomy that he speculates that, given the proper instruments and material, mankind could recreate the universe itself, as once Archimedes, and now some of Ficino's contemporaries, constructed working models thereof.

This is how Ficino built his vision of human autonomy and revealed thereby also his image of God. If in the slow process of western history human thought gradually replaced the God, whom mankind worshipped and endowed with humanly conceivable qualities, with a conception of man in which now man himself was to be worshipped because he was endowed with godlike qualities, Ficino's place in this process is a vastly important one. Thus the ancient ideal of *autarkeia* and self-sufficiency underwent a Renaissance metamorphosis.

The University of Michigan

Notes

* This essay was first published in the Acta of the Convegno, 'Marsilio Ficino e il ritorno di Platone, Studi e Documenti' by the Istituto Nazionale di Studi sul Rinascimento, Florence, 1985. It is reprinted here with the kind permission of the Istituto.

1 Max Weber, *Die protestantische Ethik und der Geist der Kapitalismus* in *Archiv für Sozialwissenschaft und Sozialpolitik*, 20-21 (1904-05), English translation by Talcott Parsons of 1930 (New York: Charles Scribner's Sons, 1958), pp. 181-82.

2 Jacob Burckhardt, *The Civilization of the Renaissance in Italy* (New York: Harper and Row, 1928; rpt. 1958), p. 143.

3 Representative of this view was certainly Erich Fromm's *Escape from Freedom* (New York: Farrar & Rinehart, Inc., 1941) and even more his *Man for Himself* (New York: Holt, Rinehart, Winston, 1947).

4 See my '*In Our Image and Likeness': Humanity and Divinity in Italian Humanist Thought* (London: Constable & Co. Ltd., Chicago; University of Chicago Press, 1970); henceforth IOIAL, Parts II and III.

5 IOIAL, Part I; for Morandi, Part II, Ch. 7.

6 See Hans Baron, *The Crisis of the Early Italian Renaissance*, revised edition (Princeton, N.J.: Princeton U.P., 1966), passim and espec. p. 419.

7 The following paper is a more focused and compact exposition than that of Ch. 11 of IOIAL. Except for the final section, it is built on other parts of Ficino's *Theologia Platonica* than those utilized in IOIAL. It follows the first part of Paul Oskar Kristeller's edition of Ficino's *Disputatio contra Iudicium Astrologorum* in his *Supplementum Ficinianum* (Florence: Leo S. Olschki, 1937, rpt 1973), Volumen Alterum, pp. 11-76; henceforth cited as *Disputatio*. Where Ficino inserted sections of his *Theologia Platonica* in his *Disputatio* (which are not re-edited by Kristeller except for listing manuscript corrections), I cite passages from these from Raymond Marcel's edition: Marsile Ficin, *Théologie platonicienne de l'Immortalité des Ames* (Paris: Les Belles Lettres, 1964) as *Theol. Plat.*, volume and page (of Marcel).

8 Ficino, *Theol. Plat.*, II, 276: 'Immo vero si Deus nullas omnino vel minimas mundi negligit partes, profecto non despicit genus humanum, quod est mundi pars adeo pretiosa ut media sit temporalium rerum et aeternarum, quantum aeterna capit, ordinat temporalia; adeo Deo proxima ut sese divinae mentis arcanis insinuans opus hoc Dei, ordinem scilicet mundi cognoscat. Mundani ordinis intelligentia eo ipso ordine est excellentior, siquidem ordo huiusmodi per intelligentiam est factus et regitur.'

9 Ficino, *Disputatio*, 12: 'Agit autem cuncta perfectissimus auctor eo actionis genere quod est omnium perfectissimum. Non igitur ad agendum ducitur necessitate nature, sed quodam potius proposito voluntatis. Quod enim voluntate agit libera prestantius est quam quod instinctu nature necessario trahitur ad agendum. Felicissima certe est actio, in qua auctor sue actionis est dominus, ut ipse modum et mensuram finemque prescribat agendi.'

10 Ficino, *Theol. Plat.*, I, 118: 'Si Deus sibi ipse placet, si amat seipsum, profecto imagines suas et sua diligit opera. Diligit faber opera sua, quae ex materia fecit externa.'

11 Ficino, *Disputatio*, 23: 'Neque a divinis compellitur, a quorum providentia liber est ab initio, neque a naturalibus cogitur ullis, quibus longe preest nec ab eis ipse dependet, immo ipsa inde moventur et iudicantur. Quamobrem mentis nostre voluntas, quando in naturale aliquod obiectum tendit, quoniam ab eo non patitur, ideo non determinatur ab illo, ergo libera proficiscitur.'

12 Ficino, *Theol. Plat.*, I, 126: 'Sicut enim praevidet te id facturum, ita praevidet te ita, id est voluntarie libereque facturum.'

13 Ficino, *Disputatio*, 23-24: 'Unde cum utrumque eque potens sit ad trahendum, si voluntas tendit in alterum non coacta sed sponte procedit. Proinde agens voluntarium est nobilius quam agens necessitate nature, quia super naturam addit intelligentiam, sue actionis est dominus, ponit actioni mensuram, prescribit finem, agit diverso modo diversa.... Proprietas autem eius quod naturaliter agit, est ut agat necessario et ut ita dicam coacte, cum fuerit materia preparata neque aliquid impediverit. Ignis enim non impeditus non potest non calefacere siccam propinquamque materiam, lapis non impeditus descendere ad inferiora non potest. Ergo proprietas voluntarii agentis erit agere ut sic loquar contin-

genter et libere, ita ut agere valeat pariter et non agere. Sed ubicumque est ratio quedam vel essentia, ibidem eius proprietas etiam reperitur. Cum ergo in homine sit voluntarii ratio, erit et ratio libertatis. Ac nisi esset contingentia ad utramque partem in agente voluntario, multo minus in agentibus naturalibus posset excogitari, atque ita non esset in mundo ordo ille contingentium inter necessaria quedam et impossibilia, quem esse debere in superioribus declaravimus. (cf. ibid. p. 19) Contingentia vero eiusmodi qui non viderit materiam esse consilii, hic solus ex omnibus videbitur vel numquam usus fuisse consilio vel semper abusus. Sane de iis solum consultare solemus que possunt aliter atque aliter se habere et acquiri a nobis vel evitari. Si necessario cuncta proveniant, frustra nimium consultabimus. Meminisse vero debemus officia propria cuiuslibet speciei vana penitus esse non posse. Quis enim dixerit apes frustra semper conficere alvearia, araneas texere telas, formicas recondere grana? Nemo. Nemo itaque audeat confiteri proprium hominis officium, quod est consilium, esse vanum. Dico autem hoc hominis proprium, in quantum homo. Siquidem omnes homines et semper et ubique consultant; atque illa que super homines sunt, consultatione non indigent; que vero infra nos sunt, nequeunt consultare.'

14 Ficino, *Theol. Plat.*, II 18-22, cit. 22: 'Natura siquidem rei cuiusque una quaedam est affixa sibi forma et certa vis ab initio insita, per quam unam similemque semper unum opus fit semper et simile.'

15 Ficino, *Theol. Plat.*, II, 23: 'Habemus enim in mente commune quoddam bonorum exemplar, ad quod singula comparantes, sive reiicimus, sive magis minusve probamus, non ipsi quidem tracti a rebus ipsis vel corpore, sed trahentes res ipsas potius ad exemplar et corpus ad mentem.... Consultatione namque fit, ut non animam rebus, sed res animae nostrae subiiciamus.'

16 Kristeller, *Supplementum Ficinianum*, I, cxl.

17 Ficino, *Theol. Plat.*, for general influence of heavens: II, 208; *spiritus*: II, 213-14. I agree with Kristeller on Ficino's astrological views: *Il pensiero filosofico di Marsilio Ficino* (Florence: Sansoni, 1953), 334-36.

18 Kristeller, *Sup. Fic.*, I, cxl.

19 Ficino, *Theol. Plat.*, II, 23: 'Cum omnia vitae studia ad animum nostrum dirigimus moribus exornandum, quis non intelligat tunc officiorum nostrorum finem esse animam, atque ideo eorundem animam esse principium? Harum actionum non humores principia sunt, quoniam humores non invitant ad aliquid contra corpus eorum et supra corpora; non caelum, quod per humores movet; corpus quippe caeli longe remotum, neque prius movet quattuor humores nostros quam moveat quattuor elementa, neque movebit animam nisi humoribus agitatis. Humorum vero agitationi animus adversatur, dum illorum impetus speculationis intentione contemnit, morum studio cohibet, artium industria frangit.'

20 Ficino, *Theol. Plat.*, 24: 'Si humoribus resistimus, obsistimus et elementis, et caelo; immo etiam si non subiicimur caelo, multo minus caeteris corporibus subdimur. Caelo vero non subiici hominis animum, ...'

21 Ficino, *Theol. Plat.*, II, 24: 'Idem rursus ita per intellectum monstramus et voluntatem. Primo sic per intellectum: Caeleste corpus formam habet corporalem, singularem, localem et temporalem. Forma per quam mens omnis intelligit est incorporalis, universalis et absoluta. Haec ergo a caelo non nascitur.... Quoniam igitur intellectus necque actionem propriam neque actionis principium habet a caelo, corpori caelesti non subditur, praesertim quia noster animus secundum eam vim qua iungitur his quae supra caelum esse dicuntur, non modo non subest caelo, sed etiam praeest.'

22 Ficino, *Theol. Plat.*, II, 25: 'Sic rursus non subiici voluntatem. Eas profecto quae natura fiunt, determinatis mediis, perducuntur ad finem, unde semper eodem pene modo proveniunt. Natura enim ad aliquid unum determinatur. Electiones autem hominis diversis viis tendunt ad finem tam in moribus quam in artificiis.'

23 Ficino, *Opera omnia* (Basel, 1572, reprinted Turin, 1983), p. 541: 'At enim sicut herbae lapidesque mirabiles quasdam ultra naturam elementa rem vires coelitus habent, sic homines quoque in artibus nonnullas habere. Mihi vero satis fuerit factum, si coelestia quomodo quasi per medicinas, sive interiores, sive exteriores ad prosperam conferant valetudinem, dummodo interea salutem corporis perquirentes iacturam nullam salutis animae faciamus.'

24 See especially Ficino, *Theol. Plat.*, II, 214-22: 'Septem vacationis genera.'

25 Ficino, *Theol. Plat.*, II, 209: 'Anima igitur per mentem est supra fatum in solo providentiae ordine tamquam superna imitans et inferiora una cum illis gubernans. Ipsa enim tamquam providentiae particeps ad divinae gubernationis exemplar regit se, domum, civitatem, artes et animalia.'

26 Ficino, *Theol. Plat.*, II, 223: 'Caetera animalia vel absque arte vivunt, vel singula una quadam arte, ad cuius usum non ipsa se conferunt, sed fatali lege trahuntur. Cuis signum est quod ad operis fabricandi industriam nihil proficiunt tempore. Contra homines artium innumerabilium inventores sunt, quas suo exsequuntur arbitrio. Quod significatur ex eo quod singuli multas exercent artes, mutant, et diuturno usu fiunt solertiores, et quod mirabile est, humanae artes fabricant per seipsas quaecumque fabricat ipsa natura, quasi non servi simus naturae, sed aemuli.' IOIAl, 482.

27 Ficino, *Theol. Plat.*, II, 224; 'Similis ergo ferme vis hominis est naturae divinae, quandoquidem homo per seipsum, id est per suum consilium atque artem regit seipsum a corporalis naturae limitibus minime circumscriptum, et singula naturae altioris opera aemulatur. Et tanto minus quam bruta naturae inferioris eget subsidio, quanto pauciora corporis munimenta sortitus est a natura quam bruta, sed ipsemet illa sua copia construit alimenta, vestes, stramenta, habitacula, suppellectialia, arma. Ideo cum ipse sua facultate se fulciat, fulcit uberius quam bestias ipsa natura. Hinc proficiscitur inenarrabilis varietas voluptatum hos quinque sensus corporis oblectantium, quas ipsimet nobis proprio ingenio machinamur. Bruta brevissimis naturae claustris concluduntur. Non solum ad corporis necessitatem noster animu respicit, sicut bestiae naturae imperio mancipatae, sed ad oblectamenta sensuum varia, quasi quaedam pabula phantasiae animus adulatur, dum quasi per iocum diversis ludis delinit quotidie phastasiam, verumetiam agit interdum cogitatrix ratio serius, et suae prolis propagandae cupida emictat foras, et quanto polleat ingenio, evidenter ostentat per variam lanificiorum sericique texturam, picturas, sculpturas et aedificia. In quibus componendis saepe nullum corporis respicit commodum, nullum sensuum blandimentum, cum aliquando sponte ex eis incommodum et molestiam patiatur, sed facundiae suae amplificationem approbationemque virtutis.' IOIAL, 482-83.

28 Ficino, *Theol. Plat.*, II, 224-25: 'In iis artificiis animavertere licet quemadmodum homo et omnes et undique tractat mundi materias, quasi homini omnes subiiciantur. Tractat, inquam, elementa, lapides, metalla, plantas et animalia, et in multas traducit formas atque figuras; quod numquam bestiae faciunt. Neque uno est elemento contenus aut quibusdam ut bruta, sed utitur omnibus, quasi sit omnium dominus. Terram calcat, sulcat aquam, altissimis turribus conscendit in aerem, ut pennas Daedali vel Icari praetermittam. Accendit ignem et foco familiariter utitur et delectatur praecipue ipse solus. Merito caelesti elemento solum caeleste animal delectatur. Caelesti virtute ascendit caelum atque metitur. Supercaelesti mente transcendit caelum.' IOIAL, 483.

29 Ficino, *Theol. Plat.*, II, 225: 'Nec utitur tantum elementis homo, sed ornat; quod nullum facit brutorum. Quam mirabilis per omnem orbem terrae cultura! Quam stupenda aedificiorum structura et urbium! Irrigatio aquarum quam artificiosa! Vicem gerit Dei qui omnia elementa habitat colitque omnia, et terrae praesens non abest ab aethere. Atqui non modo elementis, verumetiam elementorum animalibus utitur omnibus, terrenis, aquatilibus, volatilibus ad escam, commoditatem et voluptatem, supernis caelestibusque ad doctrinam magicaeque miracula. Nec utitur brutis soum, sed et imperat. . . . Non imperat bestiis homo crudeliter tantum, sed gubernat etiam illas, fovet et docet. Universalis providentia Dei, qui est universalis causa, propria est. Homo igitur qui universaliter cunctis et viventibus et non viventibus providet est quidam Deus. Deus est proculdubio animalium qui utitur omnibus, imperat cunctis, instruit plurima. Deum quoque esse constitit elementorum qui habitat colitque omnia. Deum denique omnium materiarum qui tractat omnes, vertit et format. Qui tot tantisque in rebus corpori dominatur et immortalis Dei gerit vicem est proculdubio immortalis.' IOIAL, 483-84.

30 Ficino, *Theol. Plat.*, II, 225-26: 'Sed artes huiusmodi, licet materiam mundi figurent et animalibus imperent, atque ita Deum naturae artificem imitentur, sunt tamen artibus illis inferiores, quae regnum imitatae divinum humanae gubernationis suscipiunt curam.' IOIAL, 484.

31 Ficino, *Theol. Plat.*. II, 226: 'Subtilis computatio numerorum, figurarum curiosa descriptio, linearum obscurissimi motus, superstitiosa musicae consonantia, astrorum observatio diuturna, naturalium inquisitio causarum, diuturnorum investigatio, oratorum facundia poetarumque furores. In iis omnibus animus hominis corporis despicit ministerium, utpote qui quandoque possit et iam incipiat sine coporis auxilio vivere.' IOIAL, 484-84.

Louis Valcke

Magie et Miracle chez Jean Pic de la Mirandole

I — Magie et Miracle à l'époque de la Dispute romaine (1486-7)

1. *La magie 'naturelle' dans le cadre de l'*Oratio

On sait la très grande importance que, à l'époque de la dispute romaine, Jean Pic de la Mirandole attachait à la magie. Il en fait longuement l'éloge dans l'*Oratio*; cet éloge sera repris et largement développé dans l'*Apologie* et le rang même que les Conclusions magiques occupent dans la progression des *900 Theses* atteste de l'importance que Pic leur accordait.[1] Avec les Conclusions orphiques qui leur sont liées, les Conclusions magiques constituent en effet le dernier degré initiatique, préparatoire à la révélation de l'ultime sagesse que proposent les Conclusions cabalistiques.[2] S'il la situe donc très haut sur l'échelle sapientielle, s'il insiste sur la longue préparation, la difficile initiation, et même l'ascèse, qu'elle suppose, Pic, en même temps, vise de toutes ses énergies à 'démystifier' la magie, pour mieux la légitimer et pour mieux la distinguer de sa contrefaçon diabolique, la *Goeteia* ou magie noire. Pic consacre plusieurs pages de son *Oratio* à opposer systématiquement *Magia* et *Goeteia* et cette distinction fera l'objet de ses deux premières Conclusions magiques:

Toute la magie qui est en usage chez les modernes et que l'Eglise rejette à bon droit n'a aucune solidité, aucun fondement, aucune vérité, car elle est l'oeuvre des ennemis de la vérité première, celle des puissances des ténèbres d'ici bas, qui répandent les ténèbres de la fausseté dans les intellects mal disposés.[3]

Par contre:

La magie naturelle est permise et non interdite et concernant les fondements théoriques universels de cette science, j'établis, selon ma propre opinion, les conclusions qui suivent.[4]

Ainsi, dès le départ, pour faire ressortir toute la différence qui sépare magie et sorcellerie, Pic souligne l'aspect parfaitement 'naturel, de la magie autorisée, dont il veut montrer, de plus, qu'elle appartient de plein droit au domaine des sciences humaines rationnelles. C'est ainsi qu'il voit en elle 'le parfait achèvement de la philosophie naturelle,'[5] dont, en tant que science pratique elle est 'la partie la plus noble.'[6] L'*Apologie* souligne par ailleurs que, la magie ne faisant aucunement partie des sciences révélées, la certitude qu'elle procure est cette 'certitude scientifique trouvée ou acquise par le moyen de la démonstration.'[7] De plus, si la magie est ardue, c'est précisément parce qu'elle 'présuppose une exacte et parfaite connaissance de toutes les choses naturelles.'[8]

La même intention démystifiante est sous-jacente aux nombreux textes où Pic tente une description du mode opératoire propre à la magie. C'est ainsi qu'il maintient que le Mage opère 'seulement en actuant ou en unissant les vertus naturelles,'[9] ce qui n'est qu'une paraphrase de la Conclusion magique no 5 où Pic affirme qu' 'il n'est nulle vertu dans le ciel et sur terre, à l'état séminal et séparé, que le Mage ne puisse tant actuer qu'unir.'[10] Les pouvoirs du Mage sont certes exceptionnels, ils n'en restent pas moins pleinement naturels, car, nous dit Pic, 'la magie n'enseigne rien d'autre qu'à faire des oeuvres génératrices d'étonnement, moyennant des pouvoirs naturels et l'application de ceux-ci les uns aux autres et à leurs patients naturels.'[11]

Opérer ainsi, c'est effectuer le mariage du monde (*maritare mundum*) selon ce qu'affirme la Conclusion magique no 13: 'faire oeuvre de magie n'est rien d'autre que marier le monde.'[12] Ce thème devient l'un des thèmes centraux de l'*Oratio* et c'est en quelque sorte la quintessence de sa conception de la magie que Pic expose dans un texte d'une belle venue, dont voici un bref passage:

Appelant à la lumière comme de leurs cachettes, les vertus que la divine libéralité a jetées dans le monde comme autant de semences, [la magie] ne crée pas tant les merveilles qu'elle n'assiste avec empressement la nature qui les produit. Scrutant à fond l'intime accord de l'univers, auquel les Grecs appliquaient le terme particulièrement expressif de *sumpatheia*, approfondissant la parenté réciproque des natures, appliquant ainsi à chaque chose ses attraits innés, ce qu'on appelle charmes chez les Mages, elle produit au grand jour, comme si elle était le démiurge, les miracles latents dans les replis du monde, dans le sein de la nature, dans les secrètes réserves de Dieu; et comme le cultivateur marie la vigne à l'ormeau, de même le Mage marie la terre au ciel, c'est-à-dire les êtres inférieurs aux ressources et aux vertus des êtres supérieurs.[13]

2. Conception plotinienne de la magie

C'est donc toujours en insistant sur l'aspect naturel de la magie et de ses prodiges que Pic fait la critique de leur caractère prétendument mystérieux ou démoniaque. Encore faudra-t-il évidemment que Pic, esprit rigoureux, dispose d'une conception de l'ordre naturel qui soit telle que la magie, sous tous ses aspects, s'y insère de façon harmonieuse, logique, rationnelle.

Or cette conception, ce cadre théorique précis, ce sera Plotin qui les lui fournira: on le sait, Plotin 'naturalise' la magie. Selon la cosmologie vitaliste qu'il expose en particulier dans sa quatrième *Ennéade*, l'Univers dans son ensemble est assimilé à un être vivant:

Cet univers est un animal unique qui contient en lui tous les animaux; il a une âme unique qui va dans toutes les parties, dans la mesure où les êtres qui sont en lui sont ses parties (*Enn.* IV-iv c. 32).[14]

De même qu'une âme unique anime tous les organes d'un même corps et établit entr'eux une correspondance harmonieuse, dépendant de leurs seules fonctions au sein du tout — de même règne-t-il au sein de l'Univers une sympathie réciproque des parties qui sont présentes en lui, par et pour la fonction que chacune d'elles y exerce et par l'affinité qui les relie. Toute action quelle qu'elle soit résulte de cette sympathie, qui n'est donc pas liée à la proximité physique, mais qui dépend d'une similitude ou d'une analogie de fonction. Dans les mots de Plotin:

Cet univers est donc un tout sympathique à lui-même; les parties les plus éloignées y sont proches, comme les ongles, les cornes et les doigts, dans un animal, sont proches des parties qui n'y sont pas attenantes. Malgré l'intervalle et bien que la région intermédiaire ne pâtisse pas, elles subissent l'influence des parties qui ne sont pas dans leur voisinage. Des choses semblables qui ne sont pas attenantes mais qui sont séparées par un intervalle, sympathisent en vertu de leur ressemblance. Sans être en contact, les choses agissent et elles ont nécessairement une action à distance. Comme l'univers est un animal qui arrive à l'unité, aucune de ses parties n'est en un lieu si éloigné, qu'elle ne lui soit proche à cause de la tendance à la sympathie qui existe entre toutes les parties d'un animal unique (*Enn.* IV-iv c. 32).

On aura remarqué que Plotin donne une justification rationnelle de l'action à distance. Cette justification se fonde sur le principe de participation qui figure parmi les postulats fondamentaux de sa doctrine, telle que lui-même l'expose à l'occasion de sa critique du *Parménide* de Platon (*Enn.*VI-iv).

Or, la question de l'action à distance a toujours été cruciale car c'est sur elle que repose la distinction entre *force physique* et *vertu magique*. Pour Plotin donc, qui admet l'action à distance, il ne s'agira plus d'expliquer les opérations magiques en les ramenant aux phénomènes physiques, mais au contraire, ce seront les phénomènes physiques qui seront compris comme expression des vertus occultes. Emile Bréhier rappelle que Plotin 'vise à donner une image du monde où toutes les influences quelles qu'elles soient, qui s'exercent d'une partie vers l'autre, sont de nature magique'[15] et il ajoute: 'Plotin assimile donc les forces dites naturelles aux vertus magiques, et ne les distingue que par ce caractère extérieur: elles sont habituelles ou non.'[16]

C'est bien cette conception plotinienne que l'on retrouve, à peine transposée, dans les pages que Pic consacre à la magie.[17] Une lecture attentive des textes montre qu'en bien des cas Pic ne fait que paraphraser certains passages des *Ennéades* ou en développer certaines images, ce qui suppose une fréquentation assidue des chapitres en question.

C'est ainsi que Pic se réfère explicitement à la conception plotinienne lorsqu'il affirme dans l'*Oratio* que 'Plotin . . . démontre que le Mage est le ministre de la nature, non son *artifex*.'[18] Et en effet, lorsqu'il décrit l'oeuvre magique, Plotin insiste sur le fait que, si le Mage, s'insérant dans la nature, guide les vertus naturelles, 'il ne les mène pas ailleurs que dans leur domaine propre' (*Enn.* IV-iv c. 40), qu'il ne fait qu' 'unir par des contacts les êtres déjà naturellement liés l'un à l'autre et qui ont un amour inné l'un pour l'autre' et c'est de cette manière que Plotin, en ses propres termes, 'explique les charmes de la magie' (*Enn.* IV-iv, c. 40). Or, nous avons vu que, selon Pic, la magie n'est efficace que parce qu'elle applique 'à chaque chose ses attraits innés, ce qu'on appelle charmes chez les Mages.' (Cf. ci-dessus, n. 13)

Même l'image de la greffe, par laquelle Pic illustre le 'mariage du monde,' est une métaphore qui trouve son origine chez Plotin car le Mage, nous dit celui-ci, 'joint une âme à une autre comme on attache deux plantes éloignées l'une à l'autre' (*Enn.* IV-iv, c. 40).

3. *L'impasse: essentialisme grec ou volontarisme chrétien?*

L'influence de Plotin sur la pensée de Pic, à cette époque, paraît donc déterminante, particulièrement en ce qui concerne la magie et l'arrière-plan cosmologique qui en permet l'intégration harmonieuse. Il est cependant un point, mais un point essentiel, où Pic ne peut suivre Plotin. Il s'agit précisément de ce point de doctrine où l'opposition entre la pensée grecque, d'une part, et la pensée judéo-chrétienne et islamique, d'autre part, était radicale et insurmontable.

Partant du dogme de la toute-puissance divine, la pensée biblique est volontariste, alors que la pensée grecque, donnant la primauté à l'être, est essentialiste et donc tout entière axée sur un rationalisme nécessitariste. Cette tendance culminera chez Plotin qui, dans la lignée d'Aristote et de Platon, mais plus loin qu'eux, posera, au-delà de l'être, l'unité absolue de l'Un, à partir duquel, en une émanation inéluctable, procèderont les diverses hypostases, dont notre monde sensible sera la dernière. En ce qui concerne la magie, ce nécessitarisme se traduit par un automatisme absolu, parfaitement assimilable quant à ses conséquences au déterminisme mécaniste le plus rigide.

L'ordre de la nature, dira Plotin, est rationnel, nécessaire, unique (*Enn.* IV-iv, c. 35, c. 39). Comme toutes les interactions se produisant dans cet ordre rigoureux, les opérations magiques provoqueront inévitablement l'apparition des conséquences qui leur sont proportionnées. De la même façon, les incantations, s'insérant dans la trame des choses, seront nécessairement efficaces, de même que la corde tendue d'une lyre transmet nécessairement les vibrations du bas vers le haut (c. 41). Cependant, l'univers, les dieux, les astres étant impassibles (c. 42), il n'y a pas en eux de décision volontaire et réfléchie (c. 31, c. 36). Par conséquent, il est vain de croire que nous puissions les émouvoir par nos suppliques ou qu'ils exaucent nos prières (c. 40): Plotin, comme le dit Bréhier, y verrait une 'atteinte à la rationalité de l'Univers.'[19]

Voilà qui est exclure, non seulement l'efficacité propre de la prière chrétienne, qui s'adresse à un Dieu personnel, c'est exclure la possibilité même du miracle, entendu comme intervention libre, exceptionnelle et immédiate de ce Dieu personnel dans l'ordre du monde par lui créé. Chrétien, Pic ne suivra pas Plotin en cette négation de la liberté et de la toute-puissance divines, et ce d'autant moins que c'est aussi par souci apologétique que Pic avait voulu démystifier et légitimer la magie. En effet, rendant naturelle la magie, il espérait pouvoir donner la preuve de la divinité du Christ en faisant ressortir le contraste qui distingue les miracles du Christ des prodiges magiques, même si, quant aux effets obtenus, ces prodiges sont comparables aux oeuvres miraculeuses. Tel est l'objet des célèbres conclusions magiques 7, 8 et 9:

7: Les oeuvres du Christ n'ont pu être faites, ni par la voie de la magie, ni par la voie de la Cabale.[20]

8: Ce n'est pas en raison de ce qui fut fait, mais en raison de la façon de le faire que les miracles du Christ sont la preuve la plus parfaite de sa divinité.[21]

9: Il n'y a pas de science qui nous donne plus de certitude de la divinité du Christ que la magie et la cabale.[22]

Il semble que Pic soit dans une impasse. Voulant rendre la magie naturelle pour démontrer, par contraste, l'authenticité des miracles du Christ, il fait sienne la doctrine de Plotin, mais cette doctrine, par le nécessitarisme qu'elle implique, devrait le conduire à rejeter la possibilité même du miracle.

4. Conception augustinienne du miracle

En quelque sorte, Pic se trouve ici dans une situation assez semblable à celle qu'avait connue S. Augustin. Lui aussi était passé par le néoplatonisme et il en avait subi une influence profonde. Lui aussi cependant, ne pourra intégrer cette doctrine que s'il réussit à l'harmoniser au dogme chrétien.

C'est ainsi qu'Augustin reprendra intégralement toute l'ancienne conception des raisons séminales ou semences, ces principes qui déterminent les choses à être ce qu'elles sont, leur donnant leur raison d'être et garantissant ainsi la rationalité de l'ordre du monde. Cependant, S. Augustin ajoutera une nuance importante à cet essentialisme: ces raisons séminales ne sont plus le produit aveugle d'une émanation nécessaire, elles sont le fruit de la libre décision du Dieu créateur: 'C'est bien le Créateur de toutes choses,' dit S. Augustin dans son De Trinitate, 'qui est le créateur des semences invisibles.'[23]

Dieu est tout-puissant, Dieu est libre, mais, détail significatif où l'on voit poindre une réminiscence de nécessitarisme, l'évêque d'Hippone rappelle que

Dieu est tout-puissant, non pas d'une puissance déraisonnable (*temeraria*), mais sage; et il fait de chaque chose ce qu'auparavant il a posé en elle qu'on put en faire.[24]

Et voilà qui donne à S. Augustin l'arrière-plan où il pourra développer sa conception du miracle, et on me permettra ici de faire appel à l'excellente étude que le père De Vooght lui a consacrée.[25]

Le miracle (*miraculum*) est évidemment un fait inaccoutumé, un fait exceptionnel qui éveille l'étonnement et l'admiration par son caractère étrange et par sa rareté. Toute exception, cependant, confirme une règle: il n'y aurait pas de miracle s'il n'y avait d'abord l'ordre habituel des choses, c'est-à-dire cette succession régulière de phénomènes dont l'enchaînement constitue la nature. D'autre part, un ordre absolument rigide exclurait le miracle — comme c'est le cas chez Plotin. La nature doit donc être capable d'être miraculée, elle doit posséder ce qu'on a appelé la 'puissance obédientielle.' Ce n'est là que pure tautologie ou pur verbalisme, à moins que cette 'puissance obédientielle' exprime, non pas une simple disposition passive, une non-résistance, mais bien une capacité positive, la présence d'une propriété réelle ou d'une puissance latente qui serait inscrite dans les choses mêmes. Or, c'est bien de cette dernière façon que l'entend S. Augustin. L'ordre du monde sensible, la mouvance des êtres qui naissent et disparaissent, est régi par le déploiement successif, ou par la prédominance des raisons séminales, comme le voulait également Plotin (*Enn.* V-vii, c. 1, 2 et sq.). Mais, pour S. Augustin, l'ordre du monde, en quelque sorte, se dédouble. D'une part, les raisons séminales, selon leur nature propre et les affinités qui les relient, vont interagir et par leurs multiples configurations elles feront apparaître les conséquences qui leur sont proportionnées. Cela se produit nécessairement, c'est-à-dire, dans l'optique de S. Augustin, selon le plan voulu par Dieu. Mais il existe également d'autres raisons séminales, qui, elles, n'interviennent pas spontanément dans le déroulement des phénomènes. Quoique 'naturelles', car réellement présentes dans la création, elles restent habituellement latentes, cachées au sein de l'univers à titre de pures potentialités:

Dans les éléments corporels de ce monde sont cachées des semences invisibles de tout ce qui naît corporellement et visiblement. Les unes se révèlent à nos yeux dans les fruits et les animaux, les autres sont les semences cachées des autres semences.[26]

Cette dualité permettra de comprendre, d'une part, que les animaux et les végétaux se reproduisent et s'engendrent chacun selon le mode qui lui est propre, et cet enchaînement constitue l'ordre coutumier de la nature; que, d'autre part, le début de chacune des séries corresponde à l'éclosion première de ces virtualités spéciales, de ces vertus originelles que sont les semences des semences, les *occulta seminum semina*. Celles-ci sont latentes dans la nature: l'eau des océans, par exemple, contient encore et depuis son origine, les semences des semences des espèces aquatiques. Mais pour que ces virtualités s'actualisent, il faut une intervention particulière de Dieu: le miracle de la création. Cependant, lorsque l'espèce est créée, elle se perpétue par le processus de génération habituel qui, en quelque sorte, prend la relève.

A quoi il faut encore ajouter que les raisons séminales sont capables de deux sortes de développements. Il y a le développement coutumier qui se manifeste dans le cours régulier de la nature. C'est ainsi que les raisons séminales contenues dans un rameau produiront en leur temps bourgeons et feuilles, ou que la vigne en une lente alchimie actuera les raisons de vin que contient l'eau qui baigne ses racines. Mais ces mêmes raisons seront exceptionnellement capables d'une actuation presque instantanée. C'est ainsi que la verge d'Aaron, 'coupée de terre, aride et polie,' se mit à fleurir et à porter fruit, ou que le Christ transforma l'eau en vin aux noces de Cana.

On voit donc que, pour S. Augustin, le miracle n'est pas, à proprement parler, une oeuvre surnaturelle, si on entend par là que l'intervention divine modifierait radicalement l'ordre de la création. Sans doute faut-il que Dieu se décide, qu'il intervienne de façon spéciale, mais cette intervention porte sur des virtualités réellement inscrites dans la création, exactement d'ailleurs comme pour Plotin, l'opération magique elle-même n'excède en rien le cadre de la nature. On peut ici citer le P. De Vooght:

> Si donc le miracle s'écarte des normes habituelles, il ne dépasse pas pour autant la création prise dans sa totalité. L'on dira donc avec autant de vérité que, selon saint Augustin, le miracle se maintient dans la nature ou ne s'y maintient pas, d'après qu'on désignera du nom de nature, le cours ordinaire des choses ... ou l'ensemble de toutes les choses réelles et virtuelles que Dieu créa.[27]

Ce n'est d'ailleurs pas le miracle seulement, mais tout aussi bien la magie qui trouve une place naturelle dans le schéma augustinien. En effet, Dieu peut communiquer aux anges ou à certains hommes ce pouvoir particulier leur permettant d'actuer ces *seminum semina*, ou d'accélérer le processus de maturation. En cela, selon ce qu'en dit S. Augustin dans le *De Trinitate*, ces anges et ces hommes ne feront

> que porter en pleine lumière, ces causes qui tout en n'étant pas naturelles, opèrent néamoins de façon naturelle pour faire apparaître visiblement ce qui est contenu dans le sein secret de la nature.[28]

Cela, les bons, mais aussi les méchants le peuvent. Dans le premier cas, Dieu opère un miracle par la médiation d'un ange ou d'un homme, ou même d'un animal (l'ânesse de Balaam). Dans le second cas, lorsque, se substituant à Dieu, ce sont les mauvais anges qui exercent ces pouvoirs, ils réalisent les prodiges de la magie. Et ces prodiges, quant à leurs effets, sont en tout point semblables aux miracles puisqu'ils résultent de l'actuation des mêmes semences secrètes. C'est ainsi que les démons, contre Moïse, prêtent main forte aux mages du Pharaon, les aidant à faire surgir grenouilles et serpents. La description que donne S. Augustin de ces prodiges est extrêmement intéressante:

> par leur plus grande subtilité les mauvais anges savaient de quelles semences plus secrètes naissent les grenouilles et les serpents et, les plaçant par gestes occultes en certaines conditions favorables d'eux connues, ils les firent apparaître.[29]

On est frappé par la similitude entre cette conception de la magie et celle qui fut proposée par Plotin. Conservons intacte la vision augustinienne d'une nature capable d'être miraculée, mais supprimons-en la notion d'un Dieu tout-puissant et librement créateur: le miracle augustinien sera absorbé par la magie plotinienne.

Les textes d'Augustin que l'on vient de lire sont en tout point semblables, en leur esprit, à ceux de Plotin. De part et d'autre, le concept de nature est élargi pour y inclure les vertus occultes que sont ces raisons séminales plus secrètes. De part et d'autre également, le mage, grâce à la connaissance plus parfaite qu'il en a acquise, opère sur ces vertus dont il connaît le secret, et, s'insérant dans l'ordre naturel, il fait apparaître des effets prodigieux comme s'il en était le démiurge ou le créateur, alors qu'en réalité, se soumettant à la nature, il n'en est que le ministre. De plus, il suffit de relire l'*Oratio*, et en particulier les textes déjà cités, pour qu'apparaisse la convergence entre cette conception de la magie — qu'elle soit augustinienne ou plotinienne — et celle qu'adoptera Jean Pic.

Insistons-y à nouveau: dans la conception augustinienne magie et miracle sont également 'naturels.' Opérant l'un et l'autre sur les mêmes raisons séminales secrètes, leurs effets seront évidemment semblables. Seul le mode d'opérer sera radicalement différent car, dit S. Augustin, 'Dieu seul est créateur, lui qui a inséré dans les choses, les causes propres et les raisons séminales.'[30] Il s'ensuit que l'évêque d'Hippone n'aurait eu aucune difficulté à admettre la thèse mirandolienne selon laquelle 'ce n'est pas en raison de ce qui fut fait, mais en raison de la façon de le faire que les miracles du Christ sont la preuve la plus parfaite de sa divinité.' La théorie du miracle propre à S. Augustin ne peut qu'aboutir à la même conclusion.

5. Absence d'Augustin dans l'*Apologie* de Pic

Au vu de cette profonde ressemblance, il peut sembler étonnant, non seulement que Pic ne fasse pas état de S. Augustin dans ses *900 Conclusiones*, mais surtout qu'il n'invoque pas son autorité lorsque, face à la Commission d'enquête pontificale et, par après, dans son *Apo-*

logie, il aura à défendre l'orthodoxie de ses Conclusions magiques, et plus précisément de cette neuvième conclusion, déjà citée, où il affirme que de toutes les sciences, la magie et la cabale nous donnent la meilleure preuve de la divinité du Christ.

A y voir de plus près cependant, cette omission n'a rien qui puisse surprendre. Pour S. Augustin, la possibilité du miracle entraîne certes la possibilité de la magie, l'une et l'autre relevant d'un même processus, dont le schéma fut, dès la Création, inscrit par Dieu dans l'ordre du monde. Il n'empêche que l'opération magique constituera toujours une usurpation des pouvoirs divins.

Dieu seul, en effet, directement ou par l'intermédiaire des anges et des saints peut intervenir dans l'ordre du monde: c'est le miracle. Même si, dans sa mystérieuse sagesse, Dieu donne également au démon, la science et le pouvoir d'opérer des interventions semblables, ces interventions-là, comme opération du démon, n'en resteront pas moins essentiellement lucifériennes. Or, la magie n'est possible que grâce à l'aide des démons: ce n'est pas par eux-mêmes, mais grâce aux secours des mauvais anges que les mages du Pharaon firent apparaître les grenouilles. Par conséquent, aucune forme de magie ne trouve grâce aux yeux de S. Augustin, et la condamnation qu'il en fait, dans sa *Cité de Dieu* par exemple, est sans appel.[31] Dans tous les cas, Augustin assimile la magie à la *goeteia*. Ce faisant, il récuse d'avance la distinction que Pic, et tant d'autres, voudraient opérer et qui permettrait d'opposer magie et sorcellerie.

Pic savait donc fort bien qu'invoquer la conception augustinienne de la nature et du miracle pour légitimer la magie, aurait été une arme à double tranchant, qui se serait immédiatement retournée contre lui. On peut donc supposer que c'est par simple et prudente diplomatie qu'il a jugé plus sage de ne pas invoquer l'autorité d'Augustin dans cette question.

* * *

II — Magie et Miracle dans les *Disputationes*

1. *Renversement de perspective*

On a donc pu voir à quel point l'influence et de Plotin et d'Augustin a marqué ce qu'on pourrait appeler la cosmologie du jeune Pic; on a pu voir également avec quelle habileté il a su, à partir de cette cosmologie, justifier la magie, avec Plotin, tout en adoptant une conception du miracle très semblable à celle d'Augustin.

Toute cette perspective va changer radicalement alors que, quelques années plus tard, Pic de la Mirandole entreprendra sa croisade contre l'astrologie. Ce renversement de perspective est lié à cette 'conversion' dont Jean-François Pic fait état dans la biographie de son oncle. Cette conversion, quelle qu'ait été par ailleurs sa nature et son importance, impliquait certainement sur le plan philosophique l'abandon du néo-platonisme, dont le *De ente et uno* (1491) avait déjà critiqué la thèse métaphysique maîtresse, soit l'attribution à l'Un de la primauté sur l'être.

Ce n'est pas le lieu ici de développer cette question. Je voudrais seulement, à titre de confirmation de la réalité de cette conversion philosophique, indiquer brièvement à quel point les conceptions de la magie et du miracle, telles qu'elles apparaissent dans les *Disputationes adversus astrologiam divinatrice*, diffèrent de celles que Pic avaient adoptées antérieurement.

Remarquons d'abord et d'une manière générale, que toute référence explicite au néo-platonisme a disparu des *Disputationes*. Seules subsistent, bien entendu, ces considérations générales et un certain vocabulaire qui, depuis longtemps, avaient été parfaitement intégrés au sein des tendances mêmes les plus traditionnelles de la scolastique. Ce sont là des éléments qui remontaient au Pseudo-Denys ou à S. Augustin lui-même. Pic s'appuie également, et de façon fort intéressante d'ailleurs, sur cette 'métaphysique de la lumière' qui, d'origine néo-platonicienne, avait été développée dès le treizième siècle entr'autres par Robert Grosseteste (1170-1253).[32] Mais ces traces ou résidus de néo-platonisme assimilé n'ont évidemment rien à voir avec cette renaissance de la doctrine plotinienne, dont l'académie florentine fut le foyer, et à laquelle Pic avait contribué avec tant d'enthousiasme.

2. *La magie*

En ce qui a trait à la magie, il n'y a que peu à en dire, sauf que Pic, dans les *Disputationes*, la rejette totalement. En effet, on notera d'abord que, dans son dernier ouvrage, Pic propose explicitement une critique de l'astrologie sous toutes ses formes et non pas, comme certains ont voulu le croire, de l'astrologie divinatoire seulement, ni non plus seulement dans la mesure où elle s'opposerait au libre arbitre et par là, à la religion. Pic s'exclame, invoquant ici le témoignage d'Augustin:

Comment peut-on prétendre que les docteurs de l'Eglise se refusent à approuver l'astrologie uniquement parce qu'elle élimine le libre-arbitre et introduit les contraintes du Destin? . . . Ils ne la condamnèrent pas seulement sous certains aspects mais ils s'y opposèrent et la détestèrent *omnino omne*, totalement et en bloc.[33]

Il reprendra cette idée à la toute fin de son dernier livre où il cite le témoignage de plusieurs 'mathématiciens insignes' qui, dit-il,

la détestèrent comme vaine et fausse, non seulement dans la mesure où elle est néfaste à la religion, mais *plane totam.*[34]

Or, affirme Pic, toutes les sciences occultes ont partie liée avec l'astrologie et en dépendent, au point que les mages voyaient en elles la clé de leurs arts et pratiques. Par conséquent, poursuit-il, il nous suffira de renverser l'astrologie, leur *domina ac regina*, pour arracher du même coup toute la troupe des superstitions.[35]

Comme le rejet de l'astrologie, le rejet de la magie est total et sans appel: elle n'est pas seulement interdite, elle est 'vaine et fausse.'

3. *Le miracle et la sorcellerie*

Le cas du miracle est tout différent. Pic, bien entendu, ne le rejette pas, mais, toujours dans un but apologétique, pour mieux faire ressortir le caractère divin de son origine, il le relègue en quelque sorte en dehors de la nature. Pour ce faire — cela est fort loin du néo-platonisme, loin également de S. Augustin — Pic distingue maintenant très clairement la cause première et l'ordre des causes secondes, tout en insistant sur l'auto suffisance de ces dernières:

Il y a, déclare-t-il, un ordre des choses naturelles institué par Dieu; cet ordre est maintenu en des limites précises, et il est distinct de ces choses qui se font *praeter naturam* par la volonté et la puissance divine, car ces interventions particulières n'ajoutent ni ne retranchent rien à la nature même.[36]

Tel est l'ordre naturel où, dit Pic, 'Dieu laisse la nature à ses conditions propres' (*suis conditionibus*). Voilà qui est bien proche de ce 'concours ordinaire de Dieu' dont parlera Descartes lorsqu'il voudra, lui aussi, préciser ce qu'il entend par l'ordre naturel des choses.

Le miracle, désormais, est donc bien une rupture complète par rapport à l'ordre naturel des phénomènes. Nulle part cette dichotomie n'apparaît aussi clairement que lorsque Pic étudie et rejette les présages astrologiques, sous tous leurs aspects.

La question est ancienne et Plotin l'avait posée clairement: même si on suppose que les astres ne sont pas cause efficiente des phénomènes terrestres, ne pourraient-ils néamoins les annoncer, en tant que signes:

Quel est le rôle [des astres]? Produire ou annoncer? Ou bien, par l'influence de leurs figures jointes à leur influence propre, ont-ils souvent le double pouvoir de produire et de présager, et, parfois, celui de présager seulement? (*Enn.* IV-iv, c.34)

A cette double question, Pic répond négativement, et ce sans la moindre hésitation. Mais ce qui est particulièrement intéressant pour nous, c'est qu'il prend comme exemple l'Etoile des Mages, annonciatrice de la naissance du Christ. La naissance du Christ est un miracle, mais se pourrait-il que ce miracle ait été annoncé par l'apparition naturelle d'une étoile nouvelle? Cela, Pic le rejette totalement dans le titre même du chapitre qu'il consacre à cette question:

Les divins miracles ne sont ni produits ni signifiés par le ciel, mais les miracles sont indiqués par des miracles et les choses naturelles le sont par les choses naturelles.[37]

Ce qu'il explique ainsi:

Or donc, tout ce qui est dans le ciel et le ciel lui-même, procèdent selon le cours naturel. D'où il suit que si le mouvement et la configuration des étoiles, qui sont dûs à l'ordre naturel, indiquent le futur, de telles indications doivent être comprises parmi les choses naturelles. Si nous prétendions que de tels signes indiquent quelque chose de surnaturel, il s'ensuivrait cette absurdité que si Dieu laissait la nature à elle-même et qu'il ne lui ajoutât rien, la nature elle-même deviendrait fausse et mensongère, parce que Dieu y aurait placé quelque chose de vain et de superflu . . . Si donc Dieu a déterminé de toute éternité de faire quelque miracle, ce n'est pas pour cela qu'il en aurait inséré les indices parmi les choses naturelles, de façon à ce que la nature le signifie; il a au contraire déterminé que *les choses naturelles sont annoncées par les choses naturelles, et les miracles par les miracles précédents.*[38]

L'ordre des miracles et l'ordre de la nature sont donc distincts au point de ne pas se mélanger, de ne pas même se rencontrer.

En une acception moins forte du miracle, on peut voir en celui-ci non pas, à proprement parler, une intervention divine dans l'ordre du monde, mais une convergence exceptionnelle et voulue par Dieu de phénomènes qui, eux, restent pleinement naturels. Ce fut d'ailleurs également une acception reçue par S. Augustin, même si, comme on l'a vu, ce n'en est pas l'acception première.[39] Ce sera en particulier de cette manière que nul autre qu'Albert le Grand comprendra le Déluge. Il en reconnaîtra la nature et la signification miraculeuses et il l'attribuera à la volonté divine, mais il maintiendra que, dans ce phénomène naturel qu'est le Déluge, Dieu agit par la médiation des causes naturelles.

Cette conception accorde une grande autonomie à l'ordre naturel, puisque Dieu n'y intervient pas directement, pourtant Pic la rejette explicitement, car la distinction des deux ordres n'y est pas, selon lui, assez tranchée:

En ce qui concerne le déluge universel du temps de Noé ... certains le nient, mais d'autres paraissent plus insensés encore car ils l'admettent tel qu'il est décrit, tout en lui attribuant cependant des causes naturelles, alors qu'il ne peut être plus grande folie que d'*attribuer aux forces de la nature ce qui advient de façon surnaturelle.*[40]

La position de Pic est donc claire: il reconnaît l'ordre naturel, d'une part, et le miracle, d'autre part. Le miracle, cependant, est totalement en dehors de la nature et de l'enchaînement de ses phénomènes.

Quant à la magie 'naturelle,' nous avons vu qu'avec l'astrologie, il en rejette jusqu'à la simple possibilité. Elle est une pseudo-science et ses pouvoirs sont illusoires.

Qu'en est-il cependant de la *goeteia*, cet autre paramètre de l'équation initiale? On constate que la distinction magie sorcellerie n'apparaît plus dans les *Disputationes*. On peut s'en étonner: serait-ce que Pic, maintenant, confond l'une et l'autre et que, rejetant la magie, il rejette *a fortiori* la *goeteia*, qu'il 'exécrait' déjà six ans plus tôt? Il n'en est rien: la sorcellerie, en tant qu'oeuvre du démon, est en quelque sorte l'envers du miracle, et, tout comme le miracle, elle échappe à l'ordre régulier de la nature et devient à son tour témoin du surnaturel.

Il est d'ailleurs significatif que ce soit précisément à l'intervention du démon que Pic attribue maintenant les quelques succès astrologiques qui s'avèreraient indéniables. Se référant au *De divinatione* d'Augustin, Pic dit ceci:

Il peut se faire que le devin soit conduit par hasard à la vérité, vu le grand nombre de ses tentatives. Mais ceci peut également advenir par influence démoniaque occulte et mystérieuse ... Non seulement la divine sagesse pourrait-elle permettre que cela arrive, mais même que les démons rendent la prédiction vraie en exécutant eux-mêmes l'oeuvre qui avait auparavant été faussement prédite.[41]

* * *

III. *Conclusion: distinction entre l'ordre du profane et l'ordre du sacré*

La démarche suivie par Pic et l'évolution de sa pensée auront donc été extrêmement intéressantes et significatives. On reconnaîtra sans doute qu'il n'est aucunement cet homme prométhéen qu'on a voulu voir en lui, on reconnaîtra également qu'il n'a pas été mû par un souci de libre recherche scientifique. C'est au contraire un souci apologétique qui aura guidé sa recerce philosophique. En effet, partant d'une conception néo-platonicienne, Pic aura été amené à reconnaître que dans toute vision du monde où la magie est naturelle, le caractère proprement surnaturel du miracle est oblitéré: ce qui était pour lui une incitation à intégrer le néo-platonisme devint ainsi une raison de le rejeter.

Pic fera donc la critique des sciences occultes, et pour cela il fera ressortir la distinction entre la causalité première et l'ordre des causes secondes. Insistant sur l'autonomie, toujours relative, de ces dernières, il ébauchera en fait la distinction fondamentale entre le sacré et le profane. C'est par cette voie plus que par toute autre que Jean Pic de la Mirandole a laissé de façon durable sa marque dans l'histoire de la pensée.

Centre d'études de la Renaissance
Université de Sherbrooke

Notes

1 Pic lui-méme indique que la structure des *Conclusiones* n'a pas été laissée au hasard: *Apologia Joannis Pici Mirandulani Concordiae Comitis* (Napoli: Francesco Del Tuppo (?), 1487) fol. 110: 'Et sic in omnibus meis conclusionibus semper occulta quaedam est concatenatio quam forte ipsi non advertunt.' Pour les citations françaises de l'*Oratio*, des *Conclusiones* et de l'*Apologie*, nous utilisons librement les traductions de Roland Galibois, Centre d'Etudes de la Renaissance, Université de Sherbrooke (non encore publiées).

2 Notons que la 26ième et dernière *conclusion magique* confirme, au moins implicitement, cette subordination de la magie à la cabale: 'Sicut per primis agentis influxum, si sit specialis et immediatus, fit aliquid quod non attingitur per mediacionem causarum, ita per opus cabale, si sit pura Cabala est immediata, fit aliquid, ad quod nulla Magia attingit.' Giovanni Pico della Mirandola, *Conclusiones sive Theses DCCCC*, introduction et annotations critiques par Bohdan Kieszkowski (Genève: Droz, 1973).

3 *Concl. mag.* no. 1: 'Tota Magia, que in usu est apud modernos, et quam merito exterminat ecclesia, nullam habet firmitatem, nullum fundamentum, nullam veritatem, quia pendet ex manu hostium prime veritatis, potestatum harum tenebrarum, que tenebras falsitatis, male dispositis intellectibus obfundunt.'

4 *Concl. mag.* no 2: 'Magia naturalis licita est, et non prohibita, et de huius scientie universalibus theoricis fundamentis pono infrascriptas conclusiones secundum propriam opinionem.'

5 Giovanni Pico della Mirandola, *De hominis dignitate, Heptaplus, De ente et uno*, a cura di Eugenio Garin (Firenze: Vallecchi, 1942) p. 148: '[Magia naturalis] nihil aliud est, cum bene exploratur, quam naturalis philosophiae absoluta consummatio.'

6 *Concl. mag.* no. 3: 'Magia est pars practica scientie naturalis'; *Concl. mag.* no. 4: 'Ex ista conclusione et conclusione paradoxa dogmatizante XLVI sequitur, quod magia sit nobilissima pars scientie naturalis.'

7 *Apologie*, fol. 49: '...neque in presenti conclusione loquor de certitudine scientie habite ex revelatione ... sed de certitudine scientie invente vel acquisite per demonstrationem.'

8 *Apologie*, fol. 50: 'magia ... presupponit exactam et absolutam cognitionem omnium rerum naturalium.'

9 *Apologie*, fol. 52: '... per istam magicam nihil operamur nisi solum actuando et uniendo virtutes naturales.'

10 *Concl. mag.* no. 5: 'Nulla est virtus in celo et in terra seminaliter et separata, quam et actuare et unire magus non possit.'

11 *Apologie*, fol. 49: '[Pars practica] scientiae naturalis quae nihil aliud docet quam facere opera mirabilia mediantibus virtutibus naturalibus per applicationem earum ad invicem et ad sua passa naturalia.'

12 *Concl. mag.* no. 13: 'Magicam operari non est aliud quam maritare mundum.'

13 *De hominis dignitate*, p. 152: 'Haec, inter sparsas Dei beneficio et inter seminatas mundo virtutes, quasi de latebris evocans in lucem, non tam facit miranda quam facienti naturae sedula famulatur. Haec universi consensum, quem significantius Graeci sumpatheia dicunt, introrsus perscrutatius rimata et mutuam cognationem [*] habens perspectam, nativas adhibens unicuique rei et suas illecebras, quae magorum iugges nominantur, in mundi recessibus, in naturae gremio, in promptuaris arcanisque Dei latitantia miracula, quasi ipsa sit artifex, promit in publicum, et sicut agricola ulmos vitibus, ita Magus terram caelo, idest inferiora superiorum dotibus virtutibusque maritat.' L'inspiration augustinienne de ce passage est évidente, comme il ressort d'une comparaison avec l'extrait du *De Trinitate* cité ci-dessous (cf. n. 28)

[*] Le texte d'Eugenio Garin porte *cognitionem*: *cognationem* semble préférable.

14 Nous citons les *Ennéades* dans la traduction d'Emile Bréhier (Paris: Les Belles Lettres, 1960).

15 Bréhier, *Notice* au troisième traité de la quatrième *Ennéade*, Vol. IV, p. 54.

16 Bréhier, *Notice*, p. 51.

17 L'influence de Plotin sur la pensée de Pic a récemment été mise en doute (cf. William G. Craven, *Giovanni Pico Della Mirandola, Symbol of His Age*, Genève: Librairie Droz, 1981, pp. 9 et sq., *passim*). Pourtant, l'arrière-plan plotinien de l'*Oratio* ne peut guère être méconnu, particulièrement en ce qui a trait à la magie, comme d'ailleurs en attestent les passages cités ici.

On se rappellera également le témoignage de Ficin lui-même qui affirme que ce fut à l'incitation de Pic, dès leur première rencontre, que lui, Ficin, entreprit la traduction des *Ennéades* (cf. Giovanni Di Napoli, *Giovanni Pico della Mirandola e la problematica dottrinale del suo tempo*. Roma, Parigi, Tournai, New York: Desclée et C., 1965, pp. 38 et sq.). Or, cette rencontre eut lieu lors du premier séjour de Pic à Florence, soit au début de 1484, deux ans avant la rédaction de l'*Oratio*. Le témoignage de Ficin montre que Pic avait reconnu très tôt l'importance première de l'oeuvre de Plotin. Ficin lui confiera d'ailleurs une ébauche de sa traduction, ce qui montre la haute estime qu'il portait à celui en qui il croyait voir un disciple. Le professeur P.O. Kristeller, que je remercie ici, me signale que le manuscrit de cette première traduction est conservé à Florence (Biblioteca Nazionale,

Conventi Soppressi, E 1, 2562) et qu'il porte des annotations marginales qui sont très probablement de la main de Pic. Ce manuscrit a été récemment étudié par A. Wolters, professeur au Redeemer College de Hamilton.

On sait également que Pic avait entrepris l'étude du grec dès 1482, sous la direction d'Aldo Manuzio et de Manuele Adramitteno. Ses lettres xxxiii et xxxii qui, selon Eugenio Garin, datent de l'hiver 1482-3 (*La cultura filosofica del Rinascimento italiano*: Firenze: Sansoni, 1979, p. 256) témoignent de la satisfaction que ces études apportent à Pic.

Tout ceci confirme que Pic avait pu lire et méditer les *Ennéades* bien avant la période de la dispute romaine.

Ajoutons que dans le *Commento alla Canzone d'Amore di Girolamo Benivieni*, qui est de la méme époque que l'*Oratio*, Pic fait preuve d'une connaissance précise du néo-platonisme puisqu'il n'hésite pas à critiquer Ficin, pourtant son aîné respecté, pour le manque de rigueur avec lequel ce dernier se permet d'interpréter Plotin.

Le *Commento*, probablement achevé en octobre 1486, ne sera finalement publié qu'en 1519, mais en une version légèrement modifiée. Eugenio Garin, comparant cette édition aux premiers manuscrits, affirmait que toutes les modifications apportées dans cette première impression tendaient à supprimer 'tout ce qui dans cette oeuvre était d'orthodoxie douteuse' (cf. Garin, 1942, pp. 10-18). Or, dans les passages ainsi modifiés et que Garin apporte à l'appui de ses dires, on ne relève aucune prise de position personnelle de Pic, mais seulement de vigoureuses critiques adressées à Ficin, à qui Pic reproche de donner une interprétation des textes néo-platoniciens, par laquelle ceux-ci serait rendus plus conformes aux dogmes chrétiens.

Ainsi, dès son premier écrit philosophique, Pic se révèle beaucoup plus rigoureux et exigeant que ne l'était Ficin. Pic n'est pas prêt aux concilations faciles ou purement verbales, par lesquelles on voudrait aplanir les différences qui séparent le néo-platonisme du christianisme. En cela, Pic se montre beaucoup plus respectueux de l'intégrité des doctrines.

18 *De hominis dignitate*, p. 152: 'Plotinus . . . naturae ministrum esse et non artificem Magum demonstrat.'

19 Bréhier, *Notice*, p. 53.

20 *Concl. mag.* no. 7: 'Non potuerunt opera Cristi vel per viam magie, vel per viam Cabale fieri.'

21 *Concl. mag.* no. 8: 'Miracula Cristi non racione rei facte, sed racione modi faciendi suae divinitatis argumentum certissimum sunt.'

22 *Concl. mag.* no. 9: 'Nulla est scientia, que nos magis certificet de divinitate Cristi, quam magia et cabala.'

La Commission d'enquête instituée par Innocent VIII censurera cette conclusion comme pouvant 'trahi ad malum sensum'. Les explications que Pic tentera d'en donner seront assez ambigues et le conduiront finalement à une rétraction voilée, puisqu'en son *Apologie* il lui substituera les deux conclusions suivantes:

'Miracula Cristi, quantum ad rem factam, sunt argumentum quod fuerunt facta in virtute divina'

'Miracula Cristi, quantum ad modum faciendi, sunt argumentum quod ipse Cristus faciens virtutem divinam a se habebat, non aliunde.'

23 *De Trinitate* L. III c. 8 n. 13: 'Invisibilium enim seminum creator, ipse creator est omnium rerum' (Migne, *Patrologie latine*, t. 42, c. 876).

24 *De Genesi ad litteram*, L. IX c. 17 n. 31: 'Neque enim potentia temeraria, sed sapientiae virtute omnipotens est; et hoc de unaquaque re in tempore suo facit quod ante in ea fecit ut possit' (*PL*, t. 34, c. 406).

25 Dom Paul De Vooght, O.S.B.: 'La notion philosophique du miracle chez Saint Augustin' dans *Recherches de théologie ancienne et médiévale* (Louvain: Mont-César, 1938), t. X, pp. 317-43. Venant après plusieurs autres dont elle fait la synthèse et la critique, cette étude très nuancée montre la genèse de la conception augustinienne du miracle, tout en soulignant sa fondamentale unité.

26 *De Trinitate*, L. III c. 8 n. 13: 'Omnium quippe rerum quae corporaliter visibiliterque nascuntur, occulta quaedam semina in istis corporeis mundi hujus elementis latent. Alia sunt enim haec jam conspicua oculis nostris ex fructibus et animalibus, alia vero occulta istorum seminum semina' (*PL*, t. 42, c. 875).

27 De Vooght, p. 342.

28 *De Trinitate*, L. III c. 9 n. 16: 'Adhibere autem forinsecus accedentes causas, quae tametsi non sunt naturales, tamen secundum naturam adhibentur, ut ea quae secreto naturae sinu abdita continentur, erumpant et foris creentur ... non solum mali angeli sed etiam mali homines possunt ...' (*PL*, t. 42, c. 878). Le double sens de *Nature* apparaît ici avec clarté.

29 *De Trinitate*, L. III c. 9 n. 17: '... mali angeli pro subtilitate sui sensus in occultioribus elementorum seminibus norunt unde ranae serpentesque nascantur, et haec per certas et notas temperationum opportunitates occultis motibus adhibendo faciunt creari ...' (*PL*, t. 42, c. 878).

30 *In Hept.* L. II, c. 21 'Deus vero solus verus creator est, qui causas ipsas et rationes seminarias rebus inseruit.'

31 Ainsi: '*De Civitate Dei* VII, 35; VIII, 19.

32 Voir principalement le troisième livre des *Disputationes*. Au sujet de R. Grosseteste: A.C. Crombie, *Robert Grosseteste and the Origin of Experimental Science* (Oxford: Clarendon Press, 1953) pp. 104-5, 128-34.

33 Giovanni Pico della Mirandola, *Disputationes adversus astrologiam divinatricem*, a cura di Eugenio Garin (Firenze: Vallecchi, 1946-52) *Disp.* L. I. (vol. I, pp. 84-8): 'Nam interdicere illos astrologiam non quadamtenus, sed omnino omnem prosequi, abominari, palam est ... et, cum doctores Ecclesiae utrumque pariter refellant, quomodo dici potest id eos tantum non probare quod libertatem tollet arbitrii, aut fati necessitatem inducat?'

34 *Disp.* L. XII, c. vii (vol. II, pp. 530-2): '... cum aliquot post annos honestare [astrologiam] Rogerius Bacchon et alii quadam conarentur, restiterunt eis viri doctissimi Guilelmus Alvernius episcopus Parisiensis, et post eum Nicolaus Oresmus mathematicus excellens, et Henricus ex Assia, et Joannes Caton, et Brenlanlius Britannus astrologiam, non solum qua parte laedit religionem, sed plane totam, et vanam falsamque detestantes.'

35 *Disp.* L. II, c. v (vol. I, p. 134): 'De superstitionibus nulla est controversia prodire ab astronomia omnes, et eas quasi alumnas ab illa contineri confirmat Varro ... Magi ita huius artis usum necessarium putant, ut magiae clavem astrologiam appellent ... Sed has fatuitates particulatim prosequemur cum, post eversam dominam ac reginam, reliquam omnem supertitionum turbam in cursu proteremus.'

36 *Disp.* L. IV c. xiv (vol. I, p. 508): 'Est enim ... ordo rerum a Deo pro naturali cursu institutarum ita suis finibus inclusus seiunctusque ab his rebus quae divina virtute et voluntate fiunt praeter naturam, ut haec omnia si tollantur, nihil sit in rerum natura quod desit, nihil quod supersit.'

37 *Disp.* L. IV, titre du c. xiv (vol.I, p. 506): 'Divina miracula a caelo nec fieri nec significari, sed miracula miraculis, sicut naturalia naturalibus, indicari.'

38 *Disp.* L. IV, c. xiv, (vol. I, pp. 508-10) 'Est autem caelum et quaecumque in caelo communi cursu eveniunt ex his rebus que sunt secundum naturam. Quare si quid siderum motus vel dispositio, quae ex naturali eorum conditione illis

debetur, futurum significant, debet haec significantia et indicatio inter res naturales haberi et numerari; quod si aliqua ex his signis portendere ea dicamus
quae fiunt supra naturam, sequetur illud absurdum, et, si relinquat Deus
naturam suis conditionibus, nec faciat aliquid super eam, natura iam ipsa falsa et
mendax inveniatur, in qua etiam Deus aliquid frustra superfluoque instituerit
. . . Non igitur si ab aevo miraculum aliquod facere Deux disposuit, miraculi eius
indicia naturalibus rebus inseruit, ita ut ad naturae ipsarum rationem significatio
haec pertineret, sed naturalia quidem signis naturalibus, miraculis anteceden-
tibus miracula voluit significare.'

39 On notera cependant qu'Augustin précise que l'obscurcissement du ciel à la mort
du Christ n'a pu être dû à une cause naturelle telle qu'une éclipse du soleil,
puisque la Pâque juive a lieu peu après la pleine lune (cf. *De Civ. Dei*, III, 15). Il
est étonnant que Pic n'ait pas cité cet argument.

40 *Disp*. L. IV, c. xiv (vol. I, p. 506): 'Sic et illa sub Noe totius orbis eluvionem . . . in
qua re procul dubio insanire magis videntur quam qui haec potius fuisse aliquando non concedunt, qui et fuisse credit qualia narrantur, et a naturalibus
tamen causis effecta, cum nulla maior possit insania, quam ut factum aliquid
supra naturam, naturae viribus putes.'

41 *Disp*. L. II, c. x (vol. I, p. 172): 'Porro hoc aliud non est quam . . . multa ten-
tando incidere imprudenter in veritatem. Hoc igitur idem etiam poterit occulta et
latens daemonis inspiratio . . . Sed neque hoc solum daemones posse divina
potestas et sapientia sinit, sed illud etiam ut, quod falso prius fuerat praedictum,
opere implentes ipsi verum efficiant.'

Laura Westra

Love and Beauty in Ficino and Plotinus.

The soul's relation to God and the mode of its ascent to Him are at the core of Ficino's thought; the same two themes are at the heart of Plotinus' philosophy. Does that mean that the usual connection must be made between the two thinkers and that the thought of one must be seen as no more than an extension of that of the other? Must one agree with the unidentified author of a 'Vita di Marsilio Ficino' who claimed that the Renaissance philosopher is so much in tune with Plotinus that when he cites arguments or explicates them 'non pare che si scorga differenza molta fra l'autore stesso et il commentatore' ('there appears to be no notable difference between the author himself and the commentator')?[1] This certainly represents a respectable interpretation of Ficino's thought, but this paper will argue that, just as one cannot simply agree with the anonymous writer when he states, once again, that Ficino translates Plotinus 'che si può dire sia l'anima di Platone' ('who can be called the soul of Plato'),[2] so it is also necessary to distinguish rather sharply between Ficino and Plotinus.[3] In fact, the more Platonic Ficino shows himself to be, the less Plotinian he turns out to be. Furthermore, one must take into account the undeniable religious thrust that impels him, as well as the clear influence of another Platonic thinker, namely Avicenna. Giuseppe Saitta, among others, notes Ficino's high opinion of Avicenna, 'che egli ritiene Theologorum Arabum principem' ('whom he deems the prince of Arab theologians').[4] This paper will start by discussing the two themes of love and beauty and their function and meaning within Ficino's thought in connection with the topic of the soul's ascent. Then, the same themes will be examined in the doctrine of Plotinus in order to pinpoint some of the significant differences between the two. Finally, some consideration will be given to certain aspects of Avicenna's thought on the question of the soul's ascent to God, since Avicenna's influence on Ficino does not appear as well documented by commentators as, say, that of Plotinus.

We need to consider the reason for the ascent to divine beauty in Ficino, and its mode. In a well-known passage, Ficino says:

the soul, as our Plato would have it, can fly back to the heavenly father and fatherland on only two wings, that is intellect and will . . .[5]

This passage tends to contradict the very thesis this papers proposes, since it is more Plotinian than Platonic, as Plato — to my knowledge — never speaks of flying or returning to either a heavenly father or fatherland. Let us recall, for instance, *Enneads* 1.6.8, 'On Beauty':

Let us flee then to the beloved Fatherland: this is the soundest counsel. . . . The fatherland to us is There whence we have come, and There is the Father.[6]

When one turns instead to a consideration of the 'two wings,' one is no longer within Platonic orthodoxy of the Plotinian kind. For Ficino, the 'two wings' manifest the reconciliation of philosophy and religion; that is, one needs both philosophers to stimulate the intellect for man's flight towards the Father and Country, and priests to direct his will. The two, intellect and will, interact with each other to create the best possible conditions for the flight: the intellect illuminates the will, the will embraces the intellect.[7] Thus, while the intellective faculties provide the light to direct man upwards by manifesting to the will its true aim and destination, the will on the other hand captures and holds the intellect, and becomes almost one with it in the thrust towards God. The twin aspects of the upward flight will be elaborated upon below and in that discussion the vast difference between Plotinus and Ficino will be revealed.

If one considers Plato's thought instead, one must admit that 'knowing the good' sufficed him.[8] No separate discussion or treatise on the will was required; the soul's understanding of itself and of its position and condition was sufficient to start its journey. It is on this point, then, that the theory of Ficino's Platonism weakens as his thought appears, *prima facie* at least, to be much closer to that of Plotinus, who devotes an entire treatise to 'Freewill and the Will of the One' (*Enneads* 6.7) and who describes the highest principle, the One, as possessed of a predominant aspect, that of will. The latter is totally lacking from Plato's form of the good, instead, which is eternal, but also immutable. In fact, the upper soul's return there, for Plotinus, is characterized by a progressive coming to be as much as possible like the One. Thus man's own individual freedom is yet another aspect of his kinship to the Father. Freedom, in this connection, is even more important than man's very intellective capacity which, after all, makes him only like Nous rather than like the One. The One, in turn, is more than just goodness or intellection: He is freedom itself. This aspect of Plotinian thought was perhaps adopted by Ficino because it was easier to reconcile with the Christian standpoint, and thus capable of constituting the foundation of that reconciliation between religion and philosophy which can be considered Ficino's highest priority.

The reason Ficino gives for the inception of the ascent is the first point of contrast with Plotinus. Clearly the soul itself, in line with the Christian approach which governs Ficino, is a whole entity, rather than a fraction or small part of a larger one (as Plotinus' upper soul is). Aside from its natural inclination, what impels it is unrest and an all-pervasive grief. As Kristeller explains,

Thus the grief of which we are speaking is no transitory state of mind but a basic sentiment which accompanies man in his actual living. . . . This basic sentiment of grief is not merely an expression of man's unworthiness and humiliation, but he who consciously feels it raises himself on this very account from mere vulgar existence to a higher and truer degree of life.[9]

Plotinus, on the other hand, has nothing but scorn for those who would see human embodiment as unworthiness or evil. In the treatise dedicated to a discussion of this question (*Enneads* 2.9: 'Against the Gnostics'), Plotinus manifests the true coherence of his metaphysical position in regard to man, to his soul's upper part, and to his very existence here and now as well. Man emanates from the Primals, and there can be neither ugliness nor evil in the Source. How, then, can ugliness or evil be present in those effects which are nothing other than the fulfillment, albeit copied and attenuated, of the Beauty-full master plan of the Universe?[10] The event of man's embodiment is not a descent into filth and evil; it is a testing time for souls who must recognize and remember — recognize the kinship with the copied beauty they find themselves surrounded by, and remember their Fatherland and the true Beauty there.

Thus Ficino's 'nostalgia for the celestial Fatherland'[11] is indeed an echo of Plotinus, but in his letter to Giovanni Cavalcanti on Plato's *Theaetetus* Ficino's reference to 'the pestilence of the body' ('a corporis peste') is definitely and strictly Platonic.[12] An effect of the One, no matter how far removed and meant to fulfill the Universal Plan, could never even be thought of as pestilence in itself. It is precisely because of the difference between Plato and Plotinus, mentioned at the beginning of this study, that this is so. For Plotinus, evil requires the exercise of man's freedom, in the sense of free-will; the existence of good, instead, arises from freedom understood in its true Plotinian sense of understanding one's true kinship and direction towards the One, alone. For Plato evil exists in matter itself rather than in the soul's misguided attitude towards it (as is the case for Plotinus).[13] The central notion of freedom was not part of his scenario.

Even though both Plotinus and Ficino have a somewhat similar understanding of the upward journey's import and goal and of its inception, vast differences exist between the doctrines of the two thinkers. One can expand further on this by comparing the two on the cardinally important notion of beauty. For Ficino beauty and love are intimately connected; to cite Kristeller once again,

The essence of beauty . . . consists for Ficino, according to the ancient doctrine, in proportion — that is, in the symmetric and pleasant relationship of individual parts.[14]

However, human beauty does not seem to have so important a place or function in the ascent as it did for Plotinus. In the *Theologiae Platonicae* Ficino describes the functioning of the soul which proves its immortal status through its powers of understanding. Ficino speaks of Socrates' thoughts: Socrates, knowing Plato, starts to perceive beauty, goodness, friendship, 'ideas' which he possesses intuitively already, and which therefore enable him to imagine them as well as to perceive them in reality. These are the 'conceptus phantasiae' and are more than universals, since the soul can assess and discern similarities as well as differences in these qualities, and this further implies the ability to know particulars as well as universals. At the same time, the universal character of beauty, goodness, and friendship must also be intuited in its eternal, matter-free reality.[15]

A brief physical description of Socrates by Plato is the only instance admitting a physical component to the beauty Ficino appeals to; indeed, the steady coupling of beauty with goodness and friendship would easily lend itself to a purely spiritual interpretation of the term. Elsewhere, truth is depicted as food that nourishes the soul, its most proper nourishment; is is moral virtue, intellection, and reflection which lead to 'a certain spiritual equality and harmony.'[16] Beauty *per se* is no longer mentioned in this regard.

A totally different approach characterized Plotinus' treatise 'On Beauty' (*Enneads* 1.6). The stage is already set in *Enneads* 1.3, 'On Dialectic,' which in fact offers the key to the cardinal difference between Plotinus and Ficino on the question of love. For Plotinus, a musician will accustom himself to the beauties of the senses; he is capable of being moved and excited by a particular beauty, 'but not quite capable of being moved by absolute beauty.'[17] Rather, it is the lover (ch. 2) who can go a step further and understand that beauty, since it does not originate in bodies, can also be discerned in ways of life and laws, in arts and sciences and virtues. This is very different from Ficino's view of beauty's role and function; according to Plotinus, it is not beauty *accompanied by* goodness and virtue, such as friendship, rather, it is beauty *in* goodness and virtues and laws that one needs. The best man, the philosopher, will be 'winged' by nature, thus capable of following Beauty where it leads.

Clearly, there is a great difference of approach between Plotinus and Ficino, originating possibly in their different understanding of both matter and human action. To view the physical as 'copied,' but beautiful in its own way, is perfectly consistent with Plotinus' thought.[18] Man must start from and within his embodied state, which is neither filthy nor pestilent. As the reality of the One's willed plan of the Universe, it is man's appropriate starting place, where only the recognition and appreciation of beauties *here* (and not only the spiritual ones) can stir man and spur him onward towards beauty *there*.

Turning to a consideration of beauty in itself, one finds the serious divergence already alluded to. For Plotinus beauty cannot be that harmony of parts, that 'concordantia' that Ficino espouses. If the progressive ascent is nothing but progressive uni-fication, man must be able to perceive beauty in his ascent, and especially man must be certain to find it there, in the Father and in the Fatherland to which he aspires. However, there are no parts in the One, no diversity; thus, either one abandons the Platonic concept of harmony as beauty, or one is forced to conclude that there can be no beauty in Absolute Unity. Symmetry necessarily implies duality. Ficino explicitly states in his commentary on Plato's *Symposium*:

Those senses perceive smells, tastes, heat, cold, softness and hardness and things like these. But none of those is human beauty since they are simple forms.[19]

Thus one can say without hesitation that Ficino's conception of beauty differs from that of Plotinus both in the definition of its essential nature, and in the function it plays in the ascent of the soul, although the former divergence is much clearer than the latter.

What remains to be examined is the connection between beauty and love in the thought of both philosophers. For Ficino, love or the natural desire for God appears to play the predominant role: God attracts and draws things to Himself. In man, the love of God is implanted naturally, and that is what impels him upwards; his soul loves the light which illuminates and sets him afire. Thus Ficino says:

As great is the force of love, as great its ease, as great its happiness, even greater, to speak more accurately, is the force of the beloved light. For by loving the light the mind does not so much inflame and transport itself as it is inflamed and transported and shines forth by reason of the light charmingly drawing it, strongly striking it, and interiorly penetrating it.[20]

It is important to understand that the imagery of light and fire conveys more than just love or warmth; there is within it an undeniable component of intellectual illumination. As Collins, for one, states, 'Ficino himself, not Aquinas, attributes to this desire a guiding function.'[21] Desire, then, and love remain the predominant aspects of Ficino's philosophy of the ascent. Aquinas is introduced since his understanding of the notion of 'inclinatio' appears to have inspired Ficino far more than the concept of the Plotinian upper soul. For Ficino, God's goodness itself is that which attracts the heart and the mind. Collins makes much of the Aquinas connection, and cites many parallel passages from Ficino and Aquinas to lend proof of the great respect Ficino professed for the thinking of St. Thomas. Once again, however, there is a difference caused by Ficino's overriding Platonism, not to be found in the main thrust of Aquinas' thought. For instance, 'inclinatio' in Aquinas is a pervading drive of the soul, not a source of increased direct enlightment or understanding. Kristeller captures the heart of the matter when he points to Platonism as the strongest influence on Ficino, and specifically 'that Christian Platonism which replaces Plato's intelligible reality with the concept of God and was first stated in this form by St. Augustine.'[22] For Plotinus too, as for Ficino, 'the concepts of the soul and of God' (in Plotinus' case the second *terminus* would be the One, instead) must be viewed as the 'point[s] of orientation' when attempting to understand his metaphysics.[23] However, their respective conceptions, and especially the essence of the relation between the two terms, are so different as to be more misleading than helpful as a tool of exegesis.

It is extremely illuminating to examine Saitta's treatment of Ficino's theory of love. Saitta contends that 'la teoria dell'amore dovrebbe rappresentare il mondo dell'oggettività,' which contrasts sharply with the 'soggettività del conoscere.'[24] The Ficinian vision, in which intellection and will aim at the same thing, albeit in different manners, does not appear to be too different from the Plotinian scheme until one realizes the principal difference Saitta alludes to: the intellective faculty deals with the subjective and tranforms all into its own nature ('omnia in suam transferre naturam'), whereas the will driven by love moves the soul and body to action in order that they may achieve the object of its desire ('ad res desideratas accedant').[25] The parallel Ficino draws is between the body and the soul: just as the body takes in all kinds of diverse food and converts it into its own substance ('cibos vel diversissimos in suam vertit substantiam'), so too the soul nourishes itself and grows through truth:

And so the mind becomes any true thing when it understands the things themselves by converting itself into their perpetual reasons.[26]

These are indeed the two wings through which man can fly to God. In essence,

Il Ficino . . . non è un intellettualista: egli tende al volontarismo. Ma ad un volontarismo tutto suo che ha soltanto analogie apparenti con quello agostiniano e scolastico.
('Ficino . . . is not an intellectualist: he tends to voluntarism. To a voluntarism, however, which is all his own, and whose analogies with Augustinian or Scholastic voluntarism only appear to be so.')[27]

One can easily confirm Saitta's insight with a brief glance at the text, slightly below the passage cited above:

But it lies between the intellect and the will: for each becomes indeed all things — the intellect all true things, the will all good things; but the intellect is united to things by transferring them into itself, whereas the will is united to them by transferring itself into them.[28]

Ficino explains that the intellect understands according to its mode of being, whereas the will does not return into itself in a reflective, immanent movement, but rather moves body and soul towards those things which they desire, according to their mode of being.[29] Thus the movement in the will is an outward one, while that of the intellect is essentially an inward one. Ficino concludes:

Let us conclude, therefore, that our soul, buoyed up on will and intellect as on those two Platonic wings I have spoken of, flies to God on them because on them it flies to all things. Through the first (the intellect) it applies all things to itself, whereas through the second (the will) it applies itself to all things.[30]

The parallel, yet in a sense contrasting voyage could not be defined more explicitly. This contrast is not to be found in Plotinus, and the reason is clear. Ficino affirms that even in God intellect and will are not one and the same thing, whereas Plotinus is adamant in claiming identity for will, being, and so on, in the One. Intellection, on the other hand, is primarily the attribute of Nous. The emphasis on will is Plotinian, but the division between intellect and will is not. One can now see a possible reason for the lack of emphasis on beauty *per se* in Ficino. For Plotinus the journey starts with the perception and recognition of objective beauty in actual things, and the intellectual thrust and kinship lead man onward to the appreciation of beauty in science and action — an intellectual rather than an emotion experience, though desire does have a place in the ascent. For Ficino, on the other hand, man achieves more by loving God than by striving for understanding or for intellectual satisfaction:

By loving God not only do we obtain a greater delight than by rational inquiry, but we also are made better. It befits the lover to enjoy the loved thing and to rejoice, for this is the end of love, whereas the inquirer seeks to see. Therefore joy surpasses vision in the one who is blessed.[31]

Love somehow contains knowing, but the converse does not hold true and the imaginative component of the intellect does not hold the same concrete, essential objective qualities as the will.

Not only does Ficino's thought show a marked difference from Plotinus' in this regard, but his Platonism also founders on the same rock. Contemplation entails knowing or intellection, for both; this was true perhaps for Plato even more than for Plotinus but, as Saitta states, 'per il Ficino l'amore è il culmine della spiritualità, anzi tutta quanta la realtà ne è pervasa radicalmente.'[32] It would be both anachronistic and essentially incorrect to translate 'theoria' as 'love.' For Ficino love, not Intelligible Reality, stirs the world, dispels chaos, imposes form on unformed matter, and perfects all that is.[33] Saitta envisions a 'joining' of Platonism and Neoplatonism in Ficino's understanding of 'love as the desire for beauty,'[34] but several differences have already been noted. The impossibility of beauty-in-a-body is a major difference, and so is the emphasis on the good, to which the appetite mainly aims. For Ficino, beauty is the middle term in God between goodness and justice, but it is love that attracts and returns all that is to God — a religious approach which is very close to a pantheistic conception of the universe, not to be found in either Plato or Plotinus.[35]

Finally, a great difference of emphasis can be detected between the thought of Plotinus and that of Ficino, once again on the question of the role of love. In *Enneads* 1.3 'On Dialectic,' the progression is clear: from the lowest musician, to the lover, and then to the highest, the philosopher. Love therefore is higher on the scale than sense harmony, but lower than philosophy. Love is not that 'culmination of spirituality,' previously alluded to by Saitta, and which is clear in Ficino's own work: it is better, but not best. If anything is needed to emphasize the gulf which often separates the two thinkers, surely this point cements the thesis this article presents: Ficino does indeed draw on Plotinus, but, upon careful examination, more differences than similarities come to light and the expected doctrinal correspondence vanishes.

The format of this paper does not permit an in-depth analysis of the many interwoven strands linking the thought of Ficino with that of Plotinus; therefore it has focussed on several possible points for further study and investigation. One of these concerns two main points of contact between Ficino's thought and Avicenna's Platonism. The first, and perhaps most significant one, occurs precisely within the soul's ascent, with the reason for the journey and its *terminus*. Avicenna's conception of the Agent Intellect is such that it parallels the God of the Judaeo-Christian tradition, since it appears to interact with the soul somewhat in the manner of the Christian notion of Grace, in order to lead the substantial soul to its final destination. To be sure, this could be a convincing interpretation of Avicenna, and some texts and commentators appear to suggest it; however, one must not press the parallel too closely. At any rate, the role of the Agent Intellect appears to be perhaps the most significant difference among the many one can detect between Avicenna's thought on the question of the self and its destiny, and Plotinus' thinking on the subject and, on the other hand, his (Plotinus') influence on Ficino. The ascent of the soul in Avicenna is in some ways similar to that in Plotinus, at least *prima facie*. Henry Corbin describes the soul's 'returning to its origin' as 'the most characteristic mental operation of all our [Islamic] Spiritualist, Neoplatonists' and he terms it '*Ta'wīl* or spiritual exegesis.'[36] Within such a return, the soul evolves, or rather lays itself out, as a process of return:

Ta'wīl is, etymologically and inversely, to cause to return, to lead back, to restore to one's origin and to the place where one comes from.[37]

The precise echoes of Plotinus' thinking can be readily heard here. The cardinal difference, however, is to be found in the fact that the Agent Intellect who, in the Avicennian *Recitals*, appears at a certain point of the soul's ascent and invites the soul to proceed further and higher in its company to a higher and more perfect state:

The appearance or the mental visualization of the Angel who is the Active Intelligence, simultaneously marks the *terminus* of an evolution within the soul, which has had to bring this aptitude to progressive flowering in itself, and a *point of departure*, the origin of an angelic pedagogy.[38] [my italics]

A certain duality is thus introduced at this stage, when the soul must learn to see itself 'in relation with the Angel.'[39] This helpful guide, or leader, is totally lacking in the thinking of Plotinus; in his case, there appears to be no need of anyone else. Even most aspects of one's own soul are to be discarded on the way. The only aid, if it can be termed so, is needed only towards the end of the ascent: the soul remains poised, waiting, with no further effort necessary, or even will to impel it forward. At the end, for Plotinus

we must withdraw from all extern, pointed wholly inwards; no leaning to the outer; the total of things ignored, first in their relation to us, and later in the very idea; the self put out of mind in the Contemplation of the Supreme'[40]

What we see in the Plotinian ascent to man's true self is a progressive shedding of the multiplicity or duality in any form, in a sustained striving to become more and more like that which man is aiming for: the One. Thus, as all duality is absent from Him, so too the presence of the Active Intellect or Angel posits a duality which is equally unthinkable for the soul within Plotinus' scheme. The idea of an Angel, which appears in the *Visionary Recitals*, rather than in the philosophical treatises, could possibly be considered a metaphor in Avicenna, but the external influence of the Active Intellect is unavoidable for all, with the sole exception of the rare prophets, perhaps, of whom more below. What remains, however, as a strong Plotinian point, is the understanding of the There as our country or home, and of the nature and dependency of the soul / self, understood in relation to that Higher Reality. The echoes and similarities between the thought of Avicenna and Ficino are certainly clear. Yet Saitta, who repeatedly attests to the closeness and 'sympathy' of Ficino for Avicenna, sees their basic differences on the question of love as a major Ficinian innovation, which creates a substantial break not only with the Platonism and Neoplatonism of antiquity, but also with the 'more recent one of Avicenna, Alfarabi, and

Algazali.'[41] Saitta sees Ficino's cosmogony as Christian and modern, in clear contrast with that of previous thinkers.

Finally, the role of the Agent Intellect vis-à-vis the human soul in Avicenna's philosophy is somewhat in line with some of Ficino's pronouncements. For instance, in the *Theologiae Platonicae* Ficino speaks of a 'divine ray,' containing all forms and passing 'from God in different degrees to the angelic and human intelligences to which it gives the force of knowledge.'[42] Clearly, the hierarchy of ideas, present in Plotinus, has subtly changed and is now a hierarchy of angelic intelligences. Keeping in mind the function of the Agent Intellect and its direct action on some individuals who, for Avicenna, acquired the gift of prophecy without any special effort on their part, one can see a similarity with Ficino's thought, where an almost Augustinian illumination from above appears to play a crucial role and, by the same token then, manifests a comparable departure from Plotinus. Avicenna says:

We say that the theoretical faculty in man also comes into actuality from potentiality, through the illumination of a substance whose nature it is to produce light.[43]

The 'direct ray' as well as the 'light' metaphor in general tend to remind one more of the Christian Platonism of Augustine than of the pagan Neoplatonism of Plotinus.

In conclusion, while the soul's ascent appears to be an appropriate part of Ficino's thought to search for Plotinian connections, it turns out that more often than not closer attention reveals serious divergences. Ficino's Neoplatonism is far closer to the Christian Platonism one could expect from a devout man of his time. The language he uses may indeed very often be that of Plotinus, but the depth of meaning is not. Love and beauty combine in a unique manner in his thought, and the upward flight leads, unmistakeably, to the Christian God. Therefore, the monotheistic Platonism of Avicenna appears to be closer to the spirit of Ficino's thought (albeit with the significant difference discussed above), than the pagan ascent that Plotinus outlines in the *Enneads*.

Clemson University, S.C.

Notes

1 Raymond Marcel, *Marsile Ficin* (Paris: Les Belles Lettres, 1958), appendix II, p. 707.
2 Marcel, p. 707.

3 Giuseppe Saitta, *Marsilio Ficino e la filosofia dell'umanesimo*. Studi filosofici, 20 (Florence: Le Monnier, 1943), p. 45. At the start of ch. 3, Saitta states that it is 'a common prejudice that the philosophy of Marsilio Ficino is nothing but a simple repetition of Neoplatonism' ('un pregiudizio assai diffuso che la filosofia di Marsilio Ficino non sia altro che una semplice riproduzione del neoplatonismo') (p. 45). A closer assessment reveals it as a synthesis of mediaeval Platonism instead.

4 Saitta, p. 68.

5 All English translations of Ficino are my own. 'Nam cum animus (ut Platoni nostro placet) duabus tantum aliis, id est, intellectu, et voluntate possit ad coelestem patrem et patriam revolare' Marsilio Ficino, *De Christiana Religione*, proemium; in Marsilio Ficino, *Opera Omnia*, 1st ed., 2 vols. numbered consecutively (Basel: Henricus Petri, 1561), p. 1.

6 Plotinus, *Enneads*, trans. Stephen McKenna (London: Oxford University Press, 1930), p. 63.

7 Cf. *In Philebum Platonis Commentarium, sive De Summo Bono*, c. 37; in *Opera omnia*, pp. 1250-52.

8 This point in Plato's doctrine is so well known as to need no defence here.

9 Paul Oskar Kristeller, *The Philosophy of Marsilio Ficino*, trans. V. Conant (New York: Columbia University Press, 1943), p. 208.

10 For a detailed discussion of this point in Plotinus, see Laura Westra, 'The Role of Beauty in Plotinus' Doctrine of Nature' to be published in *Neoplatonic Studies*, ed. R.B. Harris (S.U.N.Y. Press).

11 '. . . coelestis patriae desiderio . . .', *Theologiae Platonicae*, lib. 16, c. 7; in *Opera Omnia*, p. 383; quoted by Kristeller, p. 211.

12 '. . . a corporis peste . . .', *Epistolae*, lib. 1; in *Opera Omnia*, p. 633; quoted by Kristeller, p. 215; Cf. Plato, *Theaetetus*, 176a ff.

13 See John Rist, *Human Value: A Study of Ancient Philosophical Ethics* (Leiden: E.J. Brill, 1982), p. 103, and in the chapter entitled 'Plotinus,' pp. 99-104.

14 Kristeller, p. 305.

15 See *Theologiae Platonicae*, lib. 8, c. 1; in *Opera Omnia*, p. 182.

16 'Anima non quantitate crescit, sed spiritali quadam aequalitate et consonantia proficit.' *Theologiae Platonicae*, lib. 8, c. 2; in *Opera Omnia*, p. 186. On this see Marcel, p. 292.

17 Plotinus, *Enneads* 1.3. Trans. A.H. Armstrong, The Loeb Classical Library, 6 vols. (London: Harvard University Press, 1966), I, 155.

18 See Westra, 'Role of Beauty,' cit. supra.

19 'Odores, sapores, calorem, frigus, mollitiem et duritiem, horum que similia sensus isti percipiunt. Istorum nullum humana pulchritudo est dum formae simplices sint.' *In Convivium Platonis de Amore Commentarium*, oratio 1, c. 4; in *Opera Omnia*, p. 1322-23.

20 'Tanta uis est amoris, tanta facilitas, tanta felicitas, imo vero (ut rectius loquar) tanta uis est lucis amatae. Mens enim amando lucem non tam sese accendit et transfert, quam a luce blande alliciente, vehementer percutiente, penitus penetrante et accenditur, et transfertur, et lucet.' *Theologiae Platonicae*, lib. 18, c. 8; in *Opera Omnia*, pp. 1322-23.

21 Ardis Collins, *The Secular is Sacred* (The Hague: Martinus Nijhoff, 1974), p. 98.

22 Kristeller, p. 204.

23 Kristeller, p. 204.

24 Saitta, p. 277.

25 Ficino, *Theologiae Platonicae*, lib. 14, c. 3; in *Opera Omnia*, p. 310-11.

26 'Atque ita mens res quaelibet ut uera fit, quando res ipsas intelligit, se in earum rationes perpetuas conuertendo.' *Theologiae Platonicae*, lib. 14, 3. 3; in *Opera Omnia*, p. 310.

27 Saitta, p. 281.

28 'Sed interest inter intellectum et uoluntatem. Utraque enim fiunt quidem omnia, intellectus omnia uera, uoluntas omnia bona, sed intellectus res in seipsum transferendo illis unitur, uoluntas contra in res transferendo seipsam.' *Theologiae Platonicae*, lib. 14, c. 3; in *Opera Omnia*, p. 310.

29 Ficino, *Theologiae Platonicae, ibid*, in *Opera Omnia*, p. 311.

30 'Concludamus, animam nostram per intellectum et uoluntatem tamquam geminas illas Platonicas alas idcirco uolare ad Deum, quoniam per eas uolat ad omnia. Per primam omnia sibi applicat, per secundam se applicat omnibus.' *Theologiae Platonicae, ibid*, in *Opera Omnia*, p. 311.

31 '. . . amando Deum non solum maiorem percipimus uoluntatem quam perscrutando, uerum etiam meliores efficimur . . .Amanti conuenit ut re amata fruatur et gaudeat, is enim est finis amoris. Inquirenti autem ut uideat. Gaudium igitur in homine felice superat uisionem.' *Epistolae*, lib. 1; in *Opera Omnia*, p. 663.

32 Saitta, p. 299.

33 Ficino, *In Convivium Platonis de Amore Commentarium*, oratio 1, c. 3; 2, in *Opera Omnia*, p. 1322.

34 'Cum amorem dicimus, pulchritudinis desiderium intelligite' *ibid*, oratio 1, c. 4; in *Opera Omnia*, p. 322.

35 Saitta, p. 305.

36 Henry Corbin, *Avicenna and the Visionary Recital*, trans. W.R. Trask (London: Routledge and Kegan Paul, 1960), p. 28.

37 Corbin, p. 29.

38 Corbin, p. 67; see especially his chapter 2, section 8, pp. 77-93 'Angelic Pedagogy and Individuation.'

39 Corbin, p. 29.

40 Plotinus, *Enneads* 6.9.7, trans. Stephen McKenna, p. 621.

41 Saitta, p. 137.

42 Kristeller, p. 232-33; Cf. Ficino, *Theologiae Platonicae*, lib. 16, cc. 1 & 3; in *Opera Omnia*, pp. 370-71, 373.

43 F. Rahman, *Avicenna's Psychology* (Ibn Sina, *Ktab al-Najat*) (London: Oxford University Press, 1952), p. 68. Cf. also Laura Westra, 'Knowing the Self in Plato, Plotinus and Avicenna,' soon to be published.

Al Wolters

Ficino and Plotinus' Treatise 'On Eros'

It was Ficino who first coined the phrase 'Platonic love,'[1] and gave it the meaning which became so widely influential in early modern European literature and thought, and which continues to define the expression to the present day. Ultimately, of course, the idea which it embodies goes back to Plato, more specifically to the *Symposium*, but it would be a mistake to suppose that Ficino is simply reproducing Plato's thought as expressed in that dialogue. What he is in fact reproducing is not Plato's conception of love but the Neoplatonic interpretation of Plato's conception.

We touch here upon a major distortion which has dominated much of the history of Western thought: the confusion between Platonism and Neoplatonism. For a millenium and a half, Plato has been read through the glasses of Neoplatonism, notably those of Plotinus. It was not until the late eighteenth and early nineteenth centuries (when the word 'Neoplatonism' was first coined) that the distinction between Plato and Plotinus came into focus. It is not surprising, therefore, that Renaissance Platonists such as Ficino looked upon Plotinus as a reliable guide for the interpretation of the Platonic dialogues. In his eyes, as in Augustine's before him, Plotinus was simply Plato reincarnate.

To find the source of Ficino's notion of Platonic love, therefore, we must go back to the *Enneads* of Plotinus — specifically to *Enneads* III, 5, the treatise entitled 'On Eros.' It is in this treatise that Plotinus sets forth that reading of the *Symposium* which was to dominate ancient Neoplatonism and which was passed on to Renaissance Neoplatonism by Ficino.

This paper will outline the argument of 'On Eros,' sketch the history of Ficino's involvement with it, and note some significant features of his translation of and commentary on the treatise. In this way light may be shed on a small but significant link in the history of a very influential idea.

Enneads III, 5, which Porphyry entitled *Peri Erotos*, is a systematic discussion of the nature of *eros* or love, drawing on earlier philosophical discussions of the subject, but above all on relevant statements made by Plato (1.1-10).[2] The treatise is divided into two unequal sections, the first dealing with eros as *pathos* or affection (ch. 1), and the second with Eros as divinity (chs. 2-9). Interestingly enough, Plotinus treats affective eros, including sexual desire, as an inferior but legitimate expression of a longing for beautiful form, and defends it against those who see no good in it at all. Nevertheless, he does turn very quickly to a discussion of the higher Eros which is depicted in myths as a divine being, both as a god (*theos*) and as a semi-divine *daimon* (chs. 3-4).

Drawing together a number of apparently contradictory statements on this divine Eros in Plato, Plotinus harmonizes them by concluding that Eros is both a god and a daimon, and that he is born both *from* Aphrodite and *together with* her. Moreover, according to another passage in Plato, there are two Aphrodites, Aphrodite Pandemos and Aphrodite Urania, each of which has her own Eros. Plotinus then interprets the various figures allegorically: Aphrodite Urania represents the hypostasis of pure Soul in his own metaphysical system; Aphrodite Pandemos represents the embodied Soul. The *Eros* associated with the higher Soul is the *god* Eros, who represents the next highest hypostasis, Intellect. The Eros associated with the lower Soul, however, is the daimon Eros, who represents the impulse in embodied souls away from sensual pleasure and toward the good. Everywhere, consequently, Eros as divinity represents the desire of Soul for Intellect and the Good.

The stage is now set for an interpretation of Diotima's myth concerning the daimon Eros, the centrepiece of Plato's *Symposium*. Diotima's words are as follows:

[Eros] is a great spirit [*daimon*], Socrates, for all the spiritual [*pan to daimonion*] is between divine and mortal ... When Aphrodite was born, the gods held a feast, among them Plenty [*Poros*], the son of Neverataloss. When they had dined, Poverty [*Penia*] came in begging, as might be expected with all that good cheer, and hung about the doors. Plenty then got drunk on the nectar — for there was no wine yet — and went into Zeus's park all heavy and fell asleep. So Poverty because of her penury made a plan to have a child from Plenty, and lay by his side and conceived Love [*Eros*]. This is why Love has become a follower and servant of Aphrodite, having been begotten at her birthday party ...[3]

Plotinus devotes the last five chapters of the treatise (5-9) to his novel and ingenious interpretations of this passage.

After two preliminary sections in which he repudiates an earlier philosophical interpretation of Eros in the myth (ch. 5), and discusses the nature of daimons in general (ch. 6), Plotinus proceeds to his own exegesis of the *Symposium* myth. Penia, philosophically understood, represents *aoristia* (Indeterminateness) in Soul, that is, the absence of rational form. Poros, on the other hand, represents *logos* (Determinateness) in Soul, that is, the presence of rational form. As for the daimon Eros, it is the offspring, the mixture of these two opposing principles. It represents both the lack of rationality and the drive to overcome that lack. It 'wants' *logos* both in the sense of lacking it and desiring it. It is the insatiable craving of embodied soul to transcend itself in the pure rationality of Intellect. It is this craving which underlies the various kinds of human love (ch. 7).

These are the basic philosophical correlates of the personages in the *Symposium* myth according to Plotinus's interpretation. But he does not stop there. He also argues for the equivalence of Zeus with the hypostasis Intellect or *Nous* (ch. 8). Moreover, the central category of *logos* is represented in the myth not only by Poros, in his view, but also by the nectar of the gods and the park of Zeus. The novelty of this triple identification leads Plotinus to discuss briefly the nature of myth, which in his view always temporalizes and pluralizes the philosophical realities which it symbolizes (ch. 9). To this Plotinus adds a brief recapitulation of his interpretation of the myth, and so concludes his treatise.

It is immediately evident to the modern reader that Plotinus is reading into Plato's text his own elaborate ontology with its hierarchy of hypostases and its precisely defined categories of *aoristia* and *logos*. Though the interpretation of Plato's Eros as an insatiable craving for a higher aesthetic-intellectual fulfilment no doubt catches something of Plato's intention, it is put in a broader context and framework which is uniquely Neoplatonic. Plotinus thus fails to do justice not only to Plato's ontology, but also to the nature of his literary myths.

Yet it is basically this same Neoplatonic framework, somewhat adapted in the direction of an Augustinian Christianity, which is taken over by Ficino and which provides the context for his interpretation of love in Plato's *Symposium*. For the details of that framework and interpretation it is perhaps enough simply to refer to Kristeller's standard exposition of Ficino's thought.[4]

We turn now to a brief biographical sketch of Ficino's involvement with Plotinus's treatise 'On Eros'. It is well known that Ficino spent many years preparing his translation and commentary of the Platonic dialogues (published in 1484), and that it was only thereafter that he undertook the task of preparing a translation and commentary of Plotinus (published in 1492). Yet it would be a great mistake to suppose that his commentaries on Plato were written before acquainting himself with the works of Plotinus. The fact is that an intensive study of Plotinus accompanied, and in many cases preceded, Ficino's work on the Platonic dialogues.

We know that as early as 1460 Ficino not only had access to a Byzantine manuscript of the entire *Enneads* (the codex Laurentianus 87,3), but that he had the entire Greek text transcribed for his personal use (the codex Parisius graecus 1816).[5] The extensive marginalia of this personal copy of the Greek text have been carefully studied by Paul Henry, who concludes that different chronological stages in Ficino's handwriting — spanning several decades — can be distinguished, and that the marginal notes, conjectures, and scraps of translation reflect an intensive study of the difficult Greek text over a period of some thirty years.[6] Ficino's annotations are particularly copious for the treatise 'On Eros.'[7]

The fruit of this study is abundantly evident in Ficino's own major philosophical publications. This is particularly clear in his famous commentary on Plato's *Symposium* (published in 1469), in which the allusions to the *Enneads*, particularly to *Enneads* III, 5, are very plentiful indeed.[8] Not only is this commentary filled with allusions to the treatise, it is fair to say that it is substantially a Christianized restatement of the philosophical allegorical interpretation of the *Symposium* described above. A similar point can be made about Ficino's *magnum opus*, the *Theologia Platonica* (1474). Here again the text abounds in allusions, explicit and implicit, to the *Enneads*, notably including references to the treatise 'On Eros,'[9] It is not too much to say that Ficino's *Platonic Theology* could not have been written without his extensive familiarity with the Greek text of Plotinus.

What is true of Ficino's two major philosophical works applies also, though not as obviously, to many of his lesser writings and to his correspondence. My own impression is that modern scholarship has not begun to identify the many Plotinian tags and allusions scattered throughout Ficino's *oeuvre*.[10]

It is only against the background of these decades of familiarity with Plotinus that we can account for Ficino's prodigious achievement in translating the complete *Enneads* as rapidly and as accurately as he did. After completion of his giant Plato project in 1484, Ficino prepared a first draft of a translation of the entire Plotinian *corpus* in less than two years (1484-86), after which he revised the translation and added commentaries. The work was completed in 1490 and published in 1492.[11]

One of the remarkable things about Ficino's Plotinus translation is its accuracy. Leading authorities in the field of Plotinian studies, such as Paul Henry and Hans-Rudolf Schwyzer,[12] have remarked that Ficino maintains an extraordinary high standard of fidelity to the Greek, even in cases where modern translators have failed to capture the sense. This is particularly remarkable if one takes into account the state of

Greek studies in the fifteenth century. It is uncanny how often Ficino manages to discern the meaning of the sometimes elliptical Greek of Plotinus. This can only stem from years of intensive and patient struggling with the text, and from the profound philosophical congeniality of the fifteenth-century Florentine with the third-century Greek.

The treatise 'On Eros' offers many examples of Ficino's sense for the correct exegesis of the Greek text. I draw the following examples from the detailed exegetical work which I did in preparing my commentary on the treatise,[13] and in which I regularly compare Ficino's translation with the modern versions of McKenna, Armstrong, Harder, Cilento, and Bréhier. A good example of Ficino's interpretative genius occurs at III, 5, 2.7 where the Greek text is unintelligible. Literally translated, the Greek reads 'in which on Aphrodite's birthday from Poverty and Plenty'. Ficino correctly identifies this as a textually corrupt allusion to the *Symposium* myth, and translates 'ubi scribitur in Veneris natalibus amorem ex indigentia copiaque progenitum',[14] that is, 'in which *it is written that Eros was born* on Aphrodite's birthday from Poverty and Plenty.' In thus supplying a missing line Ficino anticipates modern editors of the Greek text, who all assume a lacuna which is to be filled in the way indicated by Ficino. There are other examples of tacit text-critical emendations in Ficino which later editors have been correct to follow, such as the insertion of a negative at 1.56; the change of *autē* to *hautē* at 3.30; the reading of *ho* as the relative pronoun, rather than the article. In other places Ficino impresses us with his ability to render correctly the elusive Greek particles. In the following instances he is correct where modern translations are often incorrect: 1.30 *alla gar* , 'at enim'; 1.61 *kai ouk*, 'neque tamen'; 6.8 *alla* (in apodosis), 'tamen'; 9.26 *hopou kai*, 'quandoquidem'; 9.50 *hoti kai* 'quoniam'. What is especially striking is cases where Ficino correctly interprets rare words or technical terms, such as *systoichia* at 1.22 ('ordo'), or catches grammatical subtleties such as the understood *tis* at 7.57 ('quis'), or lets the context guide him to the correct sense of a common word as 2.10 *ho logos* ('disputatio praesens').

Ficino's greatest strength, however, lies in his ability to follow Plotinus's argument; he has a rare knack for discerning the philosophical point that is being made. Even when he misconstrues the Greek, he still often captures the philosopher's line of thought, and is quite prepared to add a word or two in order to make this clear to the reader. One finds an example of this at 1.38, where the phrase *hē de pros mixin ekptōsis hamartia*, taken by itself, could be translated to mean simply 'but it is error to fall away into sexual intercourse' (so Armstrong). Given the argument of the context, however, which defends the relative legitimacy of heterosexual desire, such a translation is misleading.

Ficino translates boldly and correctly: 'lapsus vero *intemperantium* [my italics] in veneream mistionem est peccatum.'

It would be tedious to multiply examples of this kind of correct philosophical instinct in Ficino's translation of *Enneads* III, 5. For those who have sufficient Greek, philosophy and leisure, I take the liberty of referring to my recently published commentary, where many further examples are found. A particularly striking example is found in my review of the translations of III, 5.9.53-55, where it appears that none of the translators of Plotinus have correctly understood the Greek text, with the sole exception of Ficino.[15]

Before taking leave of Ficino's translation of *Enneads* III, 5, one should note that there are two versions of it extant. Not only is there the published version of 1492, but one can now also examine the unrevised first draft of the translation made in 1484-86. As I have tried to show in my paper 'The First Draft of Ficino's Translation of Plotinus', this original version can be identified with the manuscript Conv. Soppr. E.1. 2562 of the Biblioteca Nazionale Centrale of Florence.[16] It is possible, therefore, to identify precisely the revisions which Ficino made in preparing his final text. A few examples of such revisions are: at 1.17 'cognationis inrationalem perceptionem' is changed to 'et quandam sine rationis actu cognationis perceptionem'; at 1.30 the spelling of 'venereum' is corrected to 'Veneream'; at 1.47 'contentus' is expanded to 'sufficiens et contentus'; at 2.5 'indagandam' is changed to 'attingendam'; at 2.45 'fruitur' is amended to 'velut fructu vescitur', and so on.[17] It is interesting that some mistakes in the first draft are not corrected in the final version; thus at 3.14 'heros' is a scribal error for 'eros' that is repeated in the printed edition of 1492. A comparison with the Greek text is generally very instructive, but would carry us too far afield in the present context. It shows how Ficino is earnestly and honestly struggling to reproduce the sense of Plotinus' original as best he can.

A few words about the commentary which Ficino published along with his translation of *Enneads* III, 5 still remain to be said.[18] It is noteworthy that this commentary has some features which distinguish it from those which precede it in Ficino's Latin edition of Plotinus. To begin with, it is significantly shorter than the treatise itself; for the twenty-two preceding treatises the commentaries were either of about the same size as the treatises they dealt with, or else appreciably longer (II, 3, for example, is five times longer). Beginning with III, 5, however, the ratio changes. In the 1492 edition the text of 'On Eros' comprises eight pages, as compared to six pages of commentary. Secondly, the commentary of III, 5 is distinctive in that it is in the form of an *epistola* addressed to Lorenzo the Magnificent. Thirdly, the commentary is incomplete; it gives a perfunctory discussion of chapters 1-6 and the beginning of chapter 7, but it breaks off precisely at the point where the exegesis of the *Symposium* myth begins. The explanation is found in the opening and closing sentences of the commentary. Ficino begins with these words:

I judge, magnanimous Lorenzo, that you are not now going to require from your Marsilio a long discussion of love. This is both because we have discussed this at length in the *Symposium*, and especially because you your-self have discovered much concerning love by divine inspiration, and sung of it in elegant poems. Therefore I will only touch upon the high points.

Ficino concludes the commentary as follows:

The remaining matters which are discussed concerning love and the gods, seem to us to have been sufficiently established in the book *De Amore*.

In both passages Ficino is referring Lorenzo to the more extensive discussion of Eros in his commentary on the *Symposium* (which he regularly referred to as his *liber de amore*). The commentary in *Enneads* III, 5 can stay quite short, since it is already essentially contained in the *Symposium* commentary. We have come full circle, once again seeing the close link between Ficino's famous exposition of Platonic love and the Plotinian treatise *On Eros*.

As a concluding footnote it may be of interest to link this discussion of Ficino and *Enneads* III, 5 to the work of his close associate Pico della Mirandola. We know that it was Pico who first prevailed upon Ficino to undertake the Plotinus project in 1484.[19] We also know that Pico challenged Ficino's interpretation of the *Symposium* in his *Commento alla Canzone d'Amore di Girolamo Benivieni*, written in 1486.[20] Furthermore, we have seen that it is between these two dates that Ficino prepared the first draft of his Plotinus translation. In the light of these facts it is particularly striking that the codex of the first draft contains marginal annotations in a hand which has recently been identified by Sebastiano Gentile as that of Pico della Mirandola.[21] Moreover, these annotations are particularly frequent precisely in the margins of *Enneads* III, 5.[22] The conclusion seems warranted that Pico owned or had access to the copy of the first draft which still survives, and particularly studied the Plotinian passages on Eros, with a view to refuting Ficino's theory of Platonic love.[23] Further research will have to establish how plausible this conclusion is; for the moment this conclusion points to a further instance of the privileged connection in Renaissance thought between *Enneads* III, 5 and the idea of Platonic love.

Redeemer College
Hamilton, Ontario

Notes

1 P.O. Kristeller, *Eight Philosophers of the Italian Renaissance* (Stanford: Stanford University Press, 1964), p. 47. See also A.M.J. Festugière, *La Philosophie de l'amour de Marsile Ficin et son influence sur la littérature française au seizième siècle* (Paris: Vrin, 1941).
2 The references here are to chapter and line of P. Henry and H.-R. Schwyzer, eds., *Plotini Opera*. 3 vols. (Bruxelles: Desclée de Brouwer, 1951-73). The chapter divisions are common to all editions and translations of Plotinus.
3 *Symposium* 202E and 203B, quoted from *Great Dialogues of Plato*, trans. W.H.D. Rouse (New York: Mentor Books, 1956), p. 98.
4 P.O. Kristeller, *The Philosophy of Marsilio Ficino* (New York: Columbia University Press, 1943), especially section II,3.
5 See P. Henry, *Les Manuscrits des Ennéads* (Paris: Editions Universitaires, 1948), pp. 16-36, 45-62, and *idem*, 'Les manuscrits grecs de travail de Marsile Ficin, le traducteur des *Ennéades* de Plotin', in *Congrès de Tours et Poitiers* of the Association Guillaume Budé (Paris: Les Belles Lettres, 1954), pp. 323-28.
6 Henry, *Les Manuscrits*, pp. 50-62.
7 This point is made not only by Henry in the two works cited, but is confirmed by the author's personal inspection of the manuscript in question in Paris on May 22, 1984.
8 See Marsile Ficin, *Commentaire sur le Banquet de Platon*, ed. R. Marcel (Paris: Les Belles Lettres, 1956), pp. 59-62.
9 See Marsile Ficin, *Théologie Platonicienne de l'Immortalité des Ames*, ed. R. Marcel, 3 vols. (Paris: Les Belles Lettres, 1964-70), whose index lists dozens of allusions to Plotinus (on III, 5: see vol. 3, pp. 126 and 233).
10 For example, when Ficino makes a play on *Saturnus* and *satur* (*Opera* I, 238) he is alluding to the similar play of Plotinus at III, 5, 9.18 and elsewhere.
11 See R. Marcel, *Marsile Ficin (1433-1499)* (Paris:Les Belles Lettres, 1958), pp. 504, 507-08.
12 See Henry, 'Les manuscrits grecs de travail', p. 326, and Schwyzer, *Gnomon* XXXII (1960), p. 35.
13 A.M. Wolters, *Plotinus 'On Eros'* (Jordan Station, Ont.: Wedge Publishing Foundation, 1984).
14 I am quoting from the *editio princeps*: *Plotinus. Opera a Marsilio Ficino Latine reddita* (Florence: Miscomini, 1492).
15 Wolters, 'On Eros', p. 261, n. 105.
16 A.M. Wolters, 'The first draft of Ficino's translation of Plotinus,' paper delivered at the international Ficino conference in Naples and Florence, May 15-18, 1984 (forthcoming).
17 This is only a sampling, based on microfilm of the MS. Conv. Soppr. E.1. 2562 of the Biblioteca Nazionale Centrale of Florence.
18.I quote from the commentary as printed in F. Creuzer, *Plotini Opera Omnia* (Oxford, 1835), I, 522-526 (my own translation).

19. Marcel, *Marsile Ficin*, pp. 466-67.
20. See the note by S. Gentile in the printed catalogue of the 1984 Ficino exhibition, entitled *Marsilio Ficino e il ritorno di Platone. Manoscritti, Stampe e Documenti, 17 maggio-16 giugno 1984* (Florence: Le Lettere, 1984), p. 70.
21. *Marsilio Ficino e il ritorno di Platone*, p. 146.
22. *Marsilio Ficino e il ritorno di Platone*, p. 147.
23. *Marsilio Ficino e il ritorno di Platone*, p. 147.

Editors and Contributors

William R. Bowen

Dr.William R. Bowen is a Senior Fellow at the Centre for Reformation and Renaissance Studies (Victoria College, University of Toronto), and a Fellow of the Institute for Research in Classical Philosophy and Science (University of Pittsburg). He currently holds a Postdoctoral Fellowship from the Social Sciences and Humanities Research Council of Canada to study the sources of Ficino's writings on music and his impact on musical thought to 1650. Dr. Bowen completed a doctoral thesis (University of Toronto, 1984) titled 'Music and Number: An Introduction to Renaissance Harmonic Science.'

Francis Broun

Francis Broun studied art history at Princeton University, and is about to complete a Ph.D. dissertation on Sir Joshua Reynolds' collection of paintings. He is a lecturer in the Education Department of the Art Gallery of Ontario, where he has helped to organise and install such exhibitions as *William Blake: His Art and Times* and *Dutch Painting of the Golden Age*. He is currently involved with the major Reynolds retrospective at the Royal Academy in London.

Massimo Ciavolella

Massimo Ciavolella is Professor of Italian at Carleton University in Ottawa. In addition to articles on various aspects of mediaeval thought and to a book on the subject of love-as-a-disease, *La malattia d'amore dall'antichità al medio evo* (Rome: Bulzoni, 1975), he has prepared critical editions and translations of Renaissance comedies, and he co-edits the series Carleton Renaissance Plays in Translation. He is also co-editor of *Quaderni d'italianistica*, the journal of the Canadian Society for Italian Studies.

Konrad Eisenbichler

Professor Konrad Eisenbichler teaches Italian and Renaissance Studies at Victoria College in the University of Toronto, where he is also the Co-ordinator of the Renaissance Studies Programme. He has published various articles on sixteenth-century Italian theatre, a translation of Giovan Maria Cecchi's *The Horned Owl (L'Assiuolo)* and of Giovanni della Casa's *Galateo*, as well as an edition of G.M. Cecchi's lay sermons, the *Ragionamenti spirituali*.

Eva Kushner

Eva Kushner is Professor of French and Comparative Literature at McGill University. She has written on Pontus de Tyard, on the Renaissance dialogue, Montaigne and other Renaissance topics, and is editing with T. Klaniczay and A. Stegmann four volumes of comparative literary history of the Renaissance period.

Arthur M. Lesley

Professor Arthur Lesley teaches modern Hebrew language and literature at Baltimore Hebrew College, in Maryland. His comparative study of Hebrew and European literatures at the time of the Renaissance has been concentrated on rhetoric, biography, and historiography. A book on the humanist movement among Jews in Italy, with the title *All the Wisdom of Solomon*, is in preparation.

Peter V. Marinelli

Born in New York City, Professor Marinelli was educated at Fordham University (B.A., M.A.) and Princeton (Ph.D., 1964). He has been a member of the English Department of University College at the University of Toronto since 1963. With a chief interest in English and continental literature of the Renaissance, particularly the epic, he is the author of *Pastoral* (Methuen, 1971) and various articles on Renaissance epic poetry (Boiardo, Ariosto, Spenser). A work in manuscript, *Ariosto and Boiardo: The Origins of the 'Orlando Furioso'* is currently being read with a view to publication.

Dennis James McAuliffe

Professor McAuliffe teaches Italian and Literature in Translation in the Humanities Division, Scarborough College, University of Toronto. Before going to Toronto he taught at New York University, where he completed his Ph.D. in Italian Literature with a dissertation directed by Robert Clements. He is presently completing a book-length study of Vittoria Colonna's life and works.

Olga Zorzi Pugliese

Professor Pugliese teaches in the Dept. of Italian Studies (University of Toronto) and has been associated with the Renaissance Studies Programme at Victoria College, serving as a programme co-ordinator from 1983 to 1985. Her publications include articles on the Quattrocento and early Cinquecento (e.g. Castiglione) and a recent translation of two of Valla's treatises.

Riccardo Scrivano

Professor Scivano holds the chair of Italian Literature at the University of Rome II and has been Visiting Professor at various North American universities. He is the author of a dozen books written in Italian, a good number of which concern various aspects of Renaissance Italian thought and literature: classicism, mannerism, theatre, biography and autobiography.

Charles Trinkaus

Professor Emeritus of History at the University of Michigan, Prof. Trinkaus is an international scholar whose specialty is Renaissance humanism from Petrarch onwards. His two-volume opus, '*In Our Image and Likeness*': *Humanity and Divinity in Italian Humanist Thought* (1970) has become a classic on the subject of religious theory of the Quattrocento. Prof. Trinkaus was president of the Renaissance Society of America from 1973 to 1975.

Louis Valcke

A graduate of the University of Louvain, Professor Valcke teaches philosophy at the University of Sherbrooke in Quebec. His wide interests are shown in his list of publications which includes a number of titles on philosophical topics. The monograph published in 1978 is devoted to William of Ockham. Prof. Valcke is associated with the Centre d'Etudes de la Renaissance (Université de Sherbrooke).

Laura Westra

Dr. Westra obtained her doctorate in philosophy at the University of Toronto in 1983. She has worked on mediaeval and Renaissance philosophy, on Plotinus and Thomas Aquinas, as well as on Ficino. She is on staff at Clemson University, North Carolina.

Al Wolters

Dr. Wolters teaches religious studies and Greek at Redeemer College in Hamilton, Ontario. He has published (1984) a commentary on Plotinus's treatise 'On Eros' (*Enn.* III, 5) and a study of the biblical worldview entitled *Creation Regained* (Grand Rapids: Eerdmans, 1985). His study of an early manuscript of Ficino's translation of Plotinus is appearing in the Proceedings of the *Convegno ficiniano* held in Naples and Florence in 1984.